TEENAGE THUNDER

A Front Row Look at the 1950s Teenpics

by
Mark Thomas McGee

Teenage Thunder
By Mark Thomas McGee
Copyright © 2020 Mark Thomas McGee

No part of this book may be reproduced in any form or by any means, electronic, mechanical, digital, photocopying, or recording, except for inclusion of a review, without permission in writing from the publisher or Author.

Published in the USA by:

BearManor Media
4700 Millenia Blvd.
Suite 175 PMB 90497
Orlando, FL 32839
www.bearmanormedia.com

Paperback ISBN 978-1-62933-530-8
Case ISBN 978-1-62933-531-5
BearManor Media, Albany, Georgia
Printed in the United States of America
Book design by Robbie Adkins, www.adkinsconsult.com

Cover art from Movie poster for Hot Car Girl

Contents

Acknowledgements v

Foreword 1

The Movies. 34

Bibliography 243

Index. 245

For Nyla

Thank You

Some of the people who made this book possible are: Jack Arnold, William Asher, Richard Bakalyan, Albert Band, Edward Bernds, Whit Bissell, Paul Blaisdell, Herman Cohen, Gary Conway, Gene and Roger Corman, Charles "Beach" Dickerson, Mark Frank, Arthur Franz, Don Glut, Alex Gordon, Bert I. Gordon, Bob Greenberg, Charles B. Griffith, Brett Halsey, Jonathan Haze, Russell Johnson, Jackie Joseph, Steve Latshaw, Marty Kearns, Jacques Marquette, Ace Mask, Ib Melchior, Dick Miller, Luree Nicholson, Don Siegel, Gary Smith, Mike Stoller, Herbert L. Strock, Russ Tamblyn, Mamie Van Doren, Mel Welles, James Whitmore, and Albert Zugsmith.

And an extra big fine thanks to Bob Villard.

Mark McGee

FOREWORD

"*Teenagers!*" snarled Leo Gordon in **The Cry Baby Killer** (1958). "We never had 'em when I was a kid." It's a remark that isn't quite as ridiculous as it may seem. Before the marketeers took the hyphen out of the word teen-ager, young people were called "teeners" or "teensters," and they existed in a sort of twilight world in which they were expected to behave like adults while still being treated like children. It was a bum deal and, thankfully, a booming, post-war economy put an end to it. As a bi-product of an emerging middle class, the kids in 1950s America had money in their pockets for the first time in history, and were, at last, a force to be reckoned with. Manufacturers and retailers were quick to cater to these new consumers. Almost overnight, or so it seemed to their elders, it was *their* music that had climbed to the top of the charts, and *their* movies that were cleaning up at the boxoffice. Teenagers developed their own culture. Their own language. Their own fashion. Predictably, this exercise of new power frightened the bejeezus out of a lot of older folks who saw the whole business as a threat to the social fabric of America. These nervous nellies dug their heels in and declared war on just about everything that the kids liked, claiming that everything they *liked* was turning them into juvenile delinquents. "Man, I believe the older generation doesn't want the younger generation to have any fun," complained one Arizona high school student. The rise in juvenile crime reported early in the decade gave these zealots the cover that they needed to take serious action. It probably wasn't important that there had been a spike in juvenile crime in every decade since recorded history. Let the historians worry about stuff like that. Who has the time?

The so-called "Fabulous Fifties" began with the fabulous Soviet-aided army of North Korea invading South Korea, the start of a three-year "police action" that ended in a stalemate. Another bit of fabulous news—the Russians had their own Atomic Bomb. The race was on to build a bigger bomb, escalating the fabulous Cold War. In the event of an attack, children were taught to duck under their school desks and cover their heads. We all knew better and added, "And kiss your ass goodbye."

The Cold War with Russia brought with it the fear of communist infiltration. The Red scare was on, with Senator Joseph McCarthy fanning the flames of fear by claiming that our military, factories, and school systems were riddled with communists. "I don't care what kind of a crackpot some teacher might be, as long as

Mark McGee

he's an American crackpot," McCarthy insisted. As it had never been illegal to be a member of the communist party, people suddenly found themselves treated like criminals. Worse. Traitors. Suddenly, anyone with a liberal thought was suspect and a lot of lives were ruined so that Joe McCarthy, the alcoholic, junior senator from Wisconsin, could be the President of the United States. "Joe couldn't find a Communist in Red Square," wrote former UPI Reporter, George Reedy. "He didn't know Karl Marx from Groucho, but he was a United States senator." Fortunately, Joe's ambitions were thwarted by a wily old Boston lawyer who asked McCarthy on public television what a lot of folks in America wanted to ask: "At long last, have you left no sense of decency?"

The same question could have been asked of the Alabama bus driver who told 42-year old Rosa Parks to give up her seat to a white man, an incident that would mark the beginning of the Civil Rights Movement and the creation of the NAACP. "We are tired, tired of being segregated and humiliated; tired of being kicked about by the brutal feet of oppression," said Martin Luther King, the 26-year-old pastor of Dexter Avenue Baptist Church. It was decided to hit the segregationists where it hurt them the worst—their wallets. The bus boycott was the first of many non-violent protests that *slowly* but surely put an end to the Jim Crow south, at least on paper. Just remember, it took the Arkansas National Guard and a 1,000 soldiers from the 101st Airborne Division to desegregate one high school in Little Rock.

As large corporations began dominating American business, the way to success seemed to be to serve the corporation, achieved by trading one's dreams and individuality for steady employment. As one fellow observed: "If you had a college diploma, a dark suit, and anything between the ears, it was like an escalator; you just stood there and you moved up." Sloan Wilson's novel, *The Man in the Gray Flannel Suit*, was a fictionalized account of the author's own loss of identity and masculinity in his quest for corporate approval, leaving zero time to raise the children he was told that he should have.

Women, forced back into the kitchen by the men returning from war, felt the sting of oppression every bit as much as the folks struggling for their civil rights in the South. By the time *Redbook* asked its readers toward the end of the decade, "Why Young Mothers Feel Trapped," they got 24,000 answers.

With everything starting to unravel, the teenage rebellion was the last straw. Comedian George Gobel was asked if he thought the teenagers would ever grow into responsible adults. He replied, "Frankly, I don't think they'll live long enough." His tongue-in-cheek remark (almost as laugh-provoking as his trademark line, "*Well, I'll be a dirty bird,*") wasn't nearly as funny as Jackie Gleason's declaration that Elvis Presley would be a short-lived novelty.

In a 1957 issue of *Colliers* magazine, journalist Bill Davis wrote: "Never in our 180-year history has the United States been so aware of—or so confused about—our teenagers." The teenagers were equally confused by the adults, and with good cause. People tend to get a little cranky, a little irrational when they feel their power and control slipping away. As a child of the fifties, it was alarming to see the people who were supposed to be in charge—parents, teachers, civic leaders—get into a lather about the way Elvis Presley wiggled his hips. Elvis the Pelvis they called him, along with some other disrespectful things, and the outcry following his television appearances on *The Milton Berle Show* and *The Ed Sullivan Show* was absolutely and positively incomprehensible. You would have thought that the guy had unzipped his fly and let it all hang out. Quiz show host Gary Moore actually did (unknowingly) wag his weenie on network television and didn't cause the fuss and bother that Elvis did, even after Ed let him sing a couple of gospel songs, and put his arm around him, and told America what a fine, decent boy he was.

"It isn't enough to say that Elvis is kind to his parents," wrote Eddie Condon in the *New York Journal*. "That still isn't a free ticket to behave like a sex maniac in public before millions of impressionable kids." *The Catholic Sun* warned that the singer's "voodoo of frustration and defiance" was morally damaging, a sentiment shared by the writer for the *New York Times* who was afraid that Presley's gyrations might "overstimulate" 12-year olds.

"When I sing this rock and roll, my eyes won't stay open and my legs won't stand still," Presley told reporters. "I don't care what they say, it ain't nasty."

For his third appearance on Sullivan's show, the camera remained intimately close to the singer, so that the television audience would be spared the sight of his sexually-charged gyrations. But we all knew what he was up to because the girls in Sullivan's audience would scream with delight with each twitch. It might not be out of line to suggest that Elvis's hips may have single-handedly been responsible for what came to be known as the generation gap. Elvis and his music. The older generation hated rock and roll music. Some of them simply didn't like the sound of it, but there were others who didn't like it because it was black music. Race music. And Elvis sang it with the heart and soul of a black man, and he was good looking and sexy, which made him a very dangerous fellow in an era when disc jockeys routinely played homogenized versions of black songs, sung by bland white singers, as a way of keeping black singers from becoming *popular* black singers. This guy Presley was upsetting the applecart. By singing the kind of music that he loved best, he was opening the door for black singers to join the party. Segregationists believed that the music was "a plot to mongrelize America." J. Edgar Hoover, the director of the FBI, called rock and roll music "a corrupting influence," while *Time* magazine compared rock concerts to "Hitler mass meetings."

"The universality of rock and roll is proven by the fact that even though the songs are sung in English, people around the world love it," said manager and song writer Buck Ram, who collectively sold over 20 million records. "They just want the beat. It's all part of a pattern. First they called it 'rhythm and blues'—now its rock and roll. But I call 'happy music' myself. When the youngsters hear it, it breaks down barriers."

And that was the problem in a nutshell. The music broke down barriers and made people happy. There were actually black couples and white couples dancing on the same dance floor, on TV's *American Bandstand*, for everyone in the world to see. And they looked *happy!* Too happy. America was still firmly in the grip of a culture that at its core believed that too much fun was sinful. And sex... Well, what could be more fun than that? As a child I didn't know that "rock and roll" was a euphemism for sex. "Sixty-Minute Man" by Billy Ward and the Dominoes pretty much summed it up: "*Looka here girls, I'm telling you now, they call me lovin' Dan. I rock 'em, roll 'em all night long, I'm a sixty-minute man.*" But let's face it, most songs are about sex. When the very proper and very mainstream Tony Martin sang "I Get Ideas," he wasn't thinking about a night at the opera with his girl.

There is no better illustration of the explosive nature of one culture swallowing the other than in **Blackboard Jungle** (1955), when high school teacher Richard Kiley foolishly brings his prized collection of swing records to play for his students, hoping he will be able to communicate with them through music. But they don't want to hear Bix Beiderbecke, and while the soundtrack throbs with the beat of a jazzy little number, the kids toss his records around the room like Frisbees. At the end of the day, Kiley is left alone in his classroom, looking at the pieces of his broken 78s, shattered memories of a once popular culture. It was **Blackboard Jungle** that married rock and roll music to juvenile delinquency by using "Rock Around the Clock" as its main title. Glenn Ford stars in the film and it was his son who suggested they use Bill Haley's song.

Television's *Your Hit Parade* was the slow motion version of one generation giving way to the next. A radio favorite since 1935, the show came to television in 1950, with regulars Dorothy Collins, Russell Arms, Snooky Larson and Gisele MacKenzie singing the seven best-selling songs of the week. My brother and I hated the show until these mainstream maestros were forced to struggle with the likes of "Heartbreak Hotel" and "Whole Lotta Shakin' Goin' On." My brother and I laughed until it hurt, much to the dismay of our parents who didn't understand why we were laughing, which made the experience funnier still. *Your Hit Parade* became one of our favorite programs. We actually looked forward to it. Seeing the writing on the wall, NBC wisely let the show go to CBS for its final season in 1958, giving these poor people one more year to publicly humiliate themselves. If the show could have just held on for one more season, the music had been beaten back into something they could have managed.

As one sifts through all of the facts and fiction, all of the hype and hysteria, the rhetoric and moral outrage that was so much a part of these Alice in Wonderland times, one can't help but hear the collective voice of an older generation crying, "*Things aren't the way they used to be!*"

They certainly weren't for the major studios. Already shaken by the Supreme Court ruling in 1947 that forced them to sell off some of their theatres, the movie moguls staggered into the 1950s facing a lot of red ink. The people who used to go to the movies once or twice a week were staying home to watch the new one-eyed monster, television. Ticket sales in 1954 were less than half of what they'd been in 1947. The kids were the ones buying the tickets now, and they wanted to see movies that they could relate to, movies with teenage girls in "trouble," motorcycles and hot-rods, punks with switchblade knives, and monsters from outer space. The major studios turned a deaf ear, apparently assuming the whole business would blow over if given enough time, and continued to make the same kinds of movies they'd always made, only with wide screen images and stereophonic sound. Maverick filmmakers, working outside of the studio system, stepped in to fill the void, with cheaply made, black and white movies that rarely ran longer than 70 minutes which, more often than not, was plenty long enough. The scripts were written around pre-tested, catchy titles, and often financed by the exhibitors who, unlike the studio executives, knew what their audiences wanted to see. These movies were advertised in the most provocative manner—*Car crazy! Speed crazy! Boy crazy! She's hell-on-wheels…fired up for any thrill! In her eyes…desire! In her veins…the blood of a monster! They called her "JAILBAIT"! The shock story of the big city's delinquent daughters! Uncensored! Wild and wicked, living with no tomorrow! Rockin', rioting teenage fury! Explosive! Amazing! Terrifying! You won't believe your eyes!*

Alex Gordon, the producer of **Runaway Daughters**, **Shake, Rattle and Rock** and **The She-Creature** (all 1956), was a guest on journalist Paul Coates television program, *Confidential File*. (The cameraman and the director of the show would later make **Stakeout on Dope Street**.) Sitting firmly on his high horse, Coates accused Gordon of making inflammatory movies, echoing the sentiments of many parents, teachers and politicians. Gordon was convinced by the evasive nature of his remarks that Coates hadn't actually seen any of the films. All of his comments were based on what he'd heard about the films and the way they were advertised, which hardly made him a candidate for an investigative journalism award. "I told him that the pictures were actually quite moral," Gordon recalled. "The advertising was just the old come-on."

"A lot of people were uptight about those juvenile delinquency films, but we never told the true story of what was going on. We just brushed the surface," said actor Richard Bakalyan, a regular in these teenage dramas. "I never thought that kids would try to emulate us 'cuz we never glorified the characters. **Dino** [1957] certainly wasn't glorified. He was a troubled kid. That picture reflected a time."

Besieged by all of these troubled teens, *Los Angeles Times* film critic Charles Champlin took the podium at the Reiss-Davis Women's Club and wistfully asked his audience, "Whatever happened to Andy Hardy?" Andy Hardy was a teen-aged character played by Mickey Rooney, in a series of wholesome M-G-M movies that

"How long can a guy play a jerk kid?" Mickey Rooney asks Lewis Stone. "I'm twenty-seven years old. I've been divorced once and separated from my second wife. I have two boys of my own. I spent almost two years in the army. It's time Judge Hardy went out and bought me a double-breasted suit."

began in 1939 with **A Family Affair**, conceived as a one-shot film, ending ten films later with **Love Laughs at Andy Hardy** in 1946, only to resurface again in 1958 with **Andy Hardy Comes Home**. "He should have stayed where he was," said exhibitor Dave Klein. "Worst business since we opened our theatre."

Andy Hardy lived in the small but comfortable Midwestern town of Carvel, with his extremely understanding father, Judge Hardy (Lewis Stone), his unbelievably sweet mother (Fay Holden), and his older sister (Cecilia Parker). Everyone was always "nice" in the Hardy films, even Andy's girl, Polly Benedict (Ann Rutherford), who had to maintain her "niceness" during those many anxious moments when some other lass would catch Andy's wandering eye. Champlin's lamentation wasn't just for Andy Hardy, but rather for what he represented, the yardstick for the nation's young to aspire to—a decent, trustworthy, sometimes misguided but basically honest, and (most important of all) *obedient* young man. Obedient, and dangerously naïve if we are to believe this moment from **Love Finds Andy Hardy** (1938). The Judge expresses his concern to Andy that a young man he'd sent to jail for a petty crime might harbor some resentment. "Why, Dad," Andy cheerfully assures his father, "Kids don't hold any grudge against older people for punishing them. If they did, all kids'd hate their fathers—and they don't." That Rooney managed to say this line with conviction proves that the guy was one of the best actors in the business.

So taken with this idealized vision of America, free of murderers, kidnappers, child molesters, wife-beaters, delinquent parents, corrupt politicians, homeless people, street gangs, drug peddlers, drug addicts, guns and switch-blade knives, the Academy of Motion Picture Arts and Sciences honored M-G-M, and the series, with a special Academy Award for "furthering the American way of life."

It would not be going out on a limb to suggest that the teenagers of the 1940s had a lot more in common with James Dean's baffled Jim Stark, and Natalie Wood's love-starved Judy, in the film **Rebel Without a Cause** (1955), than they ever did with Andy Hardy or Henry Aldrich or Nancy Drew, or any of the other characters that appeared in what authors Michael Barson and Steven Heller call the "Kleen Teen" movies. The kids in these films were miniature adults, and even dressed in suits, only they said things like "Golly," "Gosh," and "Gee" a lot so that the audience would know the difference. It was only fitting that as Charles Champlin and his audience bemoaned the loss of Andy and his ilk, the Hardy's home was rotting on the studio's backlot.

Let's have a look at the "Kleen Teen" movies because they never really disappeared, and why should they? And movies about juvenile delinquency date back to the silent days, and the plots were pretty much the same as they were in the fifties. So let's have a look at those, too.

Canadian-born Deanna Durbin was dropped by M-G-M when the studio decided to put all of their energy into promoting Judy Garland. She found a new home at Universal, and for ten years she sang her way through a series of money-making comedies—**Three Smart Girls** (1936), **100 Men and a Girl** (1937), **It's a Date** (1940)—that helped save the studio from bankruptcy. When she retired at 29, she was the highest paid actress in Hollywood. The Academy gave her an award too, for "bringing to the screen the spirit and personification of youth."

"I represented the ideal daughter millions of fathers and mothers wished they had," Durbin remarked. Right she was. You wouldn't catch Deanna coming home with a bad report card or hanging out with the wrong crowd. Cigarettes and alcohol never touched her lips. She never had the sort of problems that would require psychiatric help, and you could bet your bottom dollar that she wouldn't turn out to be a lesbian. And there was never any danger of her becoming pregnant. Not ever! When Deanna gets a crush on worldly journalist Melvin Douglas in **That Certain Age** (1938), there's no need to fear that things might go too far, not for

Every parent's dream girl, the delightful Deanna Durbin, who once remarked: "I can't run around forever being little Miss Fix It who bursts into song."

one tiny second, not even if Deanna were to have a momentary lapse in her otherwise impeccable judgement, and gave in to temptation. Because, after all, what could a middle-aged man possibly find of interest in an adorable, beautiful, deliriously happy, eager and willing 18-year old? In the end, the sadder-but-wiser Miss Durbin returns to her dorky boyfriend, Jackie Cooper, and the two of them put on a musical benefit to send underprivileged Boy Scouts to summer camp.

Cooper was the bumbling but well-meaning 17-year old Henry Aldrich, in the first two installments of Paramount's Henry Aldrich series, based on the popular radio program, *The Aldrich Family*. Jimmy Lyndon took over the role and more or less made it his own. **Henry Aldrich Gets Glamour** (1943), written by Edwin Blum and Aleen Leslie, is considered by many to be the best of the eleven Aldrich films. Henry enters a contest and wins a date with glamorous movie star Hillary Dane (Frances Gifford). It's a farce, of course. She has lunch with him during which she spends the entire time conducting business and barely says "hello" to him. And yet, rumors spread and through no fault of his own, Henry gets a reputation for being another Hollywood wolf, which sabotages his father's political aspirations. To prove that nothing happened between them, Henry invites the actress to the

Jimmy Lyndon as the hapless Henry Aldrich, in much better company than he's used to.

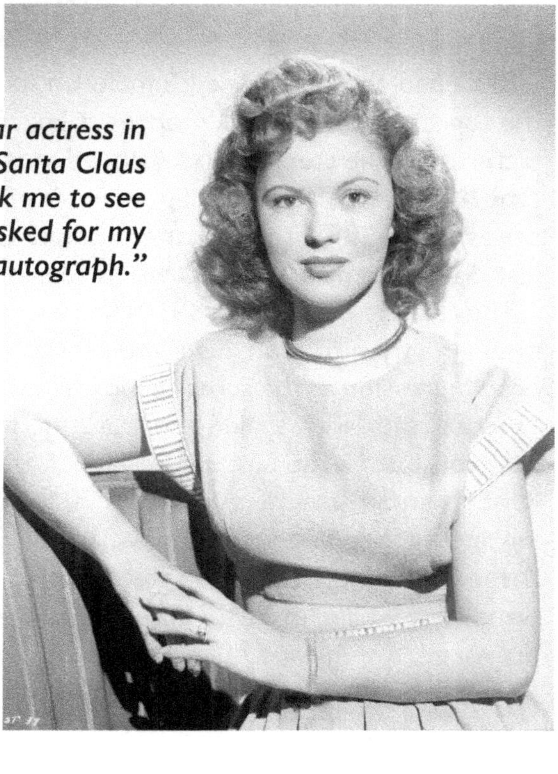

Shirley Temple, once the most popular actress in America, said she stopped believing in Santa Claus when she was six. "My mother took me to see him in a department store and he asked for my autograph."

local dance, assuming that she won't show, which will prove to everyone that he's been maligned. But she does show. Why? Miss Dane covets the role of Juliet in a new film version of Shakespeare's romance, and has been told that she's too sophisticated to play the part. Her point: "How can I be too sophisticated for Romeo, if I'm not too sophisticated for Henry Aldrich?"

Mark McGee

Kleen Teens Frankie Thomas and Bonita Granville meet two of the not-so-clean Dead End Kids, Huntz Hall and Bobby Jordan.

"We didn't have any jealousy among us," said Lyndon. "I was at Paramount, Rooney and Garland were at M-G-M, Jack Cooper was at Columbia, we were all good friends."

RKO had teenage Shirley Temple on its payroll, and though she never enjoyed the success she'd had as a moppet at Fox, she nevertheless made a couple of good pictures for the studio, **Miss Annie Rooney** (1942) and the **Bachelor and the Bobby Soxer** (1947) among them. Warner Bros. had the Nancy Drew mystery series (1938-39), with 15-year old Bonita Granville, and the less said about Columbia's Sam Katzman/Arthur Dreifuss teen-aged comedies (1946-47) the better.

The teenage rebellion of 1950s had its roots in The Roaring Twenties, when teen-aged girls tried to look like silent screen vamp Theda Bera, and the boys did their best impression of the screen's most romantic star, Rudolph Valentino. "Sheiks" and "shebas" they were called and "cat's meow" and "bee's knees" were part of their new vocabulary. The Great War had left the nation shaken and unsure of itself. The "disenchanted" *teensters* wanted to enjoy life while they could, drinking and smoking and dancing and you know what. As 19-year old Jean Harlow put it in **Hell's Angels** (1930): "I wanna be free. I wanna be gay and have fun. Life's short and I wanna live while I'm alive." In response to the moral outrage this sort of behavior provoked, the *Atlantic Monthly* published a letter by a young man named John F. Carter, who had this to say to all of those angry parents: "I would like to observe that the older generation had certainly pretty well ruined this world before passing it on to us. They give us this Thing, knocked to pieces, leaky, red-hot, threatening to blow up, and then they are surprised that we don't accept it with the same enthusiasm with which they received it."

M-G-M's **Our Dancing Daughters** (1928) was one of the first films to capture the new Jazz Age philosophy. The studio's publicity department promised the movie-goer a firsthand look at those "scandalous women" who liked fast music and fast men. Former bit player Joan Crawford got her first break playing the "sheba" in the film. Novelist and screenwriter F. Scott Fitzgerald thought she captured perfectly what he called "the girl you see at smart nightclubs, downed to the apex of sophistication, toying iced glasses with a remote, faintly bitter expression, dancing deliciously; laughing a great deal, with wide, hurt eyes." As political reporter Walter Lippmann noted, unlike the decades that would follow, the kids weren't rebelling against their parents so much as the disillusionment with their own rebellion. Said Lippmann, "It is common for young men and women to rebel, but that they should rebel sadly and without faith in their rebellion, that they should distrust the new freedom no less than the old certainties—that is something of a novelty."

The Great Depression that followed the stock market crash in 1929, left 40 million people suddenly looking poverty in the eye. The people who were thrown out of their homes by the banks took delight and made heroes

James Dean and Natalie Wood.

Samuel Goldwyn's Dead End.

out of the criminals who robbed them. During Hollywood's pre-code era, James Cagney, George Raft and Edward G. Robinson became motion picture stars playing gangsters. Pressure was applied to the studios to shift the focus from the hoodlums to the cops, and Cagney and the others found themselves enforcing the law instead of breaking it.

Warner Bros., a major player in the gangster genre, was also known for exposing social injustice wherever they found it, in as frank a manner as the Motion Picture Association of America allowed. In **Wild Boys of the Road** (1933), young Frankie Darro is charged with vagrancy and when the judge wants to know why he won't simply go home, Darro lets him have it. "Because our folks are poor. They can't get jobs, and there isn't enough to eat. What good will it do to send us home to starve? You say you got to send us to jail to get us off the streets. Well, that's a lie. You're sending us to jail 'cuz you don't want to see us. You want to forget us. Well, you can't do it. 'Cuz I'm not the only one. There's thousand just like me and more hitting the road each day."

For his trouble, Darro found himself in reform school that same year in **The Mayor of Hell** (1933), with Humphrey Bogart as the new Deputy Commissioner, determined to reform the reform school, mismanaged by a greedy superintendent, a formula that would be repeated many times.

Poverty, drug addiction, and wayward parents were to blame for bad teenagers, and poverty was the focus of Samuel Goldwyn's **Dead End** (1937), based on a successful Broadway play by Sidney Kingsley. The story takes place on a dead end street facing the river, on New York's East Side. Tired of dodging the law, weary gangster Baby Face Martin (Humphrey Bogart) returns to the slum of his childhood, hoping to find some respite. To the decent people in the neighborhood, Martin is a reminder of what they can expect from the current crop of street urchins, seen in various stages of mischief throughout the film. The young actors who played these hoodlums-in-training—Billy Halop, Leo Gorcey, Bobby Jordan, Huntz Hall, Bernard Punsley and Gabriel Dell—were known as The Dead End Kids, and were so popular that when Goldwyn was finished with them, Warner Bros. snapped them up and cast them in a series of films, opposite some of their biggest stars. The Kids quickly earned a reputation for being a collective pain in the ass. Ronald Reagan told James Cagney he had some concerns about working with them in **Hell's Kitchen** (1939). Cagney told the future president to relax. All he had to do was politely inform the lads that unless they behaved, "he'd slap hell out of them." **The Dead End Kids on Dress Parade** (1939) clearly signaled that these criminal wannabes had been whipped into military shape.

"Live fast, die young, and leave a good-looking corpse" says Nick Romero (John Derek), on trial for murder in Nicholas Ray's **Knock on Any Door** (1949). His lawyer (Humphrey Bogart) warns the jury that unless we clean up our slums, a knock on any door might find another Nick Romero. Romero is sentenced to death, much to the relief of most of the critics who felt the character would have been a bum no matter where he'd been raised. The film was a trial run for director Ray who six years later made a J.D. drama that eclipsed everything before it, and heavily influenced everything that would follow.

Writer-director Maxwell Shayne bought the screen rights to Irving Schulman's novel about gang life in the big city, *The Amboy Dukes*, and made a tepid film out of it. The lead character in Schulman's yarn is Frank Goldfarb, who spends most of his time hanging around the pool hall, occasionally running errands for some small-time hoods. On the one day Frank decides to go to school, he and his best friend, Benny, create such a disturbance the entire class is placed on suspension until the two of them bring their parents to the school. Frank and Benny beg the teacher to give them a break. They get into a scuffle and Frank shoots the teacher dead with his zip gun. Frank races home, packs a few things, and is about to make his escape over the rooftops, when he runs into "Crazy" Sacks, who has been waiting for a chance to get even with Frank for stealing his girl. The last line of the novel describes how Frank's body smacked against the rail of a third-story fire escape after Sacks threw him off of the building, bouncing off in an arc toward the street with Frank "screaming his life away."

Shayne was warned by the MPAA that it would never approve of the more shocking aspects of Shulman's novel—juveniles smoking dope, consorting with whores, committing brutal acts of violence, which in this case included the rape of a 12-year old

"The gang" from City Across the River. *Could that be Tony Curtis and Richard Jaeckel in the middle?*

girl. In Shayne's watered down screen version, **City Across the River** (1949), a mild beating replaced the rape, and the whores and the reefer were nowhere to be seen.

Taking no chances, Shayne added a prologue, in which Drew Pearson, one of the best-known news reporters of his day, once again called for the clean-up of the slums, echoed later by a shop teacher in the film. "Sometimes," said the teacher, "I think the only solution is to clear out all the people and drop an atom bomb on that whole slum."

In yet a further effort to placate the MPAA, each member of the cast portraying one of the Dukes was introduced to the audience at the end of the film, to assure everyone it was "just a movie." Nevertheless, even this weak tea proved to be too strong for PTA groups and other civic-minded people, furious over a sequence showing the students constructing zip-guns in metal shop. The film met with even more opposition after one high school teacher asked his students what they thought the film was trying to say. The general consensus: *Don't be a fink*.

"There isn't any such thing in the world as a bad boy," Father Edward Flanagan often said. "But a boy left alone, frightened, bewildered, the wrong hand reaches for him...He needs a friend. That's all he needs."

Flanagan sponsored a home for juvenile offenders and M-G-M made a film about him and his **Boys Town** (1938), with Spencer Tracy perfectly cast as the priest in an Oscar winning performance. Flanagan's problem boy is (who else?) Mickey Rooney, playing Whitey Marsh, the son of a thief. He runs for mayor of Boys Town with the slogan: Don't be a sucker. The boys don't buy Whitey's tough guy act

Mickey Rooney and Spencer Tracey.

and elect somebody else. Disappointed, Whitey takes off for the big city where he coincidentally passes by a bank being robbed by his brother's gang. Whitey is wounded and hospitalized. When his involvement in the crime reflects badly on Flanagan's school, Whitey locates the gang's hideout and demands that they clear him of any wrong-doing. The hoods turn on Whitey and his brother (Edward Norris). The kids at Boys Town hear about it and race to the rescue. **Men of Boys Town** (1946) was soon to follow.

Drug addiction comes right after poverty as being a major cause of juvenile crime, but thanks to the tireless efforts of Will Hays, the head of the MPAA, and his successor, Geoffrey M. Shurlock, moviegoers didn't hear a whole lot about it. These men set the guidelines for what the public was allowed to see. Since motion pictures appealed to every class, it became their business to protect everyone from the less sophisticated members of the audience, the nitwits who couldn't be expected to be responsible for their own actions. These impressionable people might see something wicked or evil in a movie and try it themselves. (Where do you suppose Attila the Hun got his inspiration? Or Jack the Ripper?) Under pressure from the less flexible Legion of Decency (the watchdog committee of the Catholic Church), the Hays office instigated the Production Code Administration, with Joseph Breen as the executive director. It was his job to read scripts and view completed films to make sure everyone was complying with the rules. Once passed, the films were awarded a seal of approval. Without it, no distributer would touch it. Apparently, these men believed that the best way to deal with a problem was to pretend that it didn't exist. At least, not enough to make a fuss about it. It wouldn't be out of line to suggest that the MPAA aided and abetted criminal behavior by refusing to shine a light on it. Under the law, silence gives consent.

Teenage Menace (1953), made by a little outfit called Broadway Angels, managed to play in 41 states before New York's Board of Regents banned it as "the most dangerous of its kind." Somehow, the Board concluded that watching a film about a drug addict, so desperate for his next fix that he'll lie, cheat, steal and ultimately die from it, would somehow encourage drug use. Broadway Angels took the matter to court and for the first time, the Board's decision was overturned. Producer-director Otto Preminger basically told the MPAA to sit on it when he released

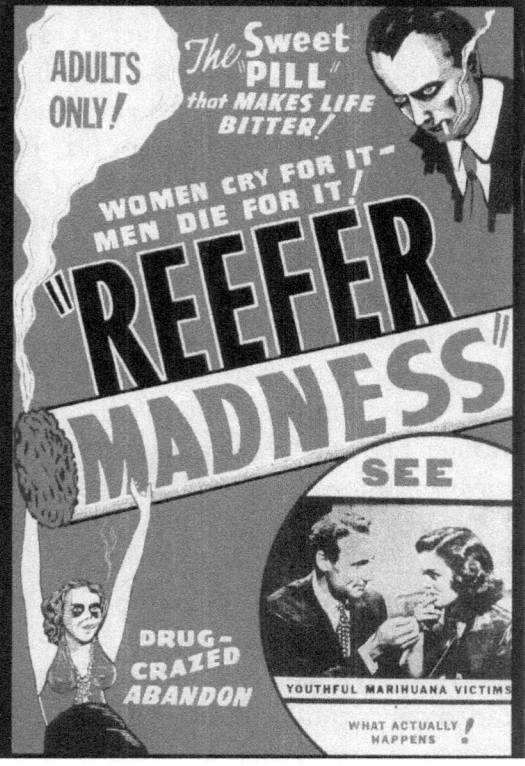

The Man With the Golden Arm (1955), based on Nelson Algren's novel about drug addiction, without their precious seal, breaking the MPAA's hold on the issue once and for all, opening the door for films such as ***A Hatful of Rain***, ***Monkey on My Back*** (both 1957) and ***The Cool and the Crazy*** (1958). This new freedom to explore subjects that had been forbidden by the code was due, in part, to the movies giving way to television as the primary source of entertainment, where censorship always exercises its strongest control.

Filmmakers who "four-walled" their movies didn't have to adhere to the motion picture code. These enterprising producers were more than happy to tackle the drug problem. They would take their "educational" productions to some rural town, rent a theatre for a couple of nights, and plaster flyers all over town. The advertising promised tales of innocent teenage girls (often seen in the buff) who become easy marks for unprincipled men seeking cheap thrills and tawdry pleasures. After smoking a little weed, these girls easily succumb to a life of prostitution, crime and shame. If the writers were feeling particularly vindictive, the girls would get a case of the clap. The most famous of these silly propaganda pieces was the church-funded ***Tell Your Children*** (1936). Bottom-feeder Dwain Esper bought the picture, added some new salacious scenes, and re-issued the film under several titles—***The Burning Question***, ***Love Madness***—but it is best-known as ***Reefer Madness***, considered high camp today, with audiences passing joints at revival screenings.

Now, we come to the third cause of delinquency—delinquent parents, the subject of a 1942 *Look* magazine article titled "Are These Our Children?" in which the author wrote that America had done a crackerjack job of producing planes, guns, and ships, but a miserable job of raising its children. Letters from their readers suggested social and community programs as a possible solution to the problem, the basis for Columbia's ***Juvenile Court*** (1938), in which Public Defender Paul Kelly struck a blow against teenage crime by organizing a Police Athletic League. Charles Koerner, RKO's vice president, wanted to make a movie based

Take a good look. This is what happens when you smoke the Devil weed. From **Reefer Madness**.

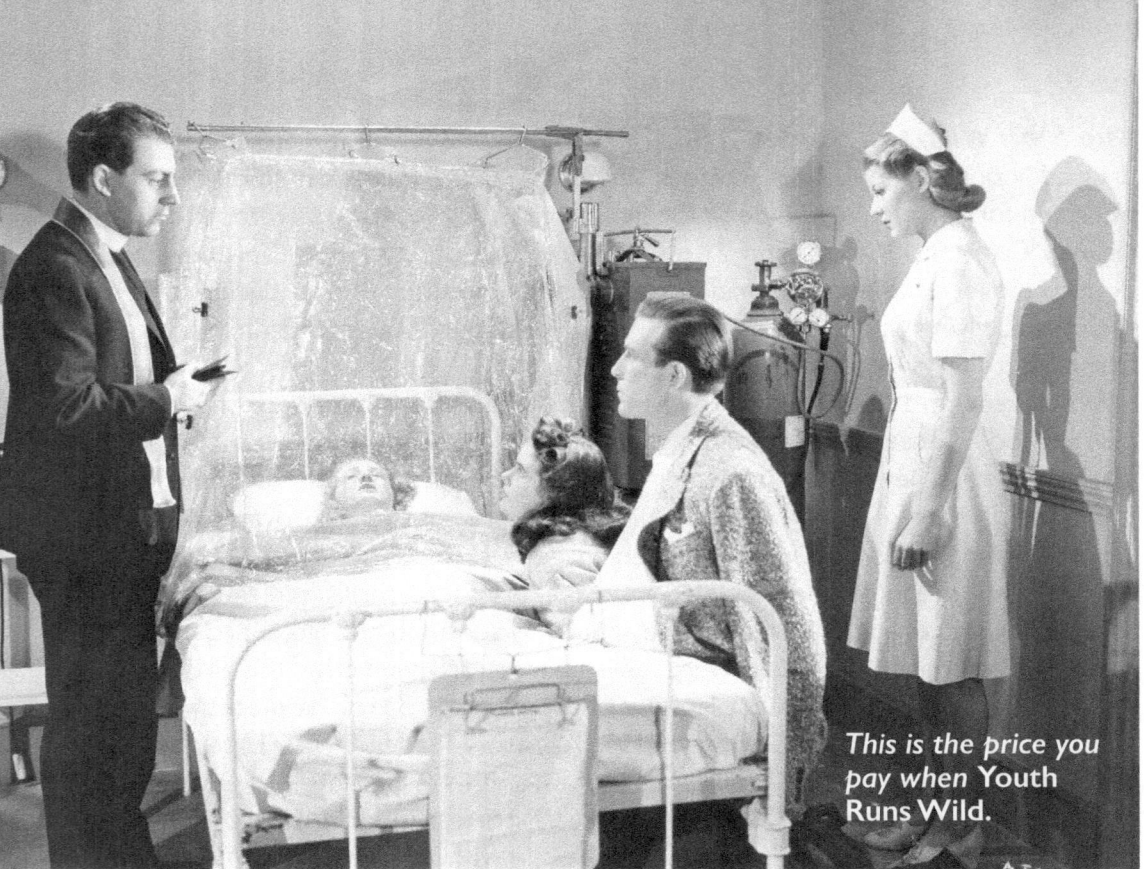

This is the price you pay when Youth Runs Wild.

on "Are These Our Children?" and said he was prepared to throw his entire production resources behind the project, then gave the assignment to Val Lewton's low budget unit.

Before production began, the State Department politely reminded the studio that such a film might give other nations the impression that the United States didn't know how to handle its youth. This was a good, all-purpose excuse to squash anything that suggested that things weren't perfect in America, used time and time again, proving that those in charge are far more interested in perception than reality. Filmmakers were able to side-step this Public Relations problem by sticking a disclaimer at the front of their pictures, basically saying that while everyone was doing a great job of doing whatever it was that they were doing, there was always room for improvement.

Looking over Lewton's script, the Hays office ordered the removal of a subplot in which a boy is forced to kill his sadistic father. Then, the people from *Look* expressed their dislike of the picture, which suggested that the studio could forget about all of that wonderful free publicity they had expected. Coupled with a bad preview, the film was pulled, re-edited and new scenes were shot. After going through several title changes it finally emerged as **Youth Runs Wild** (1944), a "banal and silly" film according to producer Lewton, whose request to have his name removed fell on deaf ears.

Monogram's **Where Are Your Children?** (1943) concluded with a probation officer reminding everyone how foolish it would be to lose the young people in the effort to win the war, and "won't the Nazis make great use of such shortsightedness in our democracy?" The month the film went into release, the *Brooklyn Daily Eagle* reported that due to the widespread lawlessness in the Bedford-Stuyvesant district, all radio stations would, every night at nine, ask the question: *Where are your children?* The film, directed by William Nigh, no stranger to short schedule pictures, finds poor Gale Storm kicked out of her home over a misunderstanding, and with nowhere else to turn, she heads for San Diego and her new boyfriend, Jackie Cooper. She accepts a ride from some of Cooper's friends who aren't the best of characters. Unbeknownst to her, the car has been stolen and one of the punks kills a gas station attendant. The film had the distinction of being the first Monogram feature to play the top half of a double bill in three Fox West Coast theatres, held over for four weeks in Chicago.

PRC's **I Accuse My Parents** (1944), was the heart-wrenching tale of a youth on trial for murder, told with the subtlety of an elephant stampede. One standout moment has the boy telling the judge about the afternoon he raced home to tell his mom that he'd won first prize in a national essay contest, with his piece "My Country, My Home." The boy throws open the door and the camera slowly moves through the living room, with ashtrays filled to overflowing, and enough empty liquor bottles strewn about the place to put the entire Marine Corps out of action for a week, until it finally finds a note from his mom: "You'll find ten dollars in the drawer. Take care of yourself until I get home." During this slice of poignancy, the soundtrack supplies the strains of "Home Sweet Home." His parents have little to say about the boy's triumph upon their return, choosing instead to plunge into their nightly argument. The boy's despondency is matched only by his embarrassment when his mother shows up at school the next day, plastered to the gills. Had he not been ashamed of his parents and his life, the boy tells the judge, he wouldn't have sought refuge in the sort of company that coerced him into trouble. The judge gives Jimmy a pass on the murder charge, and a suspended sentence for his participation in the robberies, then wheels on the boy's parents and in a burst of unbridled sermonizing, chastises them for their neglect. "I speak to parents everywhere when I say that if in the pursuit of your own pleasures and occupations, you neglect your children, realize now, before it's too late, that this might have been your boy!" In some instances, the characters delivering these cautionary warnings looked directly into the camera.

By 1953, the book racks were filled with purple prose novels about delinquent crime— *Teen-Age Mafia, The Young and the Violent, Go, Man, Go!* There was also a book by Dale Kramer and Madeline Carr, a study of *Teen-Age Gangs*, with an introduction by Senator Estes Kefauver, well-known for his televised hearings into organized crime. Kefauver was about to fire the first shot in the war on fun.

Dr. Fredric Wertham, the director of a mental hygiene clinic at New York's Bellevue Hospital, wrote a famous, best-selling book called *Seduction of the Innocent*, in which he claimed that comic books caused children to commit acts of violence, a conclusion based on the fact that all of the disturbed children he worked with liked comic books. (One might assume they also liked cartoons, ice cream and amusement parks, but then I'm no psychiatrist.) Armed with this book, Senator Kefauver headed a senate subcommittee looking into the effects of comic books on adolescents, resulting in the publishers being bullied into joining the newly established Comics Code Authority. As with the MPAA, without the Code's seal of approval, a publisher couldn't get his product distributed. This put an end to the excessive and gruesome fun of *Crime Suspense Stories, Two-Fisted Tales,* and *The Crypt of Terror,* to name just a few. The kids were left with whatever pleasure they could find in the inane innocence of *Archie* and the gang at Haverhill High, a series that began in 1941. By 1949 it was the best-selling comic book in America. The subversive *Mad* magazine would later parody Archie and his pals, turning them all into juvenile delinquents. Betty and Veronica never looked better.

With the comic book crisis solved, Kefauver set his sights on the motion picture industry. And he couldn't have picked a better time. It was an industry already under siege. No longer the primary source for cheap entertainment, the major studios were fighting for their lives when, for the second time, The House Un-American Activities Committee came looking for commies in the film industry. "I don't think I can think of a more contemptible, more despicable irony than was the House Un-American Activities Committee," said Emmy-winning comedy writer Hal Kanter. (I can. The Catholic Legion of Decency.) Kefauver was probably licking his lips. There's nothing quite like kicking somebody when they're down. Public hearings were held from April 24 to June 4 in 1954. Looking back on **City Across the River**, Kefauver's committee concluded that while the film purportedly was made as a deterrent to crime, "we have seen the delinquency rates rising since 1948, and, while we cannot say what effect this film had, if any, we may assume that it was hardly one of reducing delinquency." Having been castrated by the censors, it would have been a miracle if the film had succeeded in making any kind of statement, much less an effective one. According to Kefauver and his brood, the film was guilty because it did not succeed in doing what it wasn't allowed to do.

Someone at the committee told Jack Warner that they'd already received a disturbing call about **Rebel Without a Cause**. As the picture was still in production, Warner shrugged his shoulders and said, "The caller must be using mental radar or something because I haven't seen it yet myself." Without going into specifics, Kefauver had some disparaging things to say about **Blackboard Jungle**, a movie based on Evan Hunter's best-selling novel about an idealistic schoolteacher's struggle to communicate with his hostile students. After listening to Kefauver's vague insinuations, M-G-M's head of production, Dory Schary, wanted to know specifically what

Margaret Hayes is attacked in the library. This image was used on the poster. From **Blackboard Jungle.**

Kefauver found objectionable about the picture. Backed into a corner, the headline-seeking senator had to admit that he hadn't seen it. Schary politely suggested that there seemed to be a lack of responsibility in Kefauver's investigation. "Is that so?" said Kefauver. "Did you hear about the group of school girls who set fire to a barn after seeing **Blackboard Jungle**?" Schary fired back, "They can't pin that on us! There's no fire in the picture!" Kefauver's committee eventually published a report of their findings which amounted to 122 pages of precisely nothing.

In a speech before the National Conference of Controllers, Dory Schary told his audience that "movies seldom lead opinion, they merely reflect public opinion and perhaps occasionally accelerate it…No motion picture ever started a trend of public opinion or thinking. Pictures merely dramatize these trends and keep them going."

Paramount executive Y. Frank Freeman, MPAA head Eric Johnston, and Loew's President Nicholas M. Schneck all warned Schary not to make **Blackboard Jungle**. "Nick," said Schary, "you're suggesting I give up on a film that might earn us nine or ten million dollars." Schneck wanted to know what Schary thought it would cost to make, and when he was told just over a million, he gave Schary the green light. When the smoke cleared, the picture pulled in over eight million bucks.

No one could have possibly predicted the outrage that **Blackboard Jungle** would cause, though it had met with some opposition from Geoffrey Shurlock right from the start. Shurlock wasn't happy about words like "dago" and "nigger" in director Richard Brooks' script, nor was he thrilled with lines like "a prostitute makes more money than a school teacher." Though much of the language that Shurlock found so offensive, and some of the violence he found so objectionable was removed, Brooks refused to insert a line of dialogue that said juvenile crime was even worse in Russia.

The film went into release in late March and was immediately banned in Memphis, Tennessee, and later in Atlanta, Georgia where the city fathers labeled it "immoral, obscene and licentious," a threat to the very well-being of the community. Critics received postcards from the Institute for Public Opinion, claiming the film was "anti-public schools," and presented a completely false impression of the conditions in those schools.

The newspapers reported that the U.S. Ambassador to Italy, Clare Booth Luce, threatened to leave Venice and "cause the greatest scandal in motion picture history" unless the movie was withdrawn from the Venice Film Festival. Producer Arthur Hornblow told reporters that Miss Luce had said nothing more than she would not attend the screening. Nevertheless, the film was pulled, replaced by **The Kentuckian** (1955), a bone-headed action picture with Burt Lancaster. One weary critic pointed out that the very fact that a film like **Blackboard Jungle** could be made was a testament to a country's greatness, while **The Kentuckian** was a testament to its silliness.

"We educators who have previewed the picture have been disturbed by the picture's exaggeration and its probable effect upon the public attitude toward the students and teachers," wrote Edward N. Wallen, the principal of a vocational and technical high school in the Bronx. His feelings were echoed by Superintendent C. Frederick Pertsch who insisted that the film constituted "a grave disservice" to the nation's youth by "misrepresenting and sensationalizing the situation." Gossip columnist Hedda Hopper claimed it was the most brutal film that she had ever seen and was convinced that it would frighten many would-be teachers away from the profession, as well as giving delinquents "new ideas about how far they can go."

Desperate M-G-M executives took issue with the claim that the film was a misrepresentation by calling attention to a series of recent newspaper articles. From **New York**: "Brutal Murder by Three Youths Baffles Everyone Involved." **Los Angeles**: "Youth Beats Up Teacher in Class," a beating that left the teacher with fractures of the nose and cheekbone, and all because she reprimanded her 16-year old student for some minor infraction. **Washington, D. C.**—14-year old arrested on 14 counts of robbing his fellow junior high students. **San Francisco**:—a battle between two gangs resulted in two dead, three wounded and one boy sent to prison for life. The day prior to the opening of **Blackboard Jungle** in New York, a high school teacher was stabbed to death by a student in the Bronx.

Marlon Brando, Hollywood's number one bad boy, once remarked, "An actor's a guy who, if you ain't talking about him, ain't listening."

"Take it from a teacher whose experience has been fairly fortunate," wrote high school teacher Rose Zeitlin, "the film may be sensational, but it is hardly possible to exaggerate the conditions in the public high schools of this and presumably other cities across the country." Another champion of the film was Hazel Flynn, whose column appeared in *Daily News Life*. She said it was high time that everyone "woke up" to what was really going on among a certain slice of the nation's youth.

Los Angeles Times critic Phillip Scheuer wrote a scathing review of the movie, suggesting that it might damage our cause in foreign countries, "particularly if it ever fell into Communist hands." Directly beneath Scheuer's review was a small, four-liner about young actors auditioning for director Nicholas Ray's new movie, **Rebel Without a Cause**.

Released seven months after **Blackboard Jungle**, **Rebel Without a Cause** was an even bigger sensation. The delinquents in Ray's film weren't inner city slum kids, they were the kids from respectable middle-class families. The day the film finished, its star, James Dean, walked off of the set, got into his car and headed for a weekend race at Salinas. By 6:00 that evening he was dead, his neck broken in an auto accident outside Paso Robles, California. "What better way to die?" Dean once said about sports-car racing. "It's fast and clean and you go out in a blaze of glory." When Jack Warner heard the news he heaved a sigh and said, "Nobody will come to see a corpse."

Less than a month after the accident, **Rebel** went into release, and in a remarkable turn of events, predated only by the hysterical public reaction to the death of Rudolph Valentino, the movie went through the roof and Dean was hailed as a major star. With only three feature films to his credit, he became an iconic figure, the poster child of alienated youth. In the movie, as Jim Stark, Dean had to jump out of a car to survive. To achieve immortality, Dean had to remain behind the wheel. He never had the chance to disappoint his fans the way Marlon Brando did. "He died at just the right time," said one of the coolest actors of them all, Humphrey Bogart. "If he had lived, he'd never have been able to live up to his publicity."

Though the motorcycle hoodlums in Stanley Kramer's **The Wild One** (1954) were well past teen-age, the countless imitations of Marlon Brando's character in the J.D. films that followed, makes it an impossible film to ignore. Vic Morrow was criticized for aping Brando in his performance as Artie West in **Blackboard Jungle**, but as many real-life delinquents were doing the same, Morrow was perfectly justified. Brando's Johnny was one of the screen's first antiheroes, at times reminiscent of the lonely cowboys who drifted from town to town, righting some wrong before they rode on, but unlike those knights without armor, Johnny is contemptuous of, or indifferent to just about everything. Early in the film, as he keeps time to a jazz record playing on the jukebox, a young lady checks out the "Black Rebels" insignia on the back of his black leather jacket and jokingly asks Johnny what he's rebelling against. "What have you got?" It's the film's most famous line and pretty much reflected the sentiment of a good portion of the nation's young.

Kramer's intention had been to show the intolerance of Middle America to anyone who varied from the public norm, a concept too radical for the censors. Emphasis was shifted to the violence of the gang, and attempts to justify their actions were blunted. The hypocrisy of the businessmen who made money off of the bikers was downplayed. Even in this diluted form, the film was hardly designed to endear itself to a family audience. Harry Cohn, the head of Columbia Pictures, hated it and only released it because of Kramer's and Brando's track records. Many national magazines and newspapers panned the picture on moral grounds, seldom attempting an objective, critical evaluation. Some of the exhibitors refused to play the picture, especially after reports like this one from Frank Hughes, the manager of the Avenue Theatre in San Francisco, California. "When 200 to 300 teenagers starting 'digging that crazy jive' you have a problem. This picture is good boxoffice but it proves to the teenagers that they can do anything and get no more than a talking to. In my opinion, it should not be shown to this class of people."

The Wild One was banned in the United Kingdom for 14 years, but for all of the critical hits it took, it couldn't be accused of starting a rash of motorcycle movies. It would take Roger Corman's **The Wild Angels** (1966) to do that.

The flood of youth-oriented movies that followed the release of **Rebel Without a Cause** gave the nervous nellies even more cause to fluster and bluster. James H. Nicholson's newly formed American International Pictures began cranking out teenpics at an alarming rate. The company floundered in its first year, making westerns. Once he realized where the money was, Nicholson took on a partner, Samuel Z. Arkoff, and these two men were easily responsible for half of the teenpics in release, and became the darlings of the exhibitors who were looking at a lot of empty seats before they came along. AIP gave the exhibitors a double feature package for a fraction of the price of a single feature from the majors. They were especially popular with the owners of the outdoor theatres who often had trouble booking first-run pictures.

"At AIP, the advertising always came first," said Albert Kallis who designed his posters based on a concept that he and Nicholson would discuss. At first, Kallis watched the movies for inspiration but discovered they killed his creativity. (One exhibitor told him he wished he could put sprocket holes in his posters.) Kallis said Nicholson was a master at his game.

"Jim Nicholson was a slender man, and Sam Arkoff, who was sort of the archetypical producer, was kind of heavyset," said writer Robert Towne. "Both men were given to wearing suits. And Arkoff was always smoking a horrible cigar. It wasn't even a good cigar. And he was given to saying things like 'artsy-fartsy.' That's how he would dismiss movies that had any intelligence."

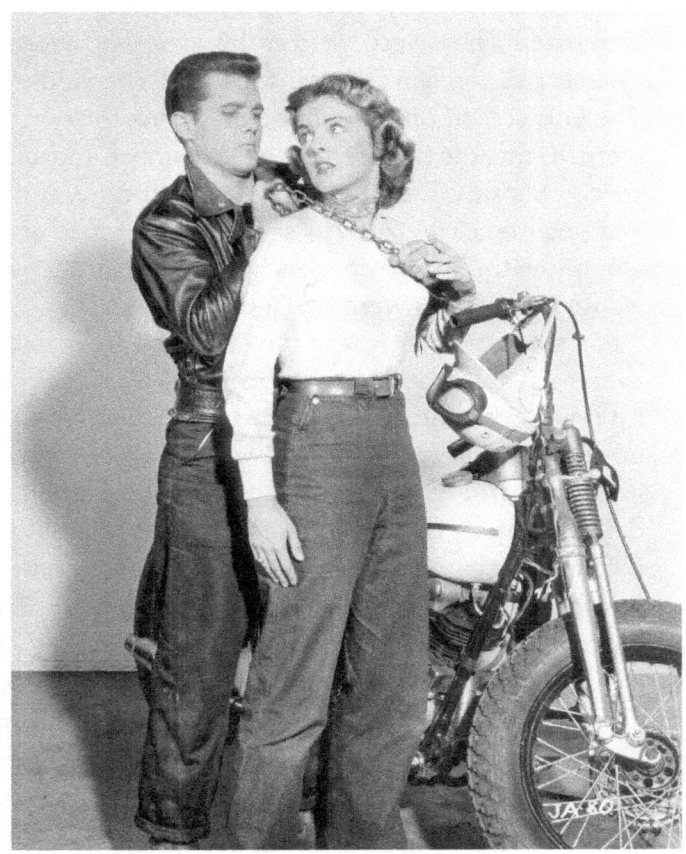

John Ashley continued to play teenage characters well into the mid-sixties. Here he is with Anne Neyland. She pronounced it "Knee-lan" but Hollywood wanted "Nay-lan."

"Jim Nicholson and Sam Arkoff went on the assumption that on their budgets, they could not make good pictures," said writer Charles B. Griffith. "They made saturation product that was in and out in five days. Skim it off the top and run, over and over again."

"Those of you who have hesitated to play these AIP pictures had better get yourselves psyhoed—they pick the themes that maybe we don't like, and they may be a bit sensational, but they are sure-fire with the teenagers, and many older as well," declared Moz Burles, the owner of the Canyon Theatre in Washington.

"I can still remember going to sneak previews of those pictures and when the audience saw that damn AIP logo, they groaned," said John Ashley, the star of **Dragstrip Girl** (1957) and **Motorcycle Gang** (1958). "I personally felt that the kids never took those pictures seriously. I think they went to those pictures and laughed at them. They didn't really get that involved because the pictures were not well-made. They were written by men who were in their late thirties or forties. The stories were pretty standard stuff. The wildness in those days was pretty mild. The kids got off on them but didn't think they were any better than I thought they were. To me, the picture that had the most impact was **Rebel Without a Cause**, strictly because Dean was so charismatic. I was no kid at the time but I went out and got me a red jacket. I saw his pictures over and over again because I could identify with Dean. Between him and Brando, if you couldn't figure out who you wanted to be, you were really out to lunch."

For the most part, these movies were an excuse to pile into a car and spend an evening at some drive-in theatre, enjoying a vicarious thumb-of-the-nose at authority. If you were lucky, you left your pals behind and brought a date. It was not for nothing that drive-in theatres were often referred to as passion pits.

When you see the same faces time and again in these dime store movies, it's difficult not to think of these actors as your little friends. John Ashley and Dick Bakalyan were front runners. Others who come to mind are Corey Allen, Edd Byrnes, William Campbell, Gloria Castillo, Gary Clark, Mark Damon, Abby Dalton, Norma Eberhardt, Frank Gorshin, June Kenney, Yvonne Lime, Scott Marlowe, Dick Miller, Kenny Miller, Barbara Morris, Mary Murphy, Fay Spain, Gloria Talbott, Steve Terrell and Mamie Van Doren. Curiously, Ann Doran was is more of these movies than anyone.

Until AIP came along, Columbia was the only studio regularly making teenpics, mostly due to the efforts of producer Sam Katzman, whose low-budget unit kept Columbia's doors open. He made pictures for a price and was proud of it. "I don't get ulcers with the type of picture I make," he would often boast.

Allied Artists, the smallest of the major studios, entered the game with their own combo programs, some of them produced by AIP's most dependable filmmakers, Roger Corman and his brother Gene. These low budget quickies were mixed with a few A-level features such as Reginald Rose's **Crime in the Streets** (1956) and **Dino**.

Producer Albert Zugsmith with the beguiling Tuesday Weld. Said Zugsmith: "What the kids of today want to see is a dramatic solution to their own problems, enacted by players of an age in which they can relate."

Albert Zugsmith was another major player with **High School Confidential** (1958), **The Beat Generation** and **Girls Town** (both 1959). "Quite a few of our Beverly Hills and Bel-Air geniuses live in too rarified an atmosphere. They don't mix with the mob," said Zugsmith. "They continue to think it is enough to put two old-time stars together." Zugsmith liked to prowl theatres to see who was in the seats. "Eighty percent are teenagers. They don't dig these old-time stars." The producer said he felt an *obligation* to give the public what it wanted to see.

Sam Katzman's **Rock Around the Clock** (1956) was the first rock and roll musical, a fictionalized account of singer Bill Haley's rise to stardom. The song, "Rock Around the Clock," written by Max C. Freedman (a postal employee) and Jimmy De Knight (a pseudonym for Jim Myers, the song's publisher), had been recorded a few years earlier by Sunny Dae with little success. Haley's version, recorded two years later, fared no better until it was used as the main title for **Blackboard Jungle**. By July it was the best-selling record in the nation and became the national anthem for the nation's young. The movie surprised everyone, including Katzman, when it became one of the studio's biggest money-makers. An exhibitor in Michigan played the picture so many times he thought the studio should let him keep the print and save the shipping costs. It was banned in some parts of England after a riot broke out at one London theatre. The kids were blocking traffic and throwing beer bottles. The police were forced to turn a hose on them. In the areas where the picture wasn't banned, nervous exhibitors kept the volume low, hoping to curb the excitement. Queen Elizabeth wanted to know what all of the fuss what about

Bill Haley, an unlikely rock 'n' roller.

and cancelled a screening of **The Caine Mutiny** (1954) and asked for Katzman's movie instead.

In Oslo, a group of overzealous Norwegians swarmed through the downtown section of the city after seeing the movie, demanding "More rock! More rock!" The military arrived and insisted on "More order! More order!" The manager of the theatre could shed no light as to the cause of the disruption, except to say that he didn't think the picture was to blame.

I saw **Loving You** (1957) the week it opened in Los Angeles at a Saturday matinee. As Elvis sang "Mean Woman Blues," we all started clapping our hands to the beat. I guess we were having too much fun because the lights came on, and they shut the movie off. An ominous voice over the P.A. system warned that the theatre would be cleared if there were any further demonstrations. I couldn't understand it then, but I believe they were afraid that we were going to tear the place apart. I hadn't heard about all of the trouble attributed to the music. I didn't know about the sailor who was repeatedly stabbed by a gang of punks just outside of the arena in Boston where disc jockey Alan Freed was having one of his rock and roll shows. In San Jose, at a Fats Domino concert, some bozo threw a beer bottle and what followed was described by the city's police chief as "the wildest riot in the history of our city." The incident nearly caused a ban on rock shows in California.

Award-winning composer Dimitri Tiomkin thought rock music was proof that the country was reverting to "savagery," evidenced by the number of rock 'n' roll concerts that had erupted in violence. "[The teenagers] will tell you they get a *charge* out of rock 'n' roll," said Tiomkin. "So do the kids who smoke marijuana and shoot H'."

In its May 12 edition, *The Evening Bulletin* (a Philadelphia newspaper) reported that two young boys stole an automobile from a dealership and seriously injured a woman after seeing **Motorcycle Gang** and **Sorority Girl**. "Stole Car After Seeing Wild Film" read the bold-faced headline on *The Inquirer*. A week later the *Upper Darby Times*, a suburban weekly, put the finger on the sloppy reporting of its big-city brothers when it revealed that the boys had stolen the key to the car a week *before* they saw the movie.

"We're getting tired of being blamed by pulpit, politician and paper for everything bad in the world," complained *Boxoffice* magazine. Hoping to bring a little sanity to the conversation, Dorothy Shensa Miller had this to say: "First of all, generally speaking, no manager blames the type of picture chosen for the delinquent behavior of a juvenile. It's true of course, that certain films excite and arouse the viewers, and may contribute to some extent to the sort of behavior which might be the result of 'high emotions'...However, assuming that such is the case, the particular type of juvenile audience which starts trouble because he is affected by what he has seen on the screen would be just as likely to react to any of hundreds of other circumstances—via subtle ad suggestions, television, books, etc."

Still, there were plenty of exhibitors who were afraid to book **Rock Around the Clock**. They wanted some assurance that their theatres would survive it. To that end, the following set of rules were enforced in many theatres across the country. (The manager in **The Young Stranger** no doubt had a hand in the creation of this list.)

1. Juvenile theatregoers must be made to recognize authority—whether in the garb of a policeman or the manager himself. No disturbance should be overlooked. For the slightest suggestion of a misdemeanor, the guilty party should be asked to leave and if necessary, forced to do. In this way, the theatre will get a reputation for being "strict," and young people, inclined to be troublemakers, will not attempt this more than once.
2. A set standard for dress should be adhered to. If boys are made to wear jackets to be admitted—even if they remove them once they are seated—and if admittance is denied to dungaree-wearing girls or boys—the general "tone" of the house will be uplifted.
3. A set of rules stating company policy as to dress, roaming around, disturbing others, etc. (such as "no smoking" signs), should be prominently displayed in the rest rooms and at various places in the theatre—and should be strictly adhered to.

4. No manager should be afraid to deny admittance to anyone if they seem to be undesirable—whether their appearance is so unkempt as to suggest a reflection of their behavior, or whether they are boisterous, or if they come as a gang—using the term restrictively to connote the meaning of organized delinquents. Law enforcement agencies will, if called upon, back up any manager denying anyone admission.
5. Generally, it is agreed that girls are by far the worst offenders and usually are at the root of most of the trouble. To offset this, the manager and ushers should constantly patrol the aisles and see that proper behavior is kept.
6. Because they are more familiar with their own audience and what might be good or bad boxoffice—not only as far as receipts are concerned—managers feel that they should have more of a "voice" in selection of features to be exhibited.

Said Texas exhibitor C.J. Otts about Katzman's film, "We played [it] once, then played it twice (only a month apart) and likely will play it once again if the youngsters keep pleading! Frankly, the teenagers were so enthusiastic that they got the personnel in the snack bar sort of swaying and rocking, too." From Missouri, Robert King reported: "Every teenager in town will be on hand to see this one when you play it. A well-made rock show that will rock the aisles of your theatre and make you feel good when the show is over." "Nothing complicated about it," explained Robert Tuttle, the owner of the Sky Drive-In in Michigan. "The teenagers were there to see it in spite of the fact that the local indoor house played it twice before we got it." Most encouraging of all was Bob Walker's take on Katzman's show. "It's a cute little programmer, and I guess I'm awfully lowbrow, cause I always loved jazz and boogie, and even this rockin' sets these old feet a-dancin'."

When Frank Sinatra called rock and roll "the most brutal, ugly, vicious form of expression" he'd ever heard, he should have added, "Especially if I try to sing it." Ol' blue eyes couldn't rock and roll to save his life. He wouldn't have been out of place on *Your Hit Parade*. And anyone over 30 remembered the afternoon in 1944, affectionately known as The Columbus Day Riot, when 30,000 of his fans (mostly female) descended upon the Paramount Theatre in New York where Sinatra was performing. The police had to be called in to restore order.

Proving that nothing ever really changes, a prominent New York psychiatrist once warned the readers of *The New York Times* about the "dangerously hypnotic influence of swing." An upstate New York preacher chastised the music for its "lawlessness, lasciviousness, and savage animalism." When "The King of Swing" was asked what he thought about rock and roll, Benny Goodman replied, "I guess it's OK man. At least it has a beat."

Estes Kefauver was probably too exhausted to take on another assignment, and so the job of ridding the world of this Godawful rock and roll music became the responsibility of Senator Owen Harris. His senate subcommittee had recently made headlines, exposing the wide-spread cheating on television's most popular quiz shows. NBC's *Twenty-One* had 25 million viewers rooting for Columbia University English professor Charles Van Doren for 15 weeks as he answered impossibly difficult questions. He was quite the celebrity until one of his opponents blew the whistle and said the show was rigged. "It was a terrible thing to do to the American people," said President Dwight Eisenhower. Van Doren told the committee he didn't think it was a big deal. It was entertainment, like wrestling.

The American Society of Composers (ASCAP) convinced Senator Harris to continue his winning streak by going after the disc jockeys who took bribes to play records, a standard practice in

> *Disc jockey Alan Freed, the most famous rock and roll deejay of them all, was unemployable after The Payola Scandal. "You can stop me," he said, "but you'll never stop rock and roll."*

the music business, but in this instance, Harris would only be going after the DJs who played rock and roll records. In all likelihood, besides the disc jockeys, the only people his investigation would inflame would be the kids. Eddie Cochran's song, "Summertime Blues," told us what we could expect should we decide to protest. *I'd like to help you, son, but you're too young to vote.*

So what was ASCAP's big interest in this? They'd made their money with sheet music, piano rolls and recordings. When radio came into its own, stations battled with ASCAP over royalty payments, and some stations refused to play anything registered with ASCAP. The Broadcast Music Incorporated (BMI) was formed to pick up the slack. They ended up with most of the rock songs because ASCAP didn't want to soil its hands with black and hillbilly music. When rock and roll turned the music business upside down, ASCAP found itself on the outside looking in. So they convinced Senator Harris to gun down the competition—legally. With zest and vigor, Harris's subcommittee went after the disc jockeys the way Senator McCarthy had chased the communists.

Dick Clark, the clean-cut host of *American Bandstand*, one of the most popular shows on television, naturally came before the committee, but Clark was a savvy businessman. He held copyrights to more than 160 songs and owned shares in more than 30 corporations, many of them in record and music publishing. He said his investments were for tax purposes, but if the government didn't think it was right, then neither did he. Clark got rid of everything but his interests in "American Bandstand." The committee left Clark alone and went after a much better target, the not so clean-cut, alcoholic Alan Freed, who looked a lot like a con man. In 1953 he had a radio program called "Rock 'N' Roll Party," the place to go for rhythm and blues. One writer called Freed the "high lama of rock 'n roll." Freed staunchly stuck to the original versions of the songs, all the while perpetuating the myth that he was just in it for the music. In truth, Freed would often insist on a writing credit on the songs he played, insuring himself a nice royalty. The subcommittee ate him up, spit him out, and left him broke and unemployable. Not wanting to follow his example, frightened disc jockeys refused to play the music, resulting in an overhaul of the music industry. Rock was out, replaced by pop music and squeaky clean, non-threatening artists. Bobby Rydell. Fabian. Frankie Avalon. In 1959, the top-selling song in the nation was "Mack the Knife" by Bobby Darin, a song that could have just as easily been a hit for Frank Sinatra or Dean Martin. Nevertheless, the kids could count on the movies to keep the spirit of rebellion alive.

Teenage Thunder takes a closer look at these movies that were made for us, movies that were frowned upon, ridiculed and held in contempt. The movies that your parents didn't want you to see. For those of us who weren't yet teenagers at the time, most of the movies dealing with juvenile delinquency were difficult to see. They mostly played the outdoor theatres and never played the kiddie matinees. Even if they had, most of my friends wouldn't have been allowed to see them. They were even worse than the science fiction pictures which were bottom of the barrel.

Young people writing about these films today often make fun of such and such a film because the so-called "teenagers" were usually around 24-years old. (One of the "teenagers" in **Earth vs. the Spider** looks like he's pushin' forty.) But you can't pick on one film without picking on them all. It was a conceit that we lived with and gave it no more thought than we did when white actors played ethnic characters. It was just the way things were done back then, like it or not. However, it posed a problem for me when it came to Andrew Stone's **The Night Holds Terror** (1955), always on the list of juvenile delinquency movies. The three young convicts in Stone's film have busted out of prison, not a juvenile facility, and with no reference to their ages (unless I missed it), they didn't look or act like teenagers to me, so you won't find it here. Likewise, **Problem Girls** (1953), where the teenagers are nothing more than background noise, though I would be remiss if I didn't mention that Norma Eberhardt, Mara Corday, Beverly Garland, Joyce Jameson, and Tandra Quinn are in the cast. It was essentially a crime film along the lines of **My**

Name is Julia Ross (1945). ***Touch of Evil*** (1958) isn't here either, though juvenile delinquents play a part in the story, it isn't about juvenile delinquency, it's about the criminal behavior of a corrupt cop, and it certainly wasn't aimed at a teenage audience. ***Running Wild*** (1956) is included because it was marketed like a J.D. movie, the delinquents do play a part in the story, and it had Mamie van Doren in it, though not nearly enough. ***Rockabilly Baby*** (1957) and ***Juke Box Rhythm*** (1959) are also included with great reluctance.

The target audience for most of the science fiction and horror movies made during this period were young people, but the only titles included here are the ones where the teenagers are front and center in the action. I had to draw the line some place or I would have had to list all of the westerns that were staples at children's matinees. There are also several American International films that don't rate an entry. ***Naked Paradise***, ***White Huntress*** (both 1957), and ***Suicide Battalion*** (1958) to name just a few, aren't teenpics and shouldn't be included just because they sport the AIP logo. Some of the movies about teenage drug addiction that *are* included maybe shouldn't have been, as the early ones were really aimed at an adult market. I won't bore you any further with my rationalizations and justifications since everyone knows that most of these matters are arbitrary and might just as well be settled by the toss of a coin. So, what are you waiting for? Let's get on with it.

Joan Lucille Olander aka Mamie Van Doren. "I was never a Monroe wannabe. I was always comfortable in my own skin."

THE MOVIES

An asterisk (*) in front of a title indicates that I have not seen the film, which absolves me from having to offer an opinion about its quality. Abbreviations used are as follows: M (music), W (writer), P (producer), D (director). The films have not been divided into categories as that can get pretty tricky when one film mixes elements from more than one genre. Listing them in the order of release would have provided the reader with a clearer picture of how these films evolved, but I chose to list them alphabetically because it makes it easier to find the title that you're looking for. This isn't the kind of a book read from start to finish. It's a bathroom book, like an expanded edition of *Leonard Maltin's Movie Guide*. Besides, listing the films alphabetically puts **April Love** right up front, which, I know, will make some of you groan, which was reason enough for me.

APRIL LOVE (February, 1958) 20th Century-Fox
M Alfred Newman, W Winston Miller, George Agnew Chamberlain, P David Weisbart, D Henry Levin.

"Thin and meandering it may be, but the flavor of country hay has it all over the dark aroma of some recent trashy switch-blade alley dramas," said *New York Times* critic Bosley Crowther. His remark suggests that he liked this color and CinemaScope remake of **Home in Indiana** (1944) simply because it *wasn't* about juvenile delinquents.

It would have been naive of me to expect much in the way of delinquent behavior from Pat Boone, but I confess that when I saw this picture back in the day, I assumed that he would at least have a chip on his shoulder, having been busted for joyriding by the Chicago police, then forced to live on his aunt's farm in Kentucky as part of his probation. And yet, he doesn't seem to be the least bit upset about it. He quickly adapts to his new environment and discovers that he loves horse racing. Wondering if he will choose Dolores Michaels over her sister, the incomparable Shirley Jones, is the only note of conflict for most of the movie.

This is a musical and Pat and Shirley sing "The Bentonville Fair," and "Do It Yourself." Solo, Pat sings "Clover in the Meadow," "Give Me a Gentle Girl," and the only memorable song, "April Love," written by Sammy Fain and Paul Francis Webster, a number one hit for the singer.

In a movie like this, one naturally expects the leading man to kiss the leading lady at some point, and it's hard to imagine how anyone could have written a romantic musical without at least including a kiss or two, or why nobody noticed, but that seems to be the case here, because at the end of a sequence with Pat and Shirley on a Ferris wheel, after they'd finished singing their song, director Henry Levin told Boone that the sequence should end with a kiss. It just seemed like the natural thing to do and Boone agreed. "But I'll have to check with my wife first," he told the director. It was something that the Boones had never discussed, and Pat wanted to be sure that his wife was okay with it. He discovered that she'd known all along, from the moment he signed his contract with Fox that he'd be obliged to make love to his leading ladies. "Just don't enjoy it too much," she cautioned.

"It was such a brouhaha that an actor refused to kiss his leading lady that, like today I'm still asked about that incident," Boone remarked. And in spite of the fact that Boone has kissed at least a half a dozen women in his films, to this day many sources report that he refused to kiss his leading ladies for religious reasons.

Parents magazine said, "Pat Boone and Shirley Jones shine delightfully in this warm-hearted story." (When *Parents* liked something, it was usually a bad sign.) "Let's have more like it," demanded *The Shreveport Journal*. Exhibitor B. Berglund urged his fellow exhibitors to play "one of the nicest family pictures ever put out."

It won't hurt one little bit if you like the two leads. They make a cute couple. But weak tea is weak tea, no matter who serves it.

Springtime! County Fair Time! First-Kiss Time! Find a better movie time!

*AS YOUNG AS WE ARE

(September, 1958) Paramount
W Meyer Dolinsky, P William Alland, D Bernard Girard

Teacher and Her Student—Too Close Too Often!

Sounds good to me, depending on which teacher we're talking about. At the

The Great White Hope—Pat Boone.

risk of sounding salacious and possibly perverse, I would have welcomed, and *badly* needed some additional instruction regarding matters between the sheets, from someone with a little experience under her skirt. The teacher in this particular instance is Kim Hutchins (Pippa Scott), fresh out of college, and eager to teach. She begs someone she knows on the State Board of Education to find her a job. She and her buddy (Majel Barrett) are sent to a high school in a small desert community. (This is not the way things are done, but we'll let it slide.) Just outside of town, they encounter a couple of jerks who get fresh. Hank Moore (Robert Hartland) comes to the rescue. It is lust at first sight between Hank and Kim. She is horrified to discover, upon walking into her classroom, that Hank is one of her students. She knows she should nip the thing in the bud, but her emotions are overriding her good sense. Two students see them kissing and the word spreads like butter on hotcakes. Everyone is outraged. Hank doesn't care. He won't give her up and threatens to kill them both if she should try to leave him. Hank has issues.

This was shot back to back with **The Party Crashers**, both pictures directed by Bernard Gerard for producer William Alland. Once a line producer at Universal, Alland cut a deal with Paramount to make two, modestly budgeted genre packages. Gerard's ability to hop from one television assignment to the next (practically nonstop), made him an ideal choice for Alland. Anyone who worked in television had to be fast on their feet, as most programs were shot in three days.

Motion Picture Herald thought the screenplay added "touches of honesty and sincerity" to the love scenes. It was lost on exhibitor W. G. Hall who remarked, "Just as my 16-year old son said, it didn't show me much."

"No one goes for that poetry stuff around here."

THE BAD SEED (September, 1956) Warner Bros.
M Alex North, W John Lee Mahin, P-D Mervyn LeRoy.

Even by the standards of the time, the performances in this film are so overwrought, "the film becomes so fantastically abnormal that it grows ridiculous and grotesque," as the *New York Times* put it. It can stand proudly alongside such camp classics as **The Oscar** (1966), **Valley of the Dolls** (1967) and **Mommy Dearest** (1981).

The studio was against Mervyn LeRoy's decision to cast the film with the actors from the play, and with good reason it seems. Some of them—Nancy Kelly and Eileen Heckart in particular—seem to be giving their stage performances, way too broad for the big screen, award-winning or not.

Like the character in the story, Patty McCormack was 8-years old when she played the sociopathic Rhoda Penmark on stage, a production that ran 334 performances. Said McCormack, "If I did something one night and the audience responded favorably, I would keep it in the next performance, provided the director approved.

So the character evolved and when it came time to film the movie, I was very comfortable with the character and my role."

Rhoda is supposed to be so charming that nobody but her mother suspects that she may be a serial-killer, like her grandmother. But she's such an obvious phony one can only conclude that the rest of the characters have suffered some sort of collective brain-damage. However, if one has no problem adjusting one's sights, and view the film as a comedy instead of a drama, McCormack's performance is spot on. Her best scenes are with Henry Jones, the sadistic handyman who seems to, but *doesn't* know that Rhoda arranged the "accidental" death of one of her classmates. He tells her about the little pink electric chairs that they have for little girls like her. He's surprised when Rhoda locks him in the barn and sets fire to it. The fool didn't know who he was dealing with.

Patty McCormack, the youngest delinquent of them all, and the youngest actress to receive a star on Hollywood's Walk of Fame.

In the novel by William March and the play by Maxwell Anderson, once Rhoda's mother is on to her, she slips her dear daughter an overdose of sleeping pills, then shoots herself in the head. Rhoda survives, with no indication that she will change her evil ways.

There was nothing about Maxwell Anderson's play that pleased censor Geoffrey Shurlock, so even though Billy Wilder had been the only one to ever express an interest in turning it into a movie, Shurlock engaged in a preemptive strike, sending letters to all of the studios, warning that the story was unacceptable. The changes that LeRoy made to get Shurlock's approval insured the film's place in the comedy hall of fame. The mother survives her suicide attempt and God kills Rhoda with a lightning bolt. Even divine intervention wasn't enough. In a "cute" curtain call, Nancy Kelly gives Patty McCormack a good old-fashioned spanking.

Nominated by the Academy for her performance, McCormack continued to be active in television, with her own short-lived series, *Peck's Bad Girl* (1959). She wanted to be a rock singer (who doesn't?) but that didn't work out. Fortunately, for those of us who think she's wonderful, she can be found in **The Explosive Generation** (1961), **Jacktown** (1962), **Born Wild**, **The Mini-Skirt Mob**, **The Young Runaways**, **The Young Animals** and **Maryjane** (all 1968).

Exhibitor Jim Fraser played **The Bad Seed** for three days of solid attendance. He called the picture "powerful entertainment." Said Jerry B. Walden, "One can say nothing but great things about this picture."

"What will you give me for a bag full of kisses?"

THE BEAT GENERATION aka THIS REBEL AGE (July, 1959) Metro-Goldwyn-Mayer

M Albert Glasser, W Richard Matheson, Louis Meltzer, P Albert Zugsmith, D Charles Haas

Contrived, unintentionally funny crime drama about a serial rapist known as "The Aspirin Kid," will leave viewers knowing exactly as much about the beatnik culture as they did before they watched the picture. Maybe less.

After leaving another victim, and his trademark bottle of aspirin behind, Ray Danton accepts a ride from Steve Cochran, the detective on his trail. Danton gets Cochran's address from the car registration, then makes Cochran's wife, played by Fay Spain, his next victim. She ends up pregnant, leading to an unusually frank and much needed discussion about unwanted pregnancies and abortion, however lurid and sensational it may be in the hands of producer Albert Zugsmith. He just couldn't help himself.

Fay Spain had auditioned for a part in an earlier Zugsmith film, and when he asked her if she could play a junkie, the actress happily replied, "Of course. I even smoked marijuana." She admitted to being pretty wild as a teenager. "I threw away two years of my life as a beachnik—just sitting on the beach in Hermosa, a few miles from Hollywood, drinking beer." Spain also appeared in Zugsmith's **The Private Lives of Adam and Eve** and later **The Great Space Adventure** (1963) with George Nader, shot in the Philippines. Zugsmith filed a $12 million dollar lawsuit against her and Nader, and nine or ten other people for slander. Apparently a few loose remarks found their way into the local newspaper. Zugsmith told reporters that he did *not* use "bad words" on the set, and he was *not* planning to leave the islands without paying his creditors. He also didn't like being called "an ugly American." Who does?

In a supporting but pivotal role is Mamie Van Doren, an absolute delight as the divorcée with a sharp tongue, used as bait by Cochran to catch Danton in the act. Mamie thought Cochran was one of the two sexiest men she'd ever met, the other being Steve McQueen. "They both possessed a kind of reckless energy that I found—er—arousing. They were also very difficult to get along with in their own ways, but one makes allowances for a good bonk."

The cast is loaded with Zugsmith regulars—Maggie Hayes, Jackie Coogan, Cathy Crosby, Ray Anthony, James Mitchum, Charles Chaplin, Jr., and Goo Goo Grabowski. Also along for the ride—Dick Contino, "Slapsie Maxie" Rosenbloom, Irish (*Sheena, Queen of the Jungle*) McCalla and Maila Nurmi, better known as Vampira, a TV horror hostess. Louis Armstrong does a number during the opening credits, and appearing without credit—Sid Melton, Paul Cavanaugh, William Schallert and Guy Stockwell.

"Out grossed a lot of 'A' pictures," Ken Christian told his fellow exhibitors. "Don't cater to this type of movie, but I like to eat." The critic for *The New York Times* said the movie was enough to make anyone "walk outside the theatre and butt his head against the wall." He thought it was "excruciating and tasteless," but never did say whether he liked it or not.

"I have been criticized for the frankness and violence of pictures like **The Beat Generation**," said Zugsmith, "but I don't have any trouble facing myself in the mirror when I shave."

"Go on. Kill me. You think I'm sorry about your wife? I'd do it again."

BERNARDINE (July, 1956) 20th Century-Fox

M Lionel Newman, W Mary Chase, Theodore Reeves, P Samuel G. Engel, D Henry Levin

Every time some clean-cut young crooner had a hit record, critics of Elvis Presley would predict this fresh talent would send Elvis into obscurity, as if salt and pepper couldn't exist in the same universe. Nobody gave these grouchy critics more hope than the wholesome, good looking Pat Boone. He had a string of hit records, his own network TV show, and was being groomed by 20th Century-Fox to be the studio's new romantic lead. But anyone who heard Pat sing "Rip It Up" or "Long Tall Sally," knew he wasn't even in the same ballpark with Elvis. He remains the source of ridicule to the baby boomers who thought of him as the anti-Elvis, but who was better suited to sing "Friendly Persuasion" than Pat Boone? Or "April Love" for that matter. He's got two good songs to sing in this film, "Bernardine" and "Love Letters in the Sand," written by the great Johnny Mercer. The latter was a last minute addition to the film, a song written strictly for the B-side of "Bernardine." "Love Letters" became the hit, a big one. Pat's okay in my book, and I liked him even better when he dressed up in leather for the cover of his 1977 album, *In a Metal Mood*. He took a lot of criticism from his fans for that, God bless him.

Buddy Adler originally bought Mary Chase's three-act play for contract player Robert Wagner. When the studio decided to turn it into a vehicle for Boone, Chase and Theodore Reeves tailored the character (played by John Kerr on stage) to suit Boone's smooth and easy manner. Neither the play nor the film have much in the way of a plot. It's more of a character study. Pat is sort of the leader of a group of upper crust teenagers who race speedboats and hang around their clubhouse, all of them longing for the mythical woman of their dreams—Bernardine. Terry Moore is the operator who makes a date with Dick Sargent when he calls, asking for Bernardine. He gets a crush on her and spends the rest of the movie whining about it. When she rejects him he joins the Army. If only he'd done it sooner. Also on board, Ronnie Burns, James Drury and Dean Jagger.

Bernardine may evoke some nostalgia in some, but the world on display in this film wasn't anything like the world I grew up in, and to this day I feel as detached from the characters as I did when I was eight years old. Other than capturing how truly miserable it can be to try to fit in when you're young, there isn't much to crow about.

Said the *New York Times,* "The original cutting edge of **Bernardine** is gone, but on the whole, you still couldn't find a nicer bunch of people." From Africa, exhibitor Dave Klein found the film "delightful," and had people "clamoring for seats at all performances." It gave Paul Rickets the best gross since his theater had become a hardtop, a "wonderful respite from the 'jump and wiggle' movies that has been the vogue too long." Audrey Thompson noted, "[It] did only half the business that **Loving You** did."

"*He has that type of shallow mind that's great for exams.*"

THE BIG BEAT (February, 1958) Universal-International
M Henry Mancini, *W* William P Harmon, *P-D* Will Cowan

In the first part of the decade, Universal kept its doors open with westerns, costume pictures, science fiction thrillers and dumbbell comedies aimed at the less sophisticated, rural audiences, so they would have been the least likely studio to live up to a title like **The Big Beat**. It's a mixed bag of music the studio offers up, a little something for everyone so to speak. Like most musicals, the plot is thin, merely something to hang the songs on. In this show, William Reynolds thinks his father is making a mistake producing the same kind of middle of the road records he always has. Reynolds wants to branch out and include calypso, rhythm and blues and rock 'n roll records. He starts his own company but quickly gets in over his head and it's up to singer Gogi Grant (who is a character in the film) to bail him out, and the absolutely stunning Andra Martin helps keep him on the straight and narrow.

Fats Domino was the heavy hitter in this line-up, one of the few rhythm and blues artists who didn't offend the oldsters, which may account for his presence in so many of these films. When a reporter asked him if he thought rock and roll music incited violence, Fats replied, "Music makes people happy. I know it makes me happy." He sings the title song and one of his biggest hits, "I'm Walking." The Del Vikings, reportedly the first integrated group, sing "Can't Wait," and The Diamonds, a Canadian group that made a career covering songs by black groups, sing their biggest hit, "Little Darlin'," originally recorded by The Gladiolas. The rest of the line-up is impressive—The Four Aces ("Take My Heart"), Gogi Grant ("Call Me," "Lazy Love," "You've Never Been in Love"), The Mills Brothers ("You're Being Followed"), The George Shearing Quintet ("As I Love You"), Jeri Southern ("I Waited So Long")—but not a single hit song from the bunch, and despite the claim that this movie is jammed with rock and roll music, there's very little of it.

Boxoffice called it a "lively, entertaining, tune-filled musical" while *Variety* felt it was important to stress that it was "not one of those rackety rock and roll offerings that drum mother and dad out of the theatre." Said exhibitor Harold Bell, "As musicals go it is fair, but was very disappointing to the younger set, as they were expecting rock 'n roll and did not get it."

The Big Beat *keeps you yawning in your seat.*

BLACKBOARD JUNGLE (March, 1955) Metro-Goldwyn-Mayer
M Charles Wolcott, *P* Pandro S. Berman, *W-D* Richard Brooks

Riveting, tense and thoroughly satisfying drama that the critic for *The New York Times* said was "as hard and penetrating as a nail." It was based on a novel by Salvatore Albert Lombino, writing as Evan Hunter, his legally adopted name. The prolific writer used at least four or five pseudonyms, but he's probably best-known as Ed McBain, the author of four decades of 87th Precinct novels. For *Blackboard Jungle*, Hunter was drawing on his own brief experience as a teacher in the unsavory south Bronx section of New York City. "I thought I was going to give these kids who want to be motor mechanics Shakespeare, and they were going to appreciate it, and they weren't buying it," said Hunter. "I went home in tears night after night."

Glenn Ford plays Richard Dadier (the kids call him Daddy-O), the idealistic teacher in Hunter's novel. He's taken the only teaching position open to him at a large vocational training school. He's heard about the school's discipline problem

Glenn Ford is wondering if he should start packing heat in this scene from Blackboard Jungle.

and quickly learns that he's more of a warden than a teacher. His classroom is full of potential hoodlums—ignorant, indifferent, disruptive and hostile. His fellow teachers have become cynical, bitter and ineffectual. "This is the garbage can of the educational system," one teacher tells him. "Our job is to sit on the lid of the garbage can and see that none of the filth overflows into the streets." "They can't all be bad kids," Dadier insists. "Why not?" the teacher replies.

On his first day, as he starts to write his name on the blackboard, a baseball zings past his head, taking a chunk of the board with it. Hefting the ball, Dadier wins a minor victory by not losing his cool. "Whoever threw this ball, you'll never pitch for the Yanks, boy." He's on his way home when he passes by the library and sees one of teachers (Margaret Hayes) being molested by one of the students (Scott Marlowe). The student becomes desperate when Dadier intervenes, and tries to leap through a closed window. He's badly cut up and the students think Dadier beat him. This creates a thicker wall (if such a thing is possible) between he and his students.

In the book, it takes Dadier almost a full page to conclude that the attack by the student wasn't somehow provoked by the teacher. It unintentionally speaks volumes about a subject that the book isn't even about. It's a frightening little page, and clearly demonstrates how men were able to successfully shift the responsibility for their bad behavior to their victims.

"Don't be a hero and never turn your back to the class," fellow teacher Jim Murdock (Louis Calhern) advises him. After he's mugged by some of his students,

Glenn Ford is ready to call it quits but Anne Francis won't let him.

Dadier takes his advice more seriously. Temptation calls when he's offered a job at a school where the students are well-mannered and eager to learn. But he knows the real test of his ability waits for him back at Mr. Warneke's horror high.

Every class has a leader, and Dadier has two. Artie West (Vic Morrow), a bigoted bully, and sensitive and intelligent Gregory Miller (Sidney Poitier). Dadier asks for Miller's help in steering the class in the right direction. West sees his power slipping away and makes anonymous calls and sends anonymous notes to Dadier's wife, Anne (Anne Francis), accusing him of having an affair with the teacher he rescued. Anne's fears and doubts cause her to lose their baby, which is more than Dadier can take.

As must happen to all idealistic characters at some point, Dadier is ready to give up, but Anne won't hear of it. "I was like one of the bad kids in your class," she tells him. "Somebody told me a lie and I believed it. One's as bad as the other." She sends him back into the classroom to finish the job he started.

In the hope of massaging ruffled feathers, the following disclaimer was added to the front of the picture: "We, in the United States, are fortunate to have a school system that is a tribute to our communities and to our faith in American youth. Today we are concerned with juvenile delinquency—its causes and its effects. We are especially concerned when this delinquency boils over into our schools. The scenes and incidents depicted here are fictional. However, we believe that public awareness is a first step toward a remedy for any problem. It is in this spirit and with this faith that **Blackboard Jungle** was produced."

Some of the city fathers insisted on personalized tags on the end of the film, such as this one:

> To our patrons: the school and situations you have just seen are not to be found in this area! We should all be proud of the facilities provided for our youth by the public schools of New Brunswick and the Middlesex County vocation and technical high school. We suggest a visit to any of the fine schools in our city and county. You will be cordially welcome.

Afraid of the bad influence the film might have, as well as concerns over the type of audience it might attract, some of the exhibitors refused to book it.

"I was expecting a madcap, rough and tumble time as [the teenagers] aped the characters in the picture. But I had the quietest audience of the year," reported Ralph Raspa. Bob Walker had the second highest gross of the year, on a picture that he would have bet would die a slow death. It did very well in Kansas, too, according to exhibitor Paul Ricketts. "Golly, what a picture!" he exclaimed. "Brought in some extra business and comments were good."

The critics were divided. *Harrison's Reports* called it "a stark, powerful melodrama, sordid, tense and disturbing." *The New Yorker* praised it for confronting the subject head on, and called it "an unsettling piece of work." *The Washington Post* claimed the movie's sensationalized approach "negated any laudable purpose its supporters claim." *The Monthly Film Bulletin* agreed. Phillip Scheuer wrote a scathing review for the *Los Angeles Times*, suggesting that the film might damage our cause in foreign countries, "particularly if it ever fell in Communist hands."

"*You ever try to fight thirty-five guys at one time, teach?*"

THE BLOB (September, 1958) Paramount
M Ralph Carmichael, W Kate Phillips, Theodore Simonson, P Jack H. Harris, D Irvin S. Yeahworth

Intelligent, reasonably believable sci-fi, made a small fortune for Paramount, one of the many studios that had refused to back the film when producer Jack Harris came knocking at their door. The studio took a seven year lease on it for $300,000 and made $4 million. A catchy main title, written by Burt Bacharach and Mack David, helped. Harris re-released the film many times when the rights returned to him.

The Blob is a shapeless creature from outer space that grows larger with each victim it eats. Teenagers Steve McQueen and Anita Corsaut (listed in the credits as Steven McQueen and Anita Corseaut, by someone with spelling issues) are the only two left alive who've seen the thing, and it's up to them to convince the cops and their friends that everyone is in danger. By the end of the show, the authority figures are working with the kids to kill it, and finally merge into one when the high school principal smashes a school window to gain access to the fire extinguishers so urgently needed to freeze the creature. The kids in the audience applauded.

McQueen was way too old (28) to be playing a teenager, but then so was James Dean. He's charismatic and charming and two years away from becoming a major star, and the movie is lucky to have him. According the people involved, he was a pain in the ass, causing delays, stealing groceries from the market where one of the most suspenseful scenes takes place. The film's finest moment has the Blob oozing out of a projection booth during a midnight spook show.

"**The Blob** just goes on and on and on," said Harris. "It's a respected movie and I've got to think of it as the best thing I've ever done."

Exhibitor Ray Moore thought the film was "pretty good of its type." M.W. Long said it was "the first horror picture to do business here!" Said Mel Danner, "Excellent attendance on this one. Done in color, an offbeat sort of thing that will draw."

"*It's kinda like a mass; it keeps getting bigger and bigger.*"

BLOOD OF DRACULA aka BLOOD IS MY HERITAGE (November, 1957) American International
M Paul Dunlap, W Aben Kandel, Herman Cohen, P Herman Cohen, D Herbert L. Strock

Miss Branding (Louise Lewis), a chemistry teacher at the Sherwood School for young ladies, uses one of her volatile students (Sandra Harrison) in her lunatic experiment. "I can release a destructive power in a human being that would make the split atom seem like a blessing," she boasts. Branding believes that if she can turn people into vampires, the military will stop making bombs. But in a world ruled by men for men, the scientific community won't even consider her thesis, if you can believe that. "They mock me and my work," she complains. So she uses the power of an ancient Carpathian amulet to hypnotize Nancy Perkins, and three murders later, the poor girl is beside herself. "I'm living a nightmare," she tells Branding. "A horrible urge comes over me. I feel a strength that's almost frightening. It takes possession of me. I must do something awful but when I try to remember, all I can see is…*you!*"

Remake of **I Was a Teenage Werewolf**, has a very good performance by Sandra Harrison in the lead role. "She was extremely easy to work with, and I think did a fairly good job," said director Herb Strock. Strock hated her transformation into a vampire, accomplished in three quick dissolves. "We had no money to really develop a technically perfect transition and therefore used the cheap dissolve method, holding Sandra Harrison as still as we could while the makeup man added makeup to her."

Good score by Paul Dunlap, with a musical interlude featuring Jerry Blaine singing "Puppy Love" to a roomful of tight sweaters that has to be seen to be believed. A number of these horror films during this period contain a song that the producers hoped would connect with their teen-aged audiences. Curiously, more often than not, as is this case here, the songs were rarely rock and roll, and were often more likely to alienate than woo.

"One critic called **Blood of Dracula** 'the worst vampire movie ever made,'" Strock told me with a grin. "He may have been right. We shot it back to back with **Teenage Frankenstein** in four weeks because Herman had some deal with AIP and they needed the two pictures for Thanksgiving."

Motion Picture Exhibitor called it "fast-moving and suspenseful" while *Boxoffice* thought

Sandra Harrison.

Sandra Harrison was "noteworthy as the blood-thirsty gal." *Time* magazine was certain it would "rank as one of the year's biggest horrors," though it is doubtful it was meant as a compliment. Exhibitor Velva Otts remarked, "Due to an overdose of horror movies, most of them have folded up for our location. However, this combination (plays with **I Was a Teenage Frankenstein**) is the best of the series boxofficewise. AIP has provided some lifesavers in 57."

"*I know what you are, and I know what you've done to me.*"

BLUE DENIM (July, 1959) 20th Century Fox
M Bernard Herrmann, W Phillip Dunne, Edith Sommer, P Charles Brackett, D Phillip Dunne

One of the few films with teenagers playing teenagers for a change. Carol Lynley and Brandon deWilde are the good kids in "trouble" in this sensitive, reasonably restrained drama, far more grounded than **Rebel Without a Cause** in its depiction of parents who don't understand their kids, and the kids who haven't been given the tools to deal with the problems that face them. And what better way to illustrate this communication gap than with the subject of sex. In my experience, the very word was enough to make parents squirm and break out in a sweat. Knowing that at some point, their children would come of age and need to know about "the birds and the bees," must have partly been responsible for all of the ulcers everybody was always talking about when I was growing up. Imagine the relief that parents must have felt when schools provided after school "sex education" classes. *"Put the Alka-Seltzer back, sweetheart, we just got a reprieve."* In my school, the nurse taught the girls and the principal taught the boys. I don't believe I've ever seen a more uncomfortable man in my life. Mr. Harrington. He stood at the front of the class, with a book in his hand, giving us the dry, clinical details of baby-making, never looking up unless somebody got out of line, which was inevitable. He was embarrassed and so were we. Making eye contact with a friend was risky, because all any of us wanted to do was laugh out loud, and it didn't take much to light the fuse. Harrington could have done himself and us a favor by pausing for a moment, just long enough to give us a wink and say, "And it feels *gooooood*." But he couldn't. He'd been brainwashed into believing that sex was shameful and dirty and that's why everyone had so much trouble talking about it. It took an act of Congress to get CBS to agree to have a pregnant woman as the star of a weekly television program. They thought it was in *bad taste*. As it turned out, *I Love Lucy* was more popular than ever. This is the climate in which **Blue Denim** was conceived.

Cautious Fox executives persuaded Joan Crawford, who was making **The Best of Everything** at the studio at the time, to do a little intro for **Blue Denim's**

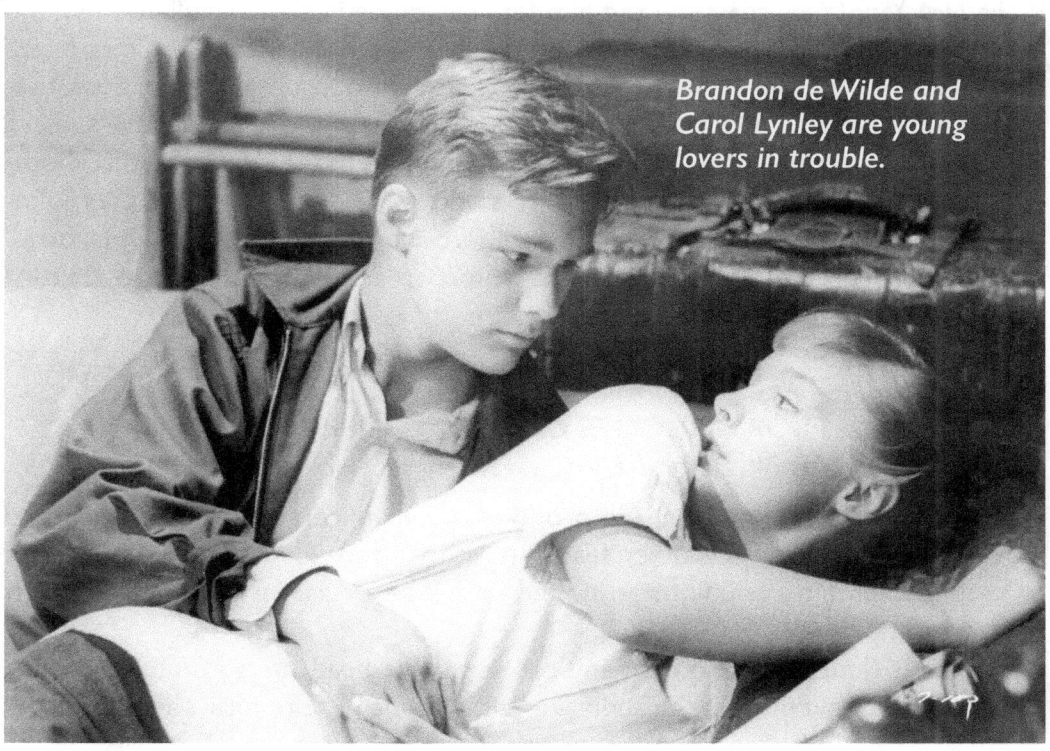

Brandon de Wilde and Carol Lynley are young lovers in trouble.

trailer, to give the picture respectability. Fox bent over backwards to assure everyone that it was not a sleazy exploitation picture.

The scene where deWilde finds Lynley in the library, with a book opened to the subject of abortion, is incredibly touching. For a few moments they are speechless, until at last she says hopelessly, "But they don't tell you how to stop it." They try to tell their parents but they just aren't listening. They're not bad people. They just don't want to admit that their kids aren't kids anymore, and the kids don't have the courage to tell them. Not knowing who else to turn to, they go to deWilde's best friend, Warren Berlinger (reprising his role from the stage play). He'd bragged about taking some sailor friend to get an abortion, but now he has to fess up and admit he made the story up. In an earlier scene, Carol Lynley asks deWilde if he'd been with other women. "Regular amount for a guy my age, I guess," he replies, and later admits that he's a virgin, like her. Insecurity runs rampant in this film until, finally, it rubs off on the audience as they watch Lynley, sitting in the backseat of the black limousine that will take her to the "doctor," as nervous and frightened as she can be, as this icy woman blindfolds her. It's a horrific moment, and as the car drives off, the audience is left with the impression that they're taking her to hell.

In the play the abortion is successful but the studio had to know, when they bought the rights (and were originally going to cast Ray Stricklyn in the lead, with Dick Powell directing) that they'd never get away with that. Lynley is rescued at the last minute.

The New York Times chastised the film for "exploiting in a shamefully clumsy and artificial way" such a "topical and delicate theme." Not having read *The Times*, *Boxoffice* feared that the film's "uncompromising treatment of pregnancy, abortions, bastardy and seduction" might earn it an Adults Only label. "A most delicate subject, handled to perfection," said exhibitor Mel Danner. Mel Kruse suggested that mothers might do well "to bring their daughters and watch it together." Murray Johnston reported that people "came from miles around to see this top adult feature."

In CinemaScope, with a terrific score from Bernard Herrmann, **Blue Denim** may be a little dated but it holds up, even after it was cleaned up.

"Maybe I could just disappear somewhere or—just kill myself."

BOP GIRL aka BOP GIRL GOES CALYPSO (July, 1957) United Artists
M Les Baxter, W Arnold Belgard, P Aubrey Schenck, D Howard W. Koch

From 1956 to 1957, as Bel-Air productions, producers Aubrey Schenck and Howard W. Koch made seventeen features, without once losing their commitment to keeping their films as uninteresting and (in this particular instance as ridiculous) as humanly possible.

Jo Thomas (Judy Tyler) is a rock and roll singer, the headliner at Club Downbeat. One night, a drunken sot in the audience yells, "I came here to hear some calypso!"

Judy Tyler is the Bop Girl. Bobby Troup watches from the stage.

Also in the audience is Professor Robert Hilton (Bobby Troup). He has a curious machine with him which measures audience reaction. After comparing notes, he and Professor Winthrop (Lucien Littlefield) have come to the conclusion that rock and roll music has peaked. Calypso music is going to be the new rage, and Hilton thinks Jo can help him prove it. (It seems to me that the best course of action would be to sit back and let nature take its course, but then I'm no psychologist.) Hilton wants her to put all of her energy into calypso music. Instead, she mixes calypso *with* rock and comes up with a new sound that sweeps the nation, as supplied by Bel-Air's favorite composer, Les Baxter.

Judy Tyler began her career as Princess Summerfall Winterspring on TV's *Howdy Doody* when she was 16. At 17 she married and after three years she quit the show and had a successful stage career. She was only 24 when she was killed while driving with her husband through Wyoming. A trucker swerved into their lane to avoid another car and hit them head on. This movie was released several months after her death. No reflection on her acting or singing ability, but as a rock and roller she is painfully out of place. Her wild gyrations when she sings are awkward and stiff and downright embarrassing. A more believable premise would have been that rock and roll would be dead if she kept singing it.

The calypso craze began with Harry Belafonte's enormously popular song, "Banana Boat (Day-O)", and lasted for about a year, more popular with adults than their offspring. It may have been the realization that it was also black music that prevented it from taking hold.

"For the fan of popular music, the picture will be a feast," said *Film Daily*. Nino Tempo gets things off to a good start with "Horn Honk." Also on board, Judy Tyler ("Rovin' Gal," "Way Back in San Francisco"), The Mary Kaye Trio ("Calypso Rock"), The Goofers ("Fools Rush In," "I'm Gonna Rock and Roll Till I Die"), and Lord Flea ("Wow," "Calypso Jamboree"). It's been so long since I've seen this movie that I can't tell you what songs The Titans or The Cubanos perform. There are only two numbers left on the soundtrack list—"Rhythm in Blues" and "So Hard to Laugh, So Easy to Cry"—that aren't written by Les Baxter, so take your pick. Baxter's contributions—"Calypso Boogie," "De Rain," Oo Ba Loo," and "Hard Rock Candy Baby"—are probably instrumentals but I wouldn't bet the farm on it.

"Oh, man, that Barney is throwing fits in Technicolor."

A BUCKET OF BLOOD (Oct, 1959) American International
M Fred Katz, W Charles B. Griffith, P-D Roger Corman

Brilliant, hilarious look at the beatnik culture, from the twisted mind of writer Charles Griffith, it remains the only accurate depiction of these disillusioned, society drop-outs, and was the inspiration for the far more successful **The Little Shop of Horrors** (1960), a less subtle comedy to say the least. Corman had always steered clear of comedy. "You have to be good to do comedy," he often said, but he figured that he couldn't possibly lose money if he was only spending $50,000.

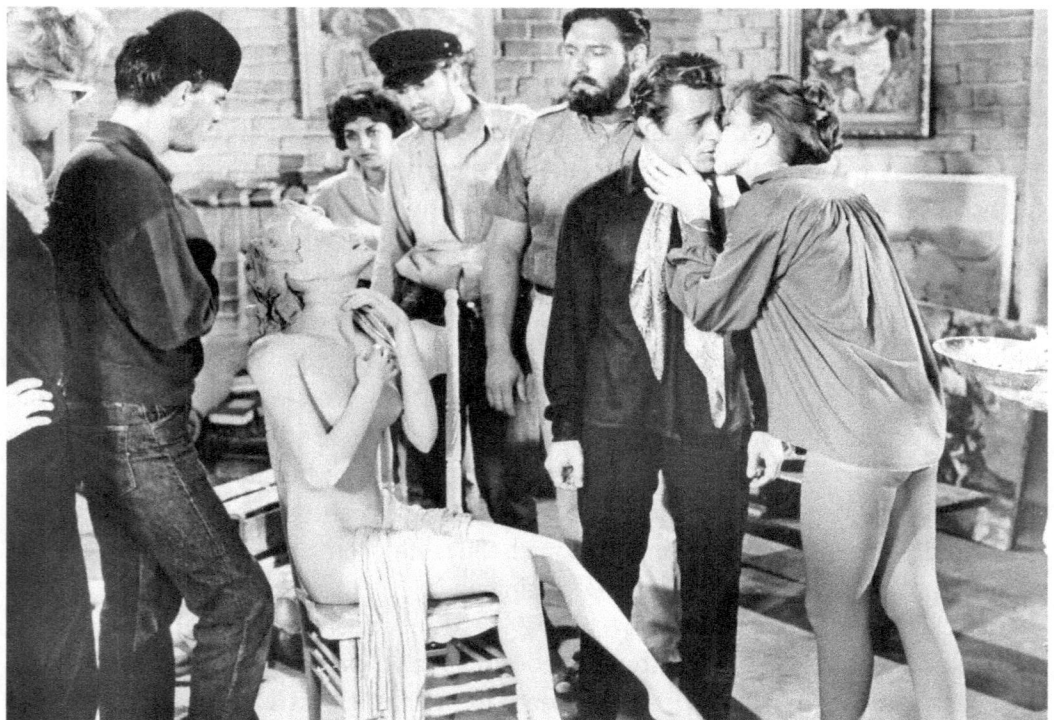

Barbara Morris gives Dick Miller an appreciation kiss for his new "statue."

In a career defining role, Dick Miller plays dim-witted Walter Paisley, a busboy at The Yellow Door, a beatnik coffee house. His idol is Maxwell Brock, the resident blowhard, bearded poet, played to perfection by Julian Burton. Brock's bitter poetry will ultimately turn the well-meaning Walter into a cold-blooded murderer.

"Julian Burton, by the way, is a psychologist now, but he doesn't have the beard anymore," said Antony Carbone, who plays Leonard de Santis, the Yellow Door's owner. "And I thought that's why he went into the field, because he had such a good beard, and all those guys have beards."

Walter wants to be an artist, in the hope of winning the heart Barbara Morris, an actress who we saw precious little of, never more charming as Carla, one of the regulars at The Yellow Door. The glitch in Walter's dream is that he has no talent. We watch him as he hopelessly attempts to create Carla's image in clay as he stares at her photograph. "Be a nose," he says in frustration. He is distracted by the cries of his landlady's cat, which has somehow become

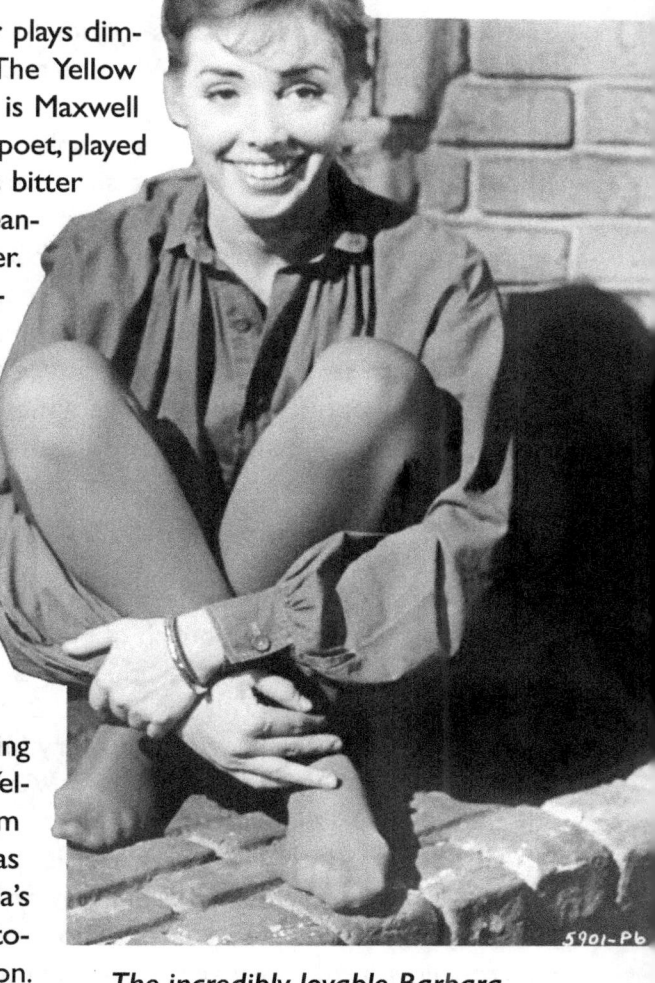

The incredibly lovable Barbara Morris.

trapped in the wall. In his attempt to rescue the cat by cutting into the wall, he accidentally stabs it. In the midst of his grief, he recalls the words from one of Brock's poems. "Let them die, and by their miserable deaths, become the clay within his hands, that he might form an ashtray or an ark." Walter covers the cat with clay, leaving the knife stuck in it, and takes it to The Yellow Door to show his boss. "What do you call it?" he asks. "Dead Cat," Walter replies, assuming his boss knows there's a real cat beneath all of that clay. "Why'd you stick a knife in it?" Leonard asks. "I didn't mean to," Walter insists.

The cat is put on display and Walter becomes a minor celebrity. One of his "fans" slips him a pack of heroin, witnessed by an undercover cop (Burt Convy). The cop is too thick-skulled to see that Walter doesn't even know what heroin is, except that he's heard it's expensive. The cop pulls a gun, Walter gets scared and splits his skull with a frying pan. The cop becomes his next statue—Murdered Man. His third victim is Alice, the awful, played by Judy Bamber. She can't believe the busboy is an artist and makes fun of him. "Why don't do you make a statue of me?" she chides. And he does.

Walter's boss becomes his accomplice. Quite by accident, Leonard discovers the truth about the cat when he sees some fur where the clay has chipped away, and is horrified when he sees Walter's new statue—Murdered Man. He's about to call the cops when an art dealer (Bruno Ve Sota) offers him $500 for the cat. He gives Walter fifty, pockets the rest, and keeps quiet. Each new "statue" plays on his guilt, until, at last, he agrees to sponsor an art show for Walter. "But first," he says, "you've got to stop making these horrible statues."

On the eve of his show, Walter gets the courage to ask Carla to marry him. But she doesn't love him. It's all been for nothing. Walter is about as low as a person can get when Brock happily reports that he'll probably make at least $25,000 on his pieces. "I thought you put money down," Walter says bitterly. "I do, Walter, but twenty-five thou!"

The audience at the sneak preview was less than enthusiastic. "This picture stinks!" one angry chap yelled. "A bunch of Hollywood nuts made this!" cried another. Sitting in the audience, Tony Carbone experienced mixed feelings. "I thought, 'Jesus, this is an awful movie. This is dumb...' But I also thought, 'This is a fun movie. It's kind of everybody making fun of everything.' It's one of those films that kind of grew on me until I felt, 'this is all right.' As a matter of fact, I now think it's one of the better films I did with Roger."

"**Bucket of Blood** is still my favorite picture," Dick Miller said. "None of these are great pictures, understand, but I always thought if **Bucket of Blood** had had another chunk of money in production, it would have ranked with any of the top horror films. It's the best script Chuck ever wrote."

"Director Roger Corman has set out to satirize both the horror film and the Beatniks," said the *Los Angeles Times*. "He succeeds rather well on a small budget." *Variety* thought it was "too comic" for a horror film, and "too explicit" for a comedy. *Monthly Film Bulletin* said Dick Miller gave a performance of "sustained poignancy." Exhibitor Arlen W. Peahl played the picture with a more prestigious film from another company and said **Bucket of Blood** saved the show. "They liked it, it's different."

"What is not creation is graham crackers."

***THE CARELESS YEARS** (September, 1957) United Artists
M Leith Stevens W John Howard Lawson, Mitch Lindemann, P Edward Lewis, D Arthur Hiller

At a party, Jerry Vernon (Dean Stockwell), a boy from the wrong side of the tracks, meets Emily Meredith (Natalie Trundy), a girl from the right side of the tracks, and the two fall in love, a relationship that neither his father, Sam (John Larch), nor her parents (Barbara Billingsley and John Stephenson) can endorse. The young couple go to Mexico to marry, with plans to spend the month in a hotel. Sam finds them and knocks his son to the floor. Seeing this, Emily realizes they've made a mistake. In the end, Jerry and Meredith decide they need a little time to think things through.

Stockwell, a former child actor, read the script, then titled **The Young Lovers**, and thought it was okay. He met with the director, Arthur Hiller, who'd come out of television to direct his first feature. Stockwell wondered, "Do I tell him about my reservations? Or do I pretend I really just love it? I didn't want to lose the job, you know."

"It does not get lost in the usual movie hokum about puppy love," said Bosley Crowther in his *New York Times* review. "It calls a spade a spade by reminding us that the problem stems from the fact that young people today mature physically long before society has prepared them for marriage. Aside from this virtue, the films falls into type." Crowther found it uninspired, naïve and repetitious. *Boxoffice* was kinder. "A tender, true-to-life depiction of the problems of teenagers (not delinquents) who fall in love." *The Mirror News* enthusiastically reported that it was "unlike most current cheap and shoddy films about teenagers which simply seek to make a quick buck through exploitation of sensational subject. **Careless Years** is expertly written, acted and directed."

Girls from the right kind of home, stumbling into the wrong kind of love!

CARNIVAL ROCK (1957) Howco International
M Walter Greene, *W* Leo Lieberman, *P-D* Roger Corman

This variation on **The Blue Angel** (1930) is one of Roger Corman's most obscure films, and certainly his most depressing. In retrospect, some critics have praised Corman for not delivering another lightweight, inane piece of nonsense where the thin story is nothing more than an excuse for the musical numbers. In all likelihood, Corman wouldn't have had any interest in making that kind of a movie, and he probably had no interest in rock and roll music. So his two rock movies, this one and **Rock All Night**, are not about the music. They're not really rock and roll movies.

Christy Christakos (David J. Stewart) is in danger of losing his nightclub, attached to a carnival. He's $3,000 in debt, business is terrible, and yet all that he can think about is the new singer that he's hired, Natalie Cook (Susan Cabot). His best friend Ben (Dick Miller) tries to get him to focus on the business but Christy won't listen, any more than he listens to Natalie when she tells him that she's in love with someone else. And when Christy realizes this "someone else" is in her dressing room, he wants to break the door down. "You go in there now and she'll hate you for the rest of her life," Ben warns him. He pulls Christy away from the door, slams him against the wall, and tries to talk sense to him.

"He kept banging his head every time I slammed him against the wall," said Miller. "One of the grips or somebody came over there and hammered one of those two-headed nails into the wall, just where his head hit. I asked them about it later, and they said they'd done it on purpose because they were tired of the guy. He'd been there two days and he was driving them crazy with his method acting. They couldn't get a shot. He had to run around the stage so he could breathe hard. I'm trying to pull him and the guy outweighed me by seventy or eighty pounds. I figured the only way to drag him was to sink my fingers in and pull. Two days later he showed me his arm. It was all purple and green. I said, 'Gee, I'm sorry.' And he said, 'It's all right. I used the pain.' When his head hit the wall on that last take, I saw blood trickling down his neck. That nail had caught him on the side of the head. I said, 'You're bleeding.' He said, 'I can use that pain. I felt something was wrong.' *Method acting!* He was doing a scene with Jonathan [Haze] where he was supposed to see the girl with her boyfriend and have a heart attack. He gave Jonathan a straight pin and told him, 'When I turn my head, stick me in the leg with that pin.' When Jonathan told me, I said, 'What! Are you kidding?' He said, 'What should I do?' I said, 'Stick the friggin' pin in him.'" They played the scene and had to pull the pin out with a pair of pliers. On the first day of the shoot, Miller and Stewart were rehearsing a scene when Stewart suddenly slapped his face. "Hey! What are you doin'?!" Miller asked. "We decided he should hit you in this scene," Corman said. Miller had no trouble making the change, but the guy didn't have to actually hit him, for Crissakes. "We rehearsed it a few times and David Stewart said, 'I don't feel it.' So Roger said, 'The guy's a Tony-Award-winner. He wants to make physical contract, otherwise he doesn't feel it. Can he hit you on the take? Just one take where he hits you.' I said, 'Okay. But this is wrong. It's not gonna look right.' By then, I'd done enough fights in pictures to know what looked good and what didn't. He hauled off and whacked me on the take, right across my ear. I tell ya, I had a ringing in my ear for six months after that."

Natalie's lover, Stanley (Brian Hutton) grows tired of Christy's stalking and plans to cheat him out of the club to get rid of him. He makes arrangements with the guy who runs "The Wheel of Fortune" to rig the wheel, but Stanley can't go through with it. During his struggle with his conscience, Christy realizes that he's Natalie's lover and insists on cutting cards for the club. He loses, then stays on as the club's comic. Under Stanley's management, the club prospers.

On the eve of her wedding to Stanley, Christy comes to Natalie's dressing room, still in his clown makeup. "Please," he pleads. "Once again I ask you to leave this boy." Of course, she can't. "Please, Christy, I don't want to hurt you. I never did." Ominously he says, "In the end, you will belong to me." He waits until after the show, grabs her and sets fire to the club. Stanley rescues them both and Christy goes off to New York, where Ben's brother has a job for him. "He was a good man," Ben remarks. "He'll be a good man again." Really?

"I don't remember it at all," Corman said. "It was not a script I was overly fond of. We finished it and turned it over to a group of people in New Orleans. Apparently, they did some pretty heavy editing after I turned it in. I was going to Europe and just gave them the film. I've never even seen it."

It's doubtful that anyone, even if they wanted to, could *heavily* edit one of these low budget quickies. There simply wasn't enough film to play with.

Said *The Hollywood Reporter*: "You do not need much story to hold together a picture of this type, but what you have should work for the musical numbers, not against them."

Had it been Natalie's story, with the focus on her love of music and her desire to sing it, with Christy as a supporting character, everything might have been all right. As it stands, **Carnival Rock** is almost an anti-musical, rather like sticking nine or ten foot-tapping numbers into **Come Back Little Sheba** (1952). Or, as another critic put it, the story is "so heavy-handed and poorly put together that it tends to suffocate even the rock-and-roll numbers that are he staple of such pictures." *Variety* had good things to say about Susan Cabot and Dick Miller, both very good in the picture. David Stewart, not so much.

Susan Cabot and Leon Tyler.

The Platters sing one of their hits, "Remember When," the only hit song in the picture. Other performers include The Shadows ("The Creep"), Bob Luman and The Shadows ("This is the Night" and "All Night Long"), Dave Houston ("Teen Age Frankie and Johnnie" and "One and Only"), The Blockbusters ("Rock-A-Boogie"), and Susan Cabot and The Blockbusters ("Ou-Shoo-Bla-D" and "There's No Place Without You").

"A couple of years later," said Miller, "I was doing a **McCloud** and I was working with one of the finest actors in the business—Joseph Wiseman. Marvelous, brilliant actor, maybe one of the ten best in the business. We're shooting on the Universal lot at night and David Stewart's name came up. And I started telling him the story about this idiot, this moron, this asshole, this imbecile. I go on and on and Wiseman looks at me as says, 'You know David Stewart is dead.' It turned out that he'd died of a heart attack three or four months prior to this night. And then Wiseman says, 'David Stewart was my dearest friend.' And I felt like crap. All night long, I kept looking over at Wiseman. When we finished shooting, we all went back to the trailers to change and he says, 'Come on in the car with me.' We got in the car and I said, 'Joseph, I really gotta apologize for what I said. I don't even know how to say this to you.' He said, 'Well, I don't know how to say *this* to *you*, but I don't know who David Stewart is.'"

"What I want, no one else will have. I promise you that."

THE COOL AND THE CRAZY (March, 1958) American International

M Raoul Kraushaar, Dave Kahn, W Richard C. Sarafian, P Elmer Rhoden Jr., D William Whitney

A must-see film about drug addiction, every bit as informative as **Reefer Madness**, with two J.D. superstars in the cast—Richard Bakalyan and Scott Marlowe. "Those early movies made me somewhat of a teen icon," Marlowe remarked. "Kids in those days enjoyed defying authority." Said Bakalyan, "I played a delinquent in **The Cool and the Crazy**, but not really. The kids in that film were actually okay. It was Scott Marlowe who led them astray. He was busy trying to get everybody hooked on marijuana and heroin. If you did the same story today, you'd do it with cocaine or heavier drugs. **The Cool and the Crazy** is a cult film today. People laugh about it. It's a fun film."

Fresh out of reform school, Bennie Saul (Marlowe) enrolls in a new school and quickly takes over a gang of toughs, then eases them into a life of drug addiction by starting them off with reefers. Bennie's supplier has nothing but disdain for his customers. The moment Bennie leaves the room, he tells his sleazy moll, "These kids. They're all the same. You pick 'em up, buy 'em a new suit—you'd think they'd play it smart and stay off the stuff. A couple of weeks and he'll want the needle." His lady remarks, "So? You gotta customer instead of a salesman."

Dick Bakalyan looks on as Scott Marlowe tries to calm Dick Jones. Jones was the voice of Walt Disney's Pinocchio *(1940), and appeared in dozens of motion pictures including* Mr. Smith Goes to Washington *and* Destry Rides Again *(1939), and performed his own stunts on TV's* The Range Rider *(1951-53) and later on his own series,* Buffalo Bill Jr.

In this film, one puff on a joint and you're hooked. Before long, everyone's banging their heads on tables and begging for more "M," which, a policeman tells us, "don't stand for Mother." And the sleazy moll was right. Bennie gets hooked and his buddy, Jackie (Bakalyan), steals a valuable antique from his girlfriend's house to get the money for Bennie's habit. Drugged out and desperate, Bennie kills the dealer and turns to the needle.

As a matter of course, it ends badly for Bennie when, in a drug-induced state, he mistakes an automobile's headlights for two motorcycle policemen. He cuts the wheel and plunges to his death over the side of a cliff. "Take a good look," a policeman says to Jackie. "It could have been any one of you. Is this what you call kicks? If you don't wise up, you're all going to wind up like this, one way or the other."

"A few weeks ago, a Brooklyn school principal committed suicide because he could not suppress the rape and hoodlumism in his institution. **The Cool and the Crazy** is a badly written sloppily edited, poorly directed low-budget film that may well inspire more such tragedies," declared *The Hollywood Reporter*. *Boxoffice* singled out Scott Marlowe's performance as the best asset "of this exaggerated and sometimes hysterical treatise on juvenile delinquency." Said Arkansas exhibitor Victor Weber, "I think every theatre, large or small, should play this picture and help itself as well as the boys and girls who will learn a lesson of great benefit." "They ate this one up," said Simon M. Cherivtch. "Should have played it three days."

"*Look at you! You're a mess! You stink!*"

CRIME IN THE STREETS (June, 1956) Allied Artists
M Franz Waxman, W Reginald Rose, P Vincent Fennelly, D Don Siegel

Beginning with *Kraft Theatre* in 1947, and ending with *Playhouse 90* in 1957, the period referred to as the "Golden Age" of television (there was an awful lot of lead in them thar hills), television audiences could look forward to original plays from some of the best writers in the business. Gore Vidal. Horton Foote. Rod Serling. These were live dramas, with three cameras running, with actors changing costumes between scenes and commercial breaks. In 1954, two producers who took more risks than anyone, Herold Hecht and Burt Lancaster, hired Paddy Chayefsky to adapt his teleplay, **Marty**, for the big screen. It won Academy Awards for the best writing, directing, acting, and walked away with the Best Picture, making TV dramas hot properties.

John Cassavetes and Mark Rydell.

Allied Artists bought Reginald Rose's **Crime in the Streets**, seen on TV's *Elgin Hour*, and hoped that the director, Sidney Lumet, would direct the feature as well. Lumet declined the offer and the film was given to Don Siegel, whose last three pictures had done very well for the studio. John Cassavetes reprised his role as Frankie Dane, the psychopathic leader of The Hornets. "I feel loose," he says. "Like I was made for getting even." He wants to get even with old man McAllister (Malcolm Atterbury), one of the people in the neighborhood, who happened to see a member of The Hornets (Jimmy Ogg) threaten a boy with a zip-gun. McAllister's call to the police resulted in the boy's arrest. Dane threatens McAllister and McAllister slaps his face. The only thing that will satisfy Dane now is to see the do-gooder dead. Sympathetic social worker Ben Wagner (James Whitmore) tries to talk him out of it.

James Whitmore was one of the most dependable and versatile supporting players in the business. He could carry a picture if he had to, and really looked good in uniform. His memory of making this movie was foggy, but he did recall that there was a lot of tension on the set. "Something was going on with the director and the writer. Reginald Rose was one of the golden boys from live television, and those gentlemen had more control over their material. I can't say for sure, but I don't think Rose realized that his word wouldn't be sacrosanct."

Considering all of the high-powered talent involved, (Sal Mineo has a major role), the film is never as good as it should be. "I blame Sidney Lumet," Siegel chuckled. "He should have taken the job. He and Rose would have gotten along fine. The two of us had trouble finding a balance between his philosophy and my philosophy."

The critic for the *New York Times* called it "cramped and flimsy," though he had some good words to say for the cast, singling out Mark Rydell's "lush performance as a shiny-faced, weed-smoking punk." Rydell would later direct one of John Wayne's best movies, **The Cowboys** (1972). Of course, John Cassavetes became a director as well, a very influential one, beginning with **Shadows** in 1959.

James Whitmore was an Emmy-Tony-Grammy Award-winner, one of the best actors in the business, who preferred stage to screen because of all of the down time. "Aren't you bored," he asked me, between takes on a show where he was a detective in pursuit of Walter Pidgeon. "No," I replied. "Then you're hooked," he told me.

Mark McGee

Exhibitor Mayme P. Muselman called **Crime in the Streets** "just another teenage delinquency picture" that her patrons resented, but C. J. Otts called it "a good bet for any house." Ken Christianson thought it might be all right for the big cities, "but small town family theatres don't dirty your screen with this blood-and-guts type of teenage showing."

"*You're garbage, Frankie Dane. I give you up.*"

THE CRY-BABY KILLER (July, 1958) Allied Artists
M Gerald Fried, W Leo Gordon, Melvin Levy, P David Kramarsky and David March, D Joe Addis

Jack Nicholson doesn't exactly set the screen on fire in his film debut. "Jeff [Corey] recommended me," Nicholson recalled. "I read for it just like every other actor in town. I screamed and yelled—I know I gave the loudest reading, if not the best."

"Jack was so strange, in those days even," Ed Nelson remarked. Nelson plays a TV news reporter in the picture. "The crew hated him. Poor Jack was defeated, I think, after that picture for two or three years—he went off to the Northwest or someplace to 'find himself.'"

Said Nicholson, "When I got the part I thought: 'This is it! I'm made for this profession!' Then I didn't work for a year."

After a particularly miserable main title song, "Cry Baby Cry," written and sung by actor Dick Kallman, we see Jimmy Wallace (Nicholson) taking a bad beating from Manny Cole (Brett Halsey) and a couple of punks. Manny stole

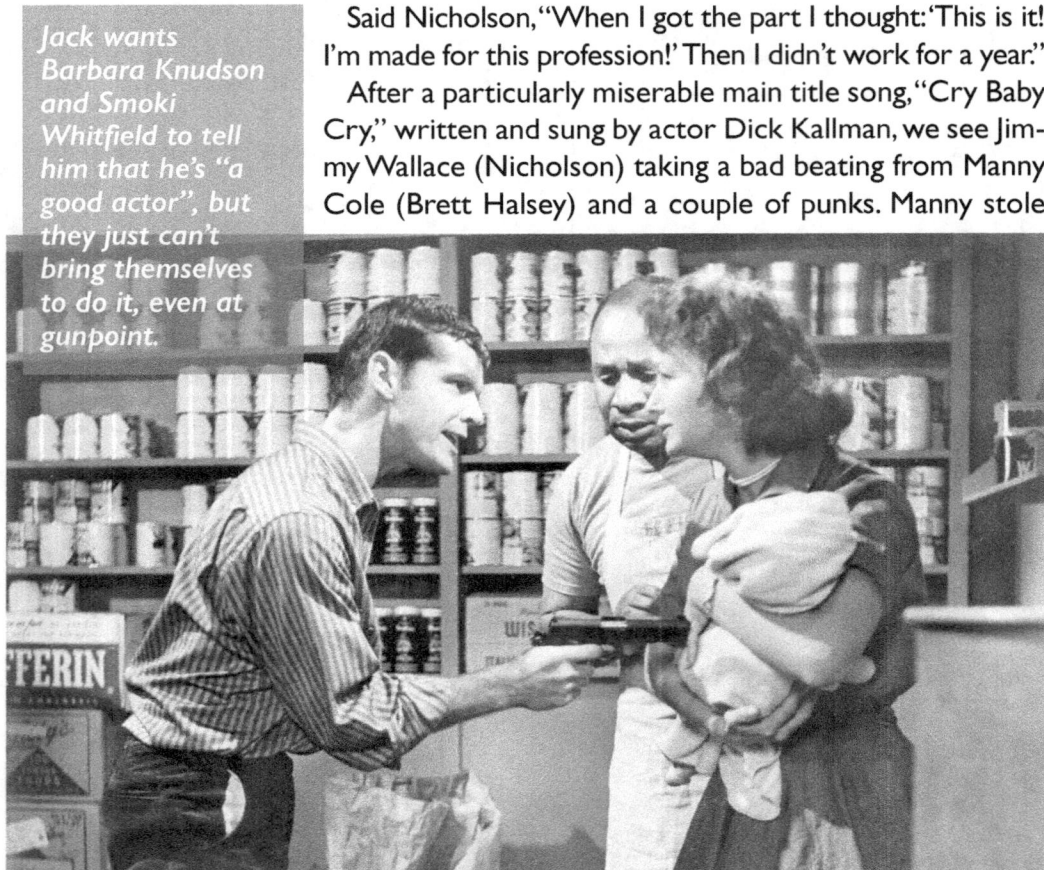

Jack wants Barbara Knudson and Smoki Whitfield to tell him that he's "a good actor", but they just can't bring themselves to do it, even at gunpoint.

Abby Dalton pleads with Jack to give up acting and find a job he can do.

Jimmy's girl, Carole (Carolyn Mitchell) and Jimmy won't leave her be. He knows Manny's a bad apple and he's afraid of the bad influence he may have on her. "Carole was a swell girl until Manny got his hands on her," Jimmy tells his buddy. "You mean until she *wanted* his hands on her," his friend says pointedly. Once we finally see Carole with Manny, it's obvious that she's nuts about him. And he's a creep, full of swagger and bluster and of himself. The few times she takes issue with his boorish behavior he quickly bends her to his will. Jimmy shows up to prove to Carole that Manny's a coward. Once again Manny and his goons are set the give Jimmy another beating when one of the punks drops a gun. Jimmy grabs it and shoots one of them in self-defense. Believing that he killed the guy, Jimmy takes refuge in a storage room and holds two people hostage.

"I went to Roger with the Goddamn story," said writer-actor Leo Gordon, who has the film's best line—*Teenagers. We never had 'em when I was a kid.* "It was probably something I saw in a newspaper article or some damn something. It was a Roman circus, for crissakes! The travesty of commercialism when human life is involved. Everything's for sale."

Gordon was a clever writer. The film is full of humorous, cynical asides, and he even manages some interesting character touches. But he runs out of steam once Jack takes those hostages. The underrated Harry Lauter, as Police Lt. Porter, has the thankless job of providing the padding for the story with his endless interrogations, making the film seem a whole lot longer than its 61 minute running time.

"*Reed, I want you to hold anyone who had anything to do with this.*"

*CRY TOUGH (August, 1959) United Artists
M Laurindo Almeida, *W-P* Harry Kleiner, *D* Paul Stanley

Irving Shulman's novel, about Jewish delinquents in the Bronx, was the basis for Harry Kleiner's screenplay about Puerto Rican delinquents in Spanish Harlem. Kleiner borrowed contract players John Saxon and Linda Cristal from Universal to play the leads. Filmmakers could often get United Artists to back a picture based on a name, and though I don't know this to be true, it's possible that Saxon, who was being groomed to be a major star, was all that U.A. needed to give this picture the green light.

Saxon plays Miguel Antonio Enrico Francisco Estrada, back in the barrio after a year in prison, determined to stay on the right side of the law. For a few anxious moments, Miguel wonders if his father (Joseph Calleia) will even let him in the house. He has shamed the family. Gang leader Carlos Mendoza (Harry Townes) wants Miguel to help him put down a rival gang but Miguel bows out. He takes a job at a laundry that turns out to be front for Juan Cortez (Joe De Santis), the leader of the rival gang that Mendoza was talking about. When Miguel discovers that one of the workers (Paul Clarke) has been paid by Mendoza to cause an explosion in the boiler, he tells him to lay off. As he walks away, Miguel sees the lovely Sarita (Linda Cristal) and before long they're married. But Sarita grows tired of him and leaves him. As you might have guessed by now, when you travel with Miguel, you're always headed in a downward direction.

Supposedly, Saxon and Cristal had some chemistry going and the director wanted to take advantage of it by shooting two versions of one of their love scenes. The version with the nudity went to the foreign markets.

"What starts out as a promising picture about poor Puerto Ricans in New York and the obviously circumscribed endeavors of one young fellow 'to belong' ends up as a routine gangster melodrama," said *The New York Times*.

"*Some guys take what they want.*"

CURFEW BREAKERS aka NARCORTICS SQUAD aka HOOKED aka TOO POOPED TO POP (March, 1957) Screen Guild
M Paul Dunlap, *P* Charles E. King, *W-D* Alexander J. Wells

Police Lt. Paul Kelly works with Coach Regis Toomey to find the dealer (Larry Getz) peddling drugs to high school students. Toomey is pretty sure he knows a student who's using, that might lead them to the dealer, but the boy isn't home. His Aunt (Cathy Downs) doesn't know where he is and laughs at the suggestion that her nephew could be into drugs. While she's being questioned, she answers the phone and tells one of her friends, "It seems Raymond is up to some boyish shenanigans." The kid dies from an overdose.

The film starts on the wrong foot, with an endless montage of an airplane taking off and landing. We have to watch the wheels drop down, and we have to see it land from every possible angle, and ever so slowly we watch it roll to a stop. If the producers could have gotten their hands on some stock of the luggage being unloaded we would have had to suffer that too before the stinking thing finally got down to business. We see this guy with an attaché case get off the plane. He goes into a phone booth and gets pumped full of lead. The headlines scream: DOPE RING FIGURE DIES IN GANGLAND GUNPLAY.

The "dope ring figure" was an undercover narcotics agent, shot by Raymond's dealer, who uses his sexy girlfriend, Sheila Urban, to entice the students into taking their first puff on a marijuana cigarette. She has some funny dialogue, but not enough to make it worth sitting through this boring, police procedural, narrated by writer-director Alexander J. Wells. He waits until the audience has forgotten about him, and suddenly, like a Jack in the Box, he's back, with a little something more to say, sometimes having the effect of someone standing behind you saying "Boo!"

"Organized narcotics traffic is big business, and to get to the top, you've got to go to the bottom."

DADDY-O aka OUT ON PROBATION aka DOWNBEAT aka DEADBEAT DADDY-O (1959) American International
M John Williams, W David Moessinger, P Elmer Rhoden Jr, D Lou Place

Elmer Rhoden Jr., the president of Commonwealth Theatres, was smitten with a hopeful young actress named Sandra Giles. Like so many of the people who owned large theatre chains, Rhoden had gone into the business of producing movies. For this film, Rhoden hired one of Roger Corman's production managers, Lou Place, to direct it. With Miss Giles in the lead, of course.

Giles had a reputation for attending more premiers and events that any other actress in town. (She should have hooked up with Cesar Romero, of whom it was said would attend the opening of a napkin.) "In my younger days," said Giles, "I never wanted to be an actress. I was shy when I came here from San Antonio, Texas, and going out was just a way of making friends. But it pays to be seen in Hollywood, if the right people see you." Her strategy finally paid off. Sort of.

Giles plays Jana Ryan, a fast-driving blonde bombshell who almost causes a three-car collision in the first three minutes of the picture. "If you were a man, baby, I'd kick your teeth out," Paul Sandifer (Dick Contino) snarls. "You touch me and I'll split your head open," she snaps. Jana challenges Paul to a drag race, during which Paul is stopped by the cops. They think he was responsible for a hit-and-run that killed Sonny Di Marco (Bob Banas). Marco was Paul's best friend. He wants to find his killer, and the trail leads to the Hi-Note Club, and its owner, Sidney Chillas (Bruno VeSota). Paul takes a job as a singer at the club, hoping to find some proof.

Sandra Giles in a hostile encounter with Dick Contino.

It just so happens that Jana is a cigarette girl at the High-Note. In no time, her initial hostility towards Paul evaporates, and we find her seething with jealousy as she helplessly watches him flirt with a big-breasted babe at the bar. He's on stage, singing a song directly to her. *"But just you wait'll I get you home, baby, wait'll I get you home. I'm gonna hold you tight. I'm gonna buzz all night, like a bee in a honeycomb."* He gets off of the stage and sings his way across the floor, and as he comes to the end of his song, he circles an arm around the woman and plants a lusty and lengthy kiss. She's very receptive. Then, he turns to the crowd, like a victorious gladiator, with a boastful "**Yeah!**" The audience goes wild and the scene fades out on Jana's humiliated face. It's a standout sequence.

Once billed as the "world's greatest accordion player," Dick Contino had a couple of hit records and had appeared on *The Ed Sullivan Show* no less than 48 times. Married to actress Leigh (**Hot Rod Rumble**) Snowden until her death in 1982, Contino was earning $4000 a week when Uncle Sam came calling. After a day at Fort Ord, with the threat of being shipped off to Korea hanging over his head, Contino went AWOL, and was sentenced to six months in the hoosegow. He finished his service with an honorable discharge, but his career had taken a hit, which is why he was available to do this ho-hum picture. A tarnished name on the marquee is better than no name at all.

Meet the 'Beat'! Daring to live...Daring to love!

DANGEROUS YOUTH (June, 1958) aka THESE DANGEROUS YEARS (1957) Warner Bros.
M Stanley Black, W Jack Trevor Story, P Anna Neagle, D Herbert Wilcox

Frankie! He's a sensation...slugging and singing his way through a great dramatic story! That's the way this film was advertised in England, where Frankie Vaughn was a well-known crooner, a regular guest on TV shows, with several hit records to his credit. He'd already made one movie before he signed on for this one. Warner Bros. bought the U.S. rights in September of '57, and changed to title to **Misguided**. Then, on March 24, 1958, Elvis Presley was inducted into the military. As far as the studio's publicity department was concerned, the timing couldn't have been better. **Misguided** was quickly changed to **Dangerous Youth** and advertised in the following manner. *What happens when the army gets its hands on the King of rock and roll!*

Anne Neagle, England's most popular singer, dancer and actress on both stage and screen for twenty years, produced this picture, the first of four with Vaughn, all of them directed by her husband, Herbert Wilcox. Unfortunately, Vaughn was too old to be a teen idol and rock and roll really wasn't his forte. The films lost money.

Vaughn is okay and so is the movie. As Dave Wyman, the son of a decorated war hero, he's a member of The Dingle Boys, a group of leather-jacketed toughs that hang out along the Liverpool shore. At night, Dave sings rock and roll. He sings the title song during a singing contest which he wins, then falls for the girl that lost, Dinah Brown (Carol Lesley). Before a romance can develop, Dave is inducted into the army and made a platoon leader. Pvt. Simpson (Michael Ripper) doesn't like Dave and gives him some bad information that causes Dave to lead his men to an active mine field where one of them is killed. Dave beats hell out of Simpson, thinks he's killed him, and goes AWOL.

Boxoffice said there was enough excitement "to hold the interest of teenagers and adult audiences alike," but *Variety* said it lacked "punch" and "the characters are unbelievable."

"You're a trouble-maker. You make trouble for yourself and everyone else."

THE DELICATE DELINQUENT (June, 1957) Paramount
M Buddy Bregman, P Jerry Lewis, W-D Don McGuire

A dangerous looking teenager stands beneath a street lamp, smoking a cigarette. As he starts across the deserted city street, wet from a recent rain, a beat cop eyes him suspiciously. The boy stops in the middle of the street, and the two stand for a moment like a couple of dogs, sizing each other up before a scrap. Two more equally dangerous looking punks round the corner and saunter toward their friend in the street. The cop continues to eyeball them, but as he has no reason to arrest them, he slowly moves on. The three toughs continue across the street and come

The Jim Carrey of his day, singer-actor-producer-director Jerry Lewis.

to a stop at the head of an alley. They wait. Before long three more punks appear at the other end of the alley. Out comes the switchblades, chains and brass knuckles. Slowly they approach each other, the tension so thick you could do chin-ups on it. They are a heartbeat away from killing one another when a door flies open and out comes Jerry Lewis with a couple of garbage cans. He sees the two gangs and goes bonkers, dropping the cans, creating pandemonium as only Lewis can, making enough noise to bring the fuzz down on all of their heads. It's a terrific opening in an otherwise tiresome exercise in mugging.

The three punks seen at the very beginning are played by Robert Ivers, Joseph Corey and, of course, Richard Bakalyan. "I knew from the beginning that I'd be typecast as an actor just as I was in real life," said Bakalyan. "I always knew that I'd have a gun or a knife in my hand, so I always tried to find a different way of presenting that kind of character. When I did **The Delicate Delinquent**, nobody had long hair yet. Trying to think like the character I was portraying, I thought to myself, 'Why should I cut my hair? They'll cut it when I'm drafted to be killed in some crazy war. The hell with them.' It was the kind of attitude that justified the long hair and the negative behavior of the character I was portraying."

After crying his way through a police lineup, Lewis is taken under the wing of a sympathetic cop, played by Darrin McGavin, a role originally written for Dean Martin. By the end of the movie, Lewis is in uniform and together with McGavin, makes quick work of three of the punks seen at the beginning of the show. When Lewis threw the first punch, the audience applauded.

If you like Jerry Lewis, you may like this film. It was his first solo effort as an actor and producer. Lewis and singer Dean Martin were the most popular comedy team in America in the early fifties, but after seventeen pictures, Martin was tired of playing the stooge to Lewis's antics, and their producer, Hal Wallis, was fed up with Lewis as well. In a last ditch effort to hold the team together, Lewis worked with Don McGuire on a script that he hoped Martin would like, though he would have had better luck with a script that gave Martin's character equal screen time. As written, the cop is a supporting character.

Comedies often break the rules of nature and reason but this film is pure nonsense. Lewis can make all of the funny faces he wants to, it won't conceal the fact that he and McGuire have fashioned a scenario that doesn't make *any* sense. Lewis isn't a juvenile, he's supposed to be 28-years old, and he isn't a delinquent, nor does he appear to be in any danger of becoming one, or even capable of being one. And yet, McGavin thinks he could fall into the wrong crowd. (As if anyone would have him.) And so, to keep him on the straight and narrow, McGavin wants to make a police officer out of him. Based on everything we've seen, and everything we are about to see, Lewis is the last guy you'd want on the force, and would make anyone think more than twice about calling the cops. Maybe that's supposed to be the funny part.

"Mr. Lewis trying hard to act a man, with a policeman's hat planted on his noggin, is a mite incredible and absurd," said *The New York Times*. "The good intention of his message may be missed in the eccentricity." Exhibitor Victor Webber said it did very well for him. "As a matter of fact, it out grossed most of Jerry's pictures when he had Dean for a buddy. The laughs were a little thin, but the people liked it."

They liked it quite a lot. **The Delicate Delinquent** was a big hit for Paramount, and was the beginning of a second career for Lewis as a writer, producer, director and (heaven help us) singer. I found a copy of his first record album, *Jerry Lewis Just Sings*, in a used record store and one Christmas, I gave it to my friend Randy Robertson, who hated Lewis. As the word "*Sings*" was against a white background, it was easy to change it to the word "Stinks." When he unwrapped the album, I never saw Randy laugh any harder, or any longer than he did that Christmas day.

Rockabye your baby with a Dixie melody.

THE DELINQUENTS (March, 1957) United Artists

M Gene Garf, Louis Palange, *P* Elmer Rhoden, Jr., *W-D* Robert Altman

First film from director Robert Altman, who'd been making documentaries and industrial films, shot on location in Kansas City in the summer of 1955, financed by Elmer Rhoden Jr. Altman was given $63,000 to make a feature about juvenile delinquents. "I wrote the thing in five days, cast it, picked the locations, drove the generator truck, got the people together, took no money, and we just did it, that's all." It took him three weeks.

Tom Laughlin, Rosemary Howard and Dick Bakalyan.

Tom Laughlin, a good boy from the wrong side of the tracks, is forbidden to see his sweetheart Rosemary Howard. His new friend, Peter Miller, pretends to be her date so that she can hook up with Tom at a party being held in an abandoned mansion. Things get too rowdy for Tom and Rosemary so they leave. When the cops show up a few minutes later, Miller and his side-kick, Richard Bakalyan (in his screen debut) think that Tom blew the whistle on them. Once they catch up with him, they force a bottle of Scotch down his throat and leave him to take the rap for murder.

Laughlin, who would later score big with his own film, **Billy Jack** (1967), was "an unbelievable pain in the ass," according to Altman. "He was a very strange guy," Dick Bakalyan remarked. "I think he thought he was Brando and Clift and Dean all rolled into one." Things got so testy between the actor and the director that Laughlin wanted to walk, and finished the last half of the picture under protest, whatever that means.

Bakalyan recalled the afternoon that he and Peter Miller went into town for a lemon ice cream soda and got quite a surprise. Suddenly, a police officer grabbed him, spun him around and slammed him against the counter. "I thought it was a gag," Bakalyan said, "that Peter had put him up to it. So I started to laugh. That made the cop angry." Once the officer was convinced that the actor wasn't the suspect he was looking for, they *all* had a good laugh. Bakalyan told the cop they were making a movie. The cop scoffed. "Nobody makes movies in Kansas City."

"[The] production, over-all, lacks the polish of professional Hollywood attention," said *Motion Picture Herald*. "Poorest Sun-Mon we've had for quite some time, and have just about decided that my kids don't want it and the adults never did," complained exhibitor Mayme P. Muselman. "If receipts continue to be as lousy as this," groused Ralph Raspa, "I'm going to be delinquent in paying off my debts."

Altman probably wasn't surprised by the negative reaction. "Nobody knew what they were doing," he said. "I don't think it has any meaning for anybody."

"Look, this has gone far enough. I'm gettin' outta here!"

DIARY OF A HIGH SCHOOL BRIDE (July, 1959) American International
M Ronald Stein, W Robert Lowell and Jan Englund, P-D Burt Topper

Teenage marriage is one of today's most controversial subjects. The producers of the picture you are about to see do not attempt to present a solution or take sides. It is a composite of several actual case histories...a story of a teenage girl who could be your daughter, your sister...or you!

Leave it to American International to produce the sleaziest motion picture about teenage love. *Does she get her lunch money from her husband or her daddy? Make up your mind...books or babies! Why can't you control yourself? You're only seventeen!* None of these questions will be answered. Instead, the writers turned the whole affair into a killer-on-the-loose yarn.

Wally Campo, an actor who often worked for AIP, recommended one of the students in his Actors Workshop for the lead in this picture. 18-year old Anita Sands was already under contract to 20th Century-Fox. Arrangements were made for her release. (I assume it wasn't difficult.) She plays 17-year old Judy Lewis, the high school bride under scrutiny. She's just married 24-year old law student Steve Redding (Ronald Foster), and during the titles we see her happily sitting next to her husband as they drive through the mountains, clutching her teddy bear, on their way back from Las Vegas. From the radio Tony Casanova sings the title song.

Judy's parents (Louise Arthur and Barney Biro) want to have the marriage annulled, and when those efforts fail, they actively work to undermine it. Judy's old boyfriend, Chuck (Chris Robinson) spreads the world that Judy had to get married, and she quickly becomes a laughingstock.

Chuck shows up at the coffee shop where Steve works part-time and makes him very uncomfortable. Steve begins to suspect that Judy is having an affair with him. But we know that even if she wanted to, she'd never be able to juggle lovers. She can't even handle the laundry. Poor, poor Judy, the object of ridicule at school and uncomfortable in her new role at home as a housewife. Watching her wrestle with her household chores is the stuff of which situation comedies are made. An argument with Steve, over whether or not she still has feelings for Chuck, sends Judy running home to mommy, leaving the audience to wonder if Steve will ever get laid. Judy phones Chuck and begs him to tell Steve there's nothing between them. Chuck gives every indication of wanting to set things right, but we know better, and so would Judy if she wasn't a complete nudnik. She agrees to meet him at his father's movie studio where Chuck has supposedly arranged for a meeting with Steve. This late night rendezvous ends up with Chuck chasing Judy all over the deserted studio, climbing atop a catwalk where a brush with a high voltage wire puts him out of commission.

"The story follows the tried-and-true pattern of 'true confession' romance magazines," said *Variety*. "We do business on these kind, but honestly I think the average intelligence rate has dropped below the 14-year old level," observed exhibitor W. E. Seaver, Jr.

"*I know I'm married. But I'm seventeen, and I'm scared.*"

DINO (July, 1957) Allied Artists
M Gerald Fried, W Reginald Rose, P Bernice Block, D Thomas Carr

Social worker Frank Mandel (Frank Faylen) begs psychiatrist Larry Sheridan (Brian Keith) to make room for Dino Minetta (Sal Mineo). He's afraid he'll lose the boy otherwise. "This kid's ready to punch you in the nose if you say 'Hello' to him," Mandel remarks. Dino gets so angry during his first session, he breaks a window. One look at his home life tells the whole story. His folks don't love him. They pretend to, but they don't even like him. "What if somebody wants to like you?" Sheridan asks. "What for?" Dino replies. "What's there to like? If they're scared of me, that's the best." Dino's dad (Joe De Santis) doesn't like the change he sees in his son and orders Dino to stop seeing Sheridan. "You can't tell me what to do," Dino tells him. "I'm not afraid of you. Go on, hit me. That's what you want to do, isn't it? Go on!" Dino's little

Brian Keith and Sal Mineo.

Susan Kohner and Sal Mineo.

brother, Tony (Pat DeSimone) comes home in time to witness his father repeatedly slapping his brother across the mouth until he's a bloody mess. Dino just stands there and lets him do it.

Low-key study of juvenile delinquency, written by Reginald Rose from his *Studio One* teleplay, with a nervous Gerald Fried score, has Sal Mineo reprising his TV role. It may be his best performance and worth watching for that reason alone. As Shirley, who knows another unloved soul when she sees one, Susan Kohner is very sweet and gives Mineo his first screen kiss. Joe De Santis is well cast as Dino's dad. And Brian Keith, as always, is letter perfect. Look for Richard Bakalyan, Rafael Campos, Molly McCart, Kenny Miller, and Cindy Robbins.

Boxoffice said **Dino** was "well done." Harold Muir did the best business he'd had in weeks. "Sal Mineo is better every time we play him, and what a following—better than Elvis!"

"How come nobody ever kissed me?"

DON'T KNOCK THE ROCK (December 1956) Columbia
W Robert E. Kent, James B. Gordon, P Sam Katzman, D Fred F. Sears

"I experienced the shock of my life when I played this picture," said Minnesota exhibitor Harry Hawkinson. He'd waited five months to get his hands on it, and when he finally did, the high school was having a class play, and two churches were having Lenten services. In a small town, an exhibitor prayed for as few distractions as possible. The place was packed. "I am falling for rock and roll just like the kids, I guess," Hawkinson admitted. "As long as I have been in the business, I have never heard so many nice comments about a show. I would like to say that Columbia is really working to keep me going, anyway."

Sam Katzman produced five pictures between **Rock Around the Clock** and **Don't Knock the Rock**. That he would make **Cha-Cha-Cha Boom** (1956) right before he made this picture, suggests that Katzman would take a gamble on any current music craze.

Rock and roll idol Arnie Haynes (Alan Dale) returns to his home town for a little rest and relaxation, and finds the townspeople divided on rock music. During an out-of-town rock show, Sunny Everett (Jana Lund) vindictively incites a brawl, angry at Haynes for not giving in to her ready-and-willing charms. This gives the rock and roll naysayers all of the ammo they need in the way of proof that the music leads to violence. With some help from disc jockey Alan Freed, Haynes convinces the old guard that the music is no more evil than the jazz music of their generation.

There is a lot of music in this picture. Alan Dale sings "Your Love Is My Love," Dave Appell and His Applejacks do "Country Dance," "Applejack," and with Alan Dale "Don't Knock the Rock," "You're So Right," "Gonna Run," and "I Cry More." The Treniers sing "Rockin' on Sunday Night" and "Out of the Bushes," and of course, Bill Hayley and the Comets are back with "Hot Dog, Buddy," "Calling All Comets," "Rip It Up" and "Don't Knock the Rock." But it's Little Richard who steals the show with "Tutti Frutti" and "Long Tall Sally."

Patricia Hardy, Alan Dale and Jana Lund.

"Tutti Frutti" was a song Richard sang when he was making twelve bucks a week washing dishes. Whenever he wanted to say something nasty to the boss, he'd launch into awop-bop-a-loo-mop-alop-bam-boom. The boss didn't know what he meant, and neither did Richard. "Long Tall Sally" was partially written by 16-year old Enortis Johnson. She walked all the way from Mississippi to California to sell Richard a song to get money for her sick Aunt Mary. The girl didn't have a melody, just a scrap of paper with the following words: *Saw Uncle John with Long Tall Sally. They saw Aunt Mary comin' so they ducked back in the alley.* The rest had to be improvised during the recording session. The shamelessly sexy lyrics were toned down by Dorothy La Bostrie, though not enough for Pat Boone. "She knows how to love me" became "She's a real gone cookie," and so on and so forth. Boone never wanted to sing the song in the first place. He knew he wasn't a rock and roller, though his version of "Tutti Frutti" outsold Richard's, simply because Richard's version didn't get the air play that Boone's did.

"I'd take one with Little Richard once a week if I could get it," said E.K. Holder, an exhibitor in Arkansas.

Richard is first seen, standing at the piano, in a flashy silver suit, large enough to house a small family, transfixed, as lifeless as a toy with a dead battery. He's introduced by Alan Freed as "that solid man of rock and roll." Richard suddenly comes to life, pounding the piano keys, making suggestive hip gyrations with one leg planted on the music shelf. He's in good form here, but he's even better in **Let the Good Times Roll** (1973).

There is a wonderful sequence in the film when director Fred F. Sears pulls his camera away from Haley and the Comets singing "Rip It Up," to watch a bunch of teenagers dancing their hearts out, the incredible Leon Tyler among them. The camera pauses to watch one couple, then moves on to the next. One pony-tailed lass takes a rather undignified spill, which remains in the film, as do the gaffers tape marks on the carpet, and the tracks left by the camera. Nevertheless, it's an ambitious number for a picture like this, besides being a lot of fun.

Boxoffice thought the picture was "tastefully done, with some imaginative touches," but an exhibitor in Waterville, Washington, W. P. Brown, thought it was "indecent and immoral," all of those teenage girls in "very scant bathing suits" and the boys in "breech cloths," dancing to rock and roll in a *public* dance hall. "Word of mouth stopped all business on second day. I was ashamed," Brown said. *Cue* didn't like anything about the movie and thought the music "(if that is the proper word) is sometimes uncomfortably akin to a jungle tom-tom." J.C. Balkcom ran it on Christmas night and was amazed. He'd been in the business for fourteen years and had never filled the house before on Christmas night.

Dig you later.

John Ashley, Judy Bamber, Fay Spain and Steve Terrell.

DRAGSTRIP GIRL (April, 1957) American International
M Ronald Stein, W Lou Rusoff, P Alex Gordon, D Edward L. Cahn

Some kids like to dance and some kids like to kill! Speed crazy! Thrill crazy! Fun-loving teenagers, free-wheeling and fast traveling in Hollywood's newest bang up, crack up, smash up double feature of fast cars and fast living! She's a dream at a dance, a darling at romance, but she's a devil on wheels. **Dragstrip Girl.** *You'll meet a teenage tantalizer with a chassis that makes all men's motors roar.* **Dragstrip Girl** *and* **Rock All Night.** *You'll meet the tough, smart little guy who's not afraid of anything, even death, just as long as he can take someone with him when he goes. And here's music for the coolest chicks and the mellowest men when the Blockbusters and The Platters blow up and sing up the stormiest sessions of sensational songs in the double rock and roll, terror thrill show* **Rock All Night** *and* **Dragstrip Girl.** *Don't miss this rockin' and rollin' double feature about teenagers, starring teenagers.*

Low octane melodrama, attempts to open strong with John Ashley straddling two hot-rods as they race through the city streets, as pictured on the poster. Unfortunately, there's no sense of danger or urgency because it's shot indoors, in front of an obvious process screen, with a background plate that's just slightly shy of being at the correct angle. It's pretty funny.

Ashley was 24-years old when he was signed to play the teenage villain in **Dragstrip Girl**. His girlfriend was auditioning for a part in the picture, and had asked him to come along. "I was waiting in the reception room when the producer walked out and asked if I was there to read for a part, and I told him I was waiting for someone. He asked me my name and wanted to know if I was an actor. Now, to be honest with you, I'd never even thought about it. I said, 'Sure. Why not?' So I read for the part and threw in an imitation of Elvis Presley which I thought was dynamite at the time. Elvis and I laughed about it later."

Fred Armstrong (Ashley) is determined to win the U.S.A. Regional Sweepstakes, and the heat of car crazy, speed crazy, boy crazy Louise Blake (Fay Spain). His rival is Jim Donaldson (Steve Terrell) who, unlike Fred, needs the prize money to continue with his education. Fred tells Louise that ever since they were kids, he and Jim went after the same thing, and somehow, Jim always got it. This time, it was going to be different.

Louise's mother warns her not to get too serious with either of the boys. "Serious is the last thing I want," Louise assures her. "All that jazz comes soon enough." Louise enjoys pitting one suitor against the other, which eventually leads to a brawl.

"Steve Terrell and I had a fight scene," said Ashley. "We took a couple of swings at each other for the close shots. Steve and I were two healthy young guys, and they brought in these two old cockers, old enough to be our fathers, to double for us."

Fay Spain and Steve Terrell.

Director Edward L. Cahn with Pin-Up girl Judy Bamber in her big screen debut. Bamber's manager negotiated contract deals with both Warner Bros. and American International. When the two companies found out about it, the deal of was off. The actress landed a few more film roles, but worked mostly in TV and in 1962 gave up.

Just before The Regional Sweepstakes, Fred swipes Jim's car for a test run. He wants to know what he's up against. He accidentally kills someone and is happy to let the police arrest Jim as the race is about to begin. Louise jumps into Jim's car and wins the race, despite Fred's attempts to run her off of the track. He knows Louise has the evidence that puts him behind the wheel of Jim's car on the night of the hit and run.

"The action moves along at a fast pace and there are plentiful chills and thrills," claimed *Harrison's Reports*. *The Los Angeles Times* thought the youngsters in the film were "very poor representatives of today's youth." *The Monthly Film Bulletin* called it "depressing and irresponsible." Oklahoma exhibitor Jess Jones admitted that the acting "may smell a little like last year's senior class play in spots, the story isn't bad, and the business was darned good."

No girl can manicure a motor or race a man's engine like the **Dragstrip Girl**.

DRAGSTRIP RIOT aka THE RECKLESS AGE (March, 1958) American International

M Nicholas Carras, W George Hodgins, P-D O'Dale Ireland

As the credits roll over scenes of fast cars zipping along the highway, we hear The Ripcords (sounding suspiciously like The Modernaires) sing "Teenage Rumble," the original title of the movie. It has everything—fast cars, fist-fights, cat-fights, and dancing—and all in the first ten minutes!

Fresh out of jail for defending a lady's honor, Rick Martin (Gary Clarke) promises his mother (Fay Wray) that his fighting days are over. He's got his work cut out for him because a troublemaker named Bart (Bob Turnbull) wants Rick's girl, Janet (Yvonne Lime). He challenges Rick to a Train Drag. (I'd never heard of it either.) "Don't go," Janet begs. "I don't make the rules," Rick tells her boldly. There's a lot of this male posturing and swaggering in this show.

A train drag is when two morons park their cars on a train track

Yvonne Lime and Gary Clarke, two veterans of teenpics, underpaid and unappreciated.

and wait for the train. The first one to bail is the loser. Bart is the loser and he's a sore one. Back at the hangout, someone laughingly remarks that after he lost the race, he took off "like a misguided missile." Feeling the fool, Bart attempts to provoke a fight between Rick and Silva (John Garwood), the leader of a motorcycle gang. Trying to keep his promise to his mother, Rick walks out, making everyone think he's a coward, including Janet. Not content with making Rick look yellow, Silva follows him outside, insults him, then manhandles Janet. The next thing Silva knows, he's on his ass, proving that he's as big a loser as Bart. In an attempt to save face, Silva says, "This is only round one."

Round two has Rick alone in his car, with Silva and his gang on motorcycles, chasing after him. (One of the bikers was injured, so Gary Clarke put on the guy's helmet, climbed on his motorcycle, and chased after himself.) Silva pulls up alongside Rick's car and hurls a wrench at him. Rick ducks and the wrench hits Silva's best buddy, Gordy (Barry Truex). Gordy loses control of his bike and ends up dead at the bottom of a ravine.

Round three takes place on the beach. "You're responsible for Gordy's death!" Silva screams. Anyone coming in on the film at this point might be terribly concerned. The hero is unarmed, in the open, with the villain standing less than eight or nine feet away, ready to pull the trigger on a spear gun. It looks pretty hopeless, but *we* know that there's nothing to worry about. Because Silva is a loser. "This is for Gordy," he says, and squeezes the trigger. The spear sails past Rick and plunges into the biggest loser of them all, Bart, standing nearby, watching with eager anticipation.

At the end of what was supposed to be a three week shoot, with very little to show for it, and with no money left, producer-director O'Dale Ireland gathered the actors together and said, "Listen, if you guys help us out, you'll all be stars. This thing is really coming together." Six months later, with the actors working for free the whole time, it finally did. David Bradley gets the credit for directing the film, but he was thrown off of the picture after a week and Ireland took over.

"The rain didn't stop this one," raved exhibitor Simon M. Cherivtch. "Turned in 200 per cent on a bill with **The Cool and the Crazy**."

"Probably one of the worst movies ever made in America," said Gary Clarke. "If not, then the second worst."

"How many times have I told you not to play with that knife when I'm not around?"

EARTH VS. THE SPIDER aka THE SPIDER (September, 1958) American International

M Albert Glasser, *W* Laszlo Gorog and George Worthing Yates, *P-D* Bert I. Gordon

Originally announced as **The Black Terror**, then **The Spider**, then **Earth vs. the Spider** as it appears on the credits, it was back as **The Spider** in the newspaper

Gene (The Party Crashers) Persson and June (Hot Car Girl) Kenney, caught in the giant spider's web.

ads, in order to take advantage of Fox's enormously successful **The Fly** (1958). I saw a marquee at the time that boasted **THE SPIDER** and **THE FLY**.

Jack Flynn (Merritt Stone) is on his way home, driving along a stretch of deserted highway at night, with a bracelet for his daughter's birthday in the seat beside him. He grins, knowing how thrilled she'll be, when his eyes go wide with horror and he hits something that cracks his windshield, and as he screams, a stream of blood comes shooting through his side window and splatters his face. At least, I assume it was supposed to be blood. One can only speculate. I get that it was the web that he hit. That's explained later. But what was that blood all about?

Flynn's daughter Carol (June Kenny), and her insensitive boyfriend Mike (Gene Persson), find Jack's truck in a ditch, and the bracelet. Carol thinks he may have gone into the nearby cave to spend the night. But there's a KEEP OUT sign and Carol has second thoughts about going in. Mike says he never believed all of "those stories" about the people who went into the cave and never came out again. Well, *somebody* must have believed them or they wouldn't have posted the sign. This is a small town. Either people are missing or they're not.

Not knowing of what speaks, Mike bravely presses on with Carol nervously at his side, and the two of them fall into a giant spider web. The giant spider appears and they barely escape with their lives. Sheriff Cagle (Gene Roth) doesn't believe their wild tale so the kids go to their high school teacher, Mr. Kingman, played by Ed Kemmer, a familiar figure to the baby boomers who knew him as Commander Buzz Corry on TV's **Space Patrol** (1950-1955). He starred in another sci-fi thriller a few months before he made this picture. Joked Kemmer, "We used to say, 'This is shit, but we'll make it the best shit we can.'" As Kingman, he persuades the sheriff to investigate. They find Carol's father, sucked dry by the spider, and then they find the spider. Kingman suggests a massive dose of DDT ought to put it out of commission. The "dead" spider is taken back to town and put on display in the high school gymnasium, awakened from its nap by some students rehearsing for the Friday sock hop. The spider busts out of the building and blows through town, stopping long enough to eat a woman who has her dress caught in her car door, does a little damage, and then heads for Kingman's home to terrorize his wife (Sally Fraser) and baby, to get even with Kingman for suggesting the DDT. Kingman drives his car into the spider's behind, then takes off with the spider on his tail. He leads it back to the cave, where Carol and Mike are looking for the bracelet that she dropped.

An ear-piercing score, a screenplay that defies logic, listless direction, and director Bert Gordon's trademark special effects all combine to create a very enjoyable waste of 73-minutes.

"A giant spider! What next?"

Mary Webster and William Campbell.

*EIGHTEEN AND ANXIOUS (1957) Republic Pictures
M Leith Stevens, W Katherine Albert and Dale Eunson, P Edmond Chevie, D Joe Parker

Nothing provoked intolerance quite like teenage pregnancy, most of it directed at the young lady involved. Yes, the young man was told to keep it in his pants, but you know how guys are. They can't help themselves. But the ladies, well, they were supposed to know better. Let them hang their heads in shame. Ship 'em out of town so they can have their babies in secret and not disgrace the family. Make them feel worse than murderers. They have it coming.

Judy Graham (Mary Webster) is the target of scorn and contempt when she becomes pregnant and can't prove (because of a typographical error) that she was secretly married in Mexico, where her husband was killed. Her father (Jim Backus) doesn't know that she's pregnant when he grabs at her housecoat and remarks, "Those double malts are showing." She decides to get an abortion and is told to "think of it just as a blemish we're removing." Sometime later, Judy gets a job and is on the cusp of having a decent relationship with Danny Fuller (Ron Hagerthy), when she falls for a sleazy trumpet player (William Campbell) who leaves her high and dry on what she thought was going to be her wedding day.

"Well, here in the middle of a deluge of screen junk about flaming youth, is a surprisingly decent and absorbing case history that rings true," said *The New York Times*. "Mr. and Mrs. Eunson have shaped an appealing, if not memorable, sermon on self-deception and selfishness." *Motion Picture Herald* found it "crude and unsuitable" for impressionable teenagers, but exhibitor Victor Weber said he was "looking for more like it."

Look for Yvonne Craig and Connie Stevens.

Parents may be shocked but…youth will understand!

ESCAPE FROM RED ROCK (December, 1957) 20th Century-Fox

M Les Baxter, *P* Bernard Glasser, *W-D* Edward Bernds

In **The Left-Handed Gun** (1958), Paul Newman plays Billy the Kid like another misunderstood delinquent. This was inevitable, with all of the focus on the teenagers, coupled with an inordinate interest in psychology at the time. (It actually became fashionable to have a psychiatrist, like one might sport a new hat.) According to one film critic, this modestly budgeted western should have been called **I Was a Teenage Desperado**.

"When we made **Escape to Red Rock**," said writer-director Edward Bernds, "there was a lot of interest in youth-oriented pictures at the time. Bob Lippert needed a western, so I took **Rebel Without a Cause** and set it in the west."

So-so western finds Cal Bowman (Gary Murray) in one scrap after another, defending his brother's name, because everyone in town thinks he's a crook. The Sheriff (J. C. Flippen) is sick of it. "Whether it's true or not, that's what everyone thinks. You can't fight them all. You're just gonna have to learn to live with it," he tells the boy.

When Cal gets home that night, he discovers the townspeople were right. Bronc Gierson (Brian Donlevy) and his outlaw gang are in his house, and his brother Judd (Rick Vallin) is dying from a bullet in his gut. Cal wants to take him to the doctor but Bronc can't let him do that. People would ask questions and there's a rope waiting for all of their necks. Bronc knows a doctor in Selano that'll keep his mouth shut.

"He's as crooked as a sidewinder's track in the sand, but he's a good doctor. He'll fix Judd up. But it takes money." And the only way for Cal to get the money is to help Bronc rob the express office. All he has to do is check the place out and give them the lay out. Naturally, things go awry because one of the members of the gang is Joe Skinner, and he's played by Myron Healey, always the badest of the bad guys, and during the hold-up he shoots a woman in the back. Judd dies and Cal takes it on the lam with Janie Acker (Eileen Janssen), who is more than happy to leave her abusive stepfather behind. "When my mother was alive, he got drunk and beat her. Now he gets drunk and beats me."

Arrangements are made to meet with someone who will take them to Mexico, but when Cal and Janie arrive at the cabin, the family has been slaughtered by the Apaches, except for a little baby girl. Bronc and the gang show up and Bronc takes a shine to the kid. "Hate to see anything happen to this little lady." When they run out of milk, Bronc tells Joe to get some. Joe doesn't want to stick his neck out. The baby can starve for all he cares. "You yellow-belly," Bronc says with disgust. "Let her go hungry, he says. Shoot a woman in the back, that's your speed. So you think I'm mush-headed, huh? Let's see you draw and find out."

"One of the lesser Regalscope pictures," declared *Boxoffice*. *Hollywood Reporter* thought it was "original and tightly-conceived," and according to *Variety*, it was "sufficiently different to warrant good suspense." Exhibitor B. Berglund thought the RegalScope pictures had "more original stories than the big pictures. Drew a good crowd and satisfied all."

"You're not a man. You're a fool kid."

THE FLAMING TEEN-AGE aka TWICE CONVICTED (June, 1956)
Truman Enterprises, Inc.
W Ethel Barrett and Jean Yeaworth, P-D Charles Edwards and Irvin S. Yeaworth

Originally released as **Twice Convicted** (who knows when or why), it was based on the life of Fred Garland, the founder of the International Fellowship of Fundamental Baptists. He is portrayed in the film by Noel Rayburn. Garland sells his candy store and heads for New York, where he hopes to become a Broadway producer. He becomes an alcoholic instead. (I understand that you can do both.)

Hoping to ride the wave of the current cycle of teenage melodramas, Irvin S. Yeaworth and Charles Edward added a second story to this tepid little tale, in which a high school dropout also becomes a victim of the devil's brew. As this new story added additional time to the film, it only made matters worse.

"If nominations are being accepted for the worst movie of the year," chimed the critic for the *Los Angeles Mirror News*, "let me submit **The Flaming Teenage**, a yawn-packed, drab and almost witless botching of screencraft."

Get ready for the shock of your life!

FOUR BOYS AND A GUN (January, 1957) United Artists
M Albert Glasser, Shorty Rogers, *W* Phillip Yordan, Leo Townsend, *P-D* William Burke

Frank Sutton, Tarry Green, William Hinnant and James Franciscus (in his film debut) commit a robbery, during which Sutton shoots and kills a policeman. Not being very good crooks, the four are quickly rounded up and taken into custody. In a flashback, we learn what led each of them to do what they did.

Sutton doesn't make much money as a runner for a small-time bookie, but the narcissistic lout sure likes to spend it, especially on women. He's gotten himself deep in debt and he needs the money desperately. Green works at the same place his girl works and discovered she's having an affair with their scummy boss. Humiliated, he slaps her and delivers a haymaker to the boss's jaw. Ergo, no girl, no job. Hinnant is too timid to do anything but go along with what everyone else wants to do. And Franciscus, still reeling from being told that his dream of being a professional boxer was never going to happen, suddenly finds his wife in need of an expensive operation.

Once captured, the four would-be candidates for the electric chair have a choice to make. If the one who actually did the shooting will confess, or if the others rat him out, the rest will get life in prison, and only the shooter will fry.

Boxoffice called it "a first rate low-budget film." It is easily the best film that director William Burke ever made and is well worth a look.

"Right now, you don't look like killers. You look like four no-good punks."

FRANKENSTEIN'S DAUGHTER aka SHE MONSTER OF THE NIGHT (December, 1958) Astor
M Nicholas Carras, *W* H. E. Barrie, *P* Marc Frederic, *D* Richard E. Cunha

Wonderfully deranged, contemptable piece of junk, has Oliver Frankenstein (Donald Murphy) carrying on the family tradition in the home of his employer, Carter Morton (Felix Locher), who is working on a drug that he hopes will wipe out all disease. Frankenstein tests it on Carter's teenaged ward, Trudy (Sandra Knight). It turns her into a monster.

Frankenstein has the hots for Trudy, but she wants nothing to do with him, and when her trashy friend, Suzie Lawler (Sally Todd), gives him the brush-off, it's more than he can take. He kills Suzie and plants her brain in the monster's skull. I don't know about you, but I'd think twice about bringing someone back to life that I'd just murdered.

"I knew when we were making the film that it didn't seem very frightening," said star John Ashley, easily the best actor in it. Donald Murphy is delightfully over-the-top and Felix Locher's "incredibly weak performance" (according to the *Monthly Film Bulletin*) "adds an unintentionally humorous note."

Harry Wilson, John Ashley, Sandra Knight and Donald Murphy, caught with their pants down.

"I think they were all talented [actors], it's just that the movie stunk," Sally Todd told author John O'Dowd. "Let me tell you, any one of us could have written better lines than we were given."

Page Cavanaugh and His Trio perform two numbers, "Special Date" and "Daddy Bird," at a pool party in Carter's backyard, actually the backyard of Harold Lloyd, Jr. who sings with them. At the end of the number someone, apparently a music critic, pushes him in the pool.

Called "a dismal clinker" by *The Los Angeles Examiner*, **Frankenstein's Daughter** has far too many magic moments to list them all here, so I will use restraint and focus only on one. The monster finds its way out of the lab and smacks the front door off its hinges. Sometime later, Trudy hears a knock at the front door, which has somehow healed itself. She opens it and there (gadzooks!) is the monster, so confused by this indestructible, self-healing door that he felt the need to knock this time. Trudy screams and faints, and is later told that it was all in her mind.

"*I need a brain! I need a brain!*"

GHOST OF DRAGSTRIP HOLLOW aka THE HAUNTED HOT-ROD (July, 1959) American International
M Ronald Stein, W-P Lou Rusoff, D William Hole Jr.

Incomprehensible, lame-brained sequel to **Hot Rod Gang** (1958), will leave viewers exhausted. Jody Fair, who was cast in John Frankenheimer's **The Young Savages** (1961) because of her association with films like this, returns as Lois Cavendish, a member of The Zeniths, a gang of law-abiding teens who dig racing fast cars, like Miss Fair herself. "Someone once told me I drove like a parking lot attendant." The Zeniths can't pay the rent on their clubhouse, so Lois's Aunt Anastasia

(Dorothy Newman) opens the old family house to them, perfect for their Halloween party.

Lots of songs in this one. None of them good. The performers: Nick Venet and the Vettes ("Geronimo," "Charge," "Ghost Train"), Charlotte Breson ("He's My Guy"), Jimmy Maddino ("Tongue Tied"), Bruce Johnson and Judy Harriet ("I Promise You"), and Ronald Stein composed the bouncy main title, recorded in stereo.

Swan song for Paul Blaisdell, the creator of such memorable monsters as the Tabonga and the saucer-men, dons his she-creature costume one last time to appear as a monster-maker on his way out. As this was actually the case, it is an embarrassing and uncomfortable to scene to watch.

"It's virtually impossible to assess individual actors since the script is so poor and the directing so perfunctory," declared *Variety*. "Why teens like these, I'll never know," groused exhibitor W. E. Seaver. Jim Fraser didn't care. "Ran this alone on a kiddie matinee, and, brother, did it pull them in. Very funny and a little scary. The kids yelled their lungs out and had a bang-up time."

"*He's got static in the attic.*"

GIANT GILA MONSTER (June, 1959) McClendon Radio Pictures
M Jack Marshall, W Jay Sims, P Ken Curtis, D Ray Kellogg

First feature produced by Gordon McClendon, who for over twenty years wrote radio campaigns for United Artists and American International. The owner of radio stations and a theatre chain in Texas, one afternoon it struck McClendon that if he could sell pictures he could make them. A package of horror pictures sounded like the best bet. "I am going very quietly crazy, getting ready to shoot our two epic productions starting here in January," McClendon wrote to a friend. "These are turning out to be horror pictures in every sense of the word, but we are looking for tremendous grosses in Southern Tibet." It cost him a little over $100,000 to make **The Killer Shrews** and **Giant Gila Monster**.

Jay Simms loads his screenplay with all of the things he thinks the kids want to see—hot-rods, sock hops, misunderstood teenagers, and the Gila monster, of course. His script is long on talk and short on action. Worse, there isn't a single scene of the monster and the people in the same shot. We watch the critter move across obvious miniature sets with nary a human in sight. One dramatic moment finds the Gila monster making its way toward a Lionel train, overturned in a gully. As it crawls past a pathetic little twig (doing its best to look like a mighty Oak), the lizard knocks it over. We hear the splintering of wood, loudly supplied by the soundtrack, suddenly making it all so believable. Director Ray Kellogg was once the head of the special effects unit at 20th Century-Fox. The studio would never have let him get away with what he was doing here.

"I loved the movie," said Don Sullivan, the film's star. "It was a tour de force. I got to play and sing my songs, and do the lead in a movie."

Sullivan is good in the picture. *The Los Angeles Times* called him "a rather skilled young actor, who must graduate from these little efforts sometime soon." He plays Chase Winstead, an auto mechanic who supports his mother and his crippled sister since the death of his father. He also writes songs in his spare time and has a girlfriend, Lisa (Lisa Simone). It's a safe bet that Chase has never so much as copped a feel. He's pretty much of an Andy Hardy kind of a guy. He helps the Sheriff (Fred Graham) search for the missing people the Gila monster has eaten. He picks up a drunk (Ken Knox) and lets him sleep it off on a cot in the back room of his repair shop and won't let the guy pay him for his trouble. But this kind deed pays off. The drunk turns out to be "Steamroller Smith," a popular disc jockey. He's awakened from his sleep when Chase starts pounding a fender into submission while he sings "My Baby She Rocks," one of his own compositions. Steamroller sets up a recording session and shows up at the big barn dance to introduce Chase's new record, "I Ain't Made That Way." The kids go wild. He also sings, for the second time, "The Mushroom Song," which he sang to his crippled sister in an earlier, shamelessly sentimental sequence. "His vocal assets don't match even his minor acting talents," said *Variety*. *The Los Angeles Examiner* noted: "It seems that a big theatre exhibitor in Dallas got together some money and after bowing three times in the direction of Hollywood (the producing company is actually called Hollywood Pictures Corp.) turned out these features. They're not very much, I'm afraid."

"*Let me have some of that there sody-pop.*"

James (Rumble on the Docks) *Darren and Sandra* (The Restless Years) *Dee.*

GIDGET (May, 1959) Columbia
M Fred Karger, W Gabrielle Upton, P Lewis J. Rachmil, D Paul Wendkos

Charming romantic comedy with a big heart and a little sex, but they didn't want to stress it. Based on Frederick Kohner's novel, *Gidget: The Little Girl with Big Ideas*, it was a fictionalized account of the stories that his daughter Kathy told him. "I was sixteen," she recalled. "I didn't want to be the girl on the beach looking at the men. I wanted to surf. It was not a competitive sport. I was competing against myself. I felt I could do this. I could be like one of them."

Kathy is number seven on *Surfer Magazine*'s list of the twenty-five most influential people in surfing. You'll also find her on the Surfing Walk of Fame in Huntington Beach, California. **Gidget** introduced the world to surfing and its culture, which is why the song, "Gidget," written by Fred Karger and Patti Washington, should be on any collection of surf music. You can always pretend Dick Dale is playing somewhere in the background.

On screen Kathy Kohner is Francine Lawrence, who the surfers nickname Gidget (girl plus midget), played by 15-year old Sandra Dee. She is perfect. The absolute ultimate! Dee manages to be naïve without being stupid. When Lover Boy (Tom Laughlin) tries to take advantage of her, while pretending to teach her how to surf, she thinks nothing of it when he lets his hands run across her body. The thought would never cross her mind that he was any more interested in sex than she is. The reason she's there in the first place is because the girls she used hang with during summer vacations have become "man-hunters." Gidget wanted no part of that. Surfing looks like fun to her, and she just wants to be one of the guys.

At first, she is the object of ridicule, a clumsy, awkward girl in a bathing suit that looks like something out of Max Sennett comedy. The guys don't want her but their objections are overridden by their idol, a charismatic beach bum called The Kahuna, real name Burt Vail (Cliff Robertson). He likes Gidget. And her determination ultimately wins everyone's respect. Along the way she falls for Moondoggie, real name Jeffrey Matthews (James Darren). Instead of going to college like his father expects him to do, Moondoggie thinks he wants to be like The Kahuna, living in a shack, never stopping in any one place for long, looking for the next wave, owing nothing to anyone. He plans to go with The Kahuna to surf in Peru. Kahuna knows he's only adopting this pose to tick off his father. But it's of no concern to him.

Gidget takes a spill and is rescued by Moondoggie. He carries her into The Kahuna's shack and out of the blue, the movie becomes surreal as Moondoggie breaks into the same song about Gidget that we heard The Four Preps sing during the main title. It's a little odd. Imagine James Dean suddenly breaking into a song about Natalie Wood when the two of them are alone in the big empty mansion in **Rebel Without a Cause**.

"They were gonna use somebody else's voice and I told them I could sing," Darrin said. "I'm not saying I had to sing well for 'Goodbye Cruel World,' but when I did 'There's No Such Thing' for **Gidget**, that happened to be a real good song. John Williams was conducting. Billy May did the arrangements for both songs. These were the people who would make a difference to me if they told me I couldn't sing. Then, maybe I wouldn't sing."

Once Gidget realizes that she's in love with Moondoggie, she pays someone to play up to her at the big luau, hoping to make Moondoggie jealous. Moondoggie shows up in the guy's stead. Thinking fast, Gidget tells Moondoggie she's after The Kahuna. Moondoggie betrays himself when he asks, "Don't you find Kahuna to be

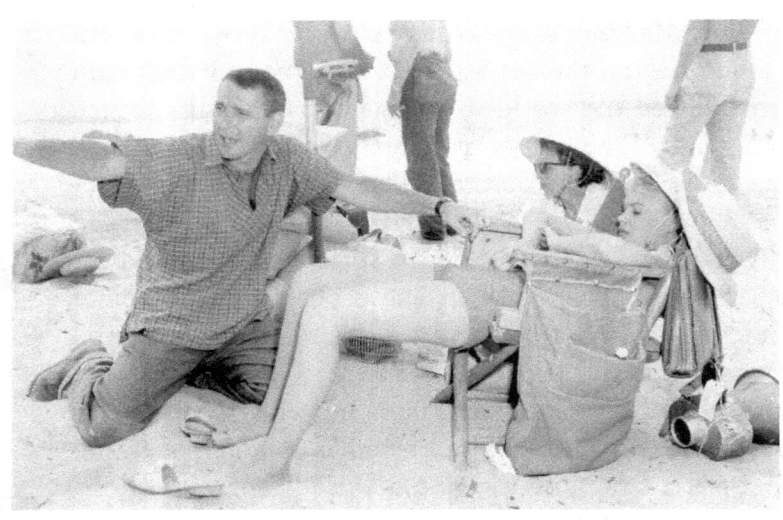
Director Paul Wendkos and Sandra Dee.

a little on the lazy side?" She replies, "Love makes room for fault." When Moondoggie hears that Gidget has gone off with The Kahuna for one of his "private parties," he jumps into his car and burns rubber. Gidget hopes (kind of) to lose her virginity to The Kahuna, believing then Moondoggie will quit thinking of her as a kid. In the film's only dark moment, Kahuna pretends to take her seriously, hoping to call her bluff, but as he looks at her sweet, innocent face, resting in his lap, he has a moment, brief though it may be, of giving her what she's asking for. Angry at himself, he throws her out. She's in tears, running out the back way as Moondoggie knocks at the door. She assumes the boys will have a good laugh at her expense, but The Kahuna has something else in mind. He's going to give Gidget what he knows she really wants—Moondoggie. He unbuttons his shirt, musses his hair and opens the door. Moondoggie barges in and is ready to trade blows. "Bringing a broad to a place like this is one thing," he says reproachfully, "but the Gidget…" Kahuna smiles. "Personally, I found her delightful company and a very good sport," giving the impression that he deflowered their cute little mascot. Gidget sadly tells her mom (Mary LaRoche) that after all of her efforts, "I came home as pure as the driven snow."

We baby boomers were lucky enough to be on the tail end of the ballyhoo days of the movie going experience, when an exhibitor would do something more than change their marquee to announce the arrival of a new attraction. In Glens Falls, New York, the manager of the Rialto held a contest to select their own "Gidget." Any girl from grades 10 through 12 was eligible, so long as they weren't over five feet and had been chosen by their classmates. The girls were outfitted in gowns from one of the local merchants, treated to a hotel dinner, and then driven to the theatre in a parade of small sport cars, supplied by another local merchant, with a motorcycle escort. The red carpet was rolled out and the young ladies entered the theatre in style. Now that's ballyhoo, my friend.

Gidget was a big hit for Columbia, and Darren was back for the sequels—**Gidget Goes Hawaiian** (1961), with Deborah Walley as Gidget, and **Gidget Goes to Rome** (1963) with Cindy Carol taking over the role. Sally Field played Gidget in a short-lived TV series, and in 1969, Karen Valentine starred in a movie made for TV, **Gidget Grows Up**, followed by **Gidget Gets Married** (1972), **Gidget's Summer Reunion**, and yet another sitcom, **The New Gidget** (1986) starring Caryn Richman. But without Sandra Dee, what was the point? Small wonder that when William Asher was getting ready to make **Beach Party** (1963), it wasn't Annette Funicello that he wanted. It was Sandra Dee.

"*To get this date, I had to fork over hard cash.*"

THE GIRL CAN'T HELP IT (December, 1956) 20th Century-Fox
M Lionel Newman, *W* Frank Tashlin and Herbert Baker, *P-D* Frank Tashlin

This splashy, colorful rock and roll extravaganza began as a modest, black and white satire of the jukebox racket, from a story by Garson Kanin called *Do Re Mi*. Tom Ewell and Sheri North were slated for the lead roles, with Nunnally Johnson producing and directing. It was still in the butt-scratching stage three months later, when Columbia's *Rock Around the Clock* went into release and within a few months grossed three million dollars. The figure was still climbing when Fox switched gears and turned *Do Re Mi* into a vehicle for rock and roll music and its new star, Jayne Mansfield.

Mansfield made a name for herself by lampooning Marilyn Monroe in the smash Broadway play, *Will Success Spoil Rock Hunter?* She reprised her role in the hit movie of the same name, produced and directed by Frank Tashlin. Which is the reason Tashlin was put in charge of producing and directing *The Girl Can't Help It*. He once remarked that there was nothing funnier than a big-breasted woman. As Mansfield

Tom Ewell and Jayne Mansfield.

Little Richard, the Queen of rock 'n roll.

struts down the street, with Little Richard singing the title song (written by Bobby Troup), eyeglasses crack and ice melts and milk boils out of bottles.

"A forty-one inch bust and a lot of perseverance will get you more than a cup of coffee—a lot more," Mansfield once remarked. When she walked into Tashlin's office for the first time, he thought her breasts were fake until she peeled away her tight-fitting, striped sweater. In the film she's Jerri Jordan, the girlfriend of mobster Fats Murdock (Edmond O'Brien), who hires a heart-broken, drunken promotor (Tom Ewell) to make her a singing sensation.

The studio probably had more faith in Miss Mansfield than in it did in the music, for during nearly every performance, the camera cuts away to give the actress another opportunity to thrust her bountiful chest across the CinemaScope screen. A projectionist in Ohio was so mesmerized by her bazooms that he "plum forgot to change the reels."

"Amid such comments as, 'Dig that crazy music,' 'Go, man, go' 'Cu-razy man!' 'It's the most,' we happily counted the boxoffice," wrote exhibitor F. A. Phillips, the owner of the Nortown Theatre in Flint, Michigan. "Miss Mansfield drew the usual cat-calls and whistles, especially when walking, but it was the music they came for."

The movie features rock legends Little Richard ("She's Got It," "Rip It Up," "The Girl Can't Help It"), Fats Domino ("Blue Monday"), Eddie Cochran ("20 Flight Rock"), and Gene Vincent ("Be Bop a Lula"), in their prime, and in color. (The studio would have added Elvis Presley to the line-up but his manager wanted too much money.) Also on board, the most popular singing group of the era, The Platters ("You'll Never Know"), sultry Julie London singing what became her trademark number, "Cry Me a River," The Chuckles ("Cinnamon Sinner") Eddie Fontaine ("Cool It Baby"), Abbey Lincoln ("Spread the Word"), Johnny Oleen ("I Ain't Gonna

Cry No More," "My Idea of Love"), Nino Tempo ("Tempo's Tempo"), and The Treniers ("Rockin' Is Our Bizness"). But it's Edmond O'Brien who unexpectedly steals the show with his spirited rendition of "Rock Around the Rock Pile."

The critic for the *New York Times* found the picture "as meager and witless as a cheap pin-up magazine joke." *The Hollywood Reporter* called it a rock and roll comedy with class, "as effervescent as New Year's Eve and as goofy and gay as somebody else's funny paper hat." *The Los Angeles Mirror* said Miss Mansfield "makes the big beat sound better." From Seagoville, Texas, exhibitor Jerry B. Walden reported: "Our town has gone nuts, and I mean nuts, over rock and roll, and we have a filled theatre every time we show that kind of film. This was even more than they could have asked for—color, CinemaScope, good story, with Jayne Mansfield to hold the men's attention. Fellow exhibitors, do not miss showing this one. It's the most!"

"No one thinks I'm equipped for motherhood."

GIRL GANG (1954) Screen Classics
W Robert C. Dertano and George Weiss, P George Weiss, D Robert C. Dertano

It had been several decades since this movie had graced the movie palaces on skid row, and one Christmas day, after all of the presents had been opened, and with a glass of egg nog in hand, Mary Lou O'Connor's family gathered around the television to watch this old movie she was in a long time ago for the very first time, a film not quite as popular at Christmas time as **It's a Wonderful Life**, but rest assured that **Girl Gang** is rapidly gaining ground.

It's in focus! You can't take that away from it. Other than that, there is a complete absence of screen craft. Even the notorious Edward Wood, often called the worst filmmaker in Hollywood's history, is far more talented than the writer-director of this film.

Most of the picture takes place in the home of Joe, the Big Boss, played by Timothy Farrell, a staple in these Z-grade melodramas. Joe and his accomplice, June (Joanne Arnold) get teenage girls hooked on drugs and turn them into prostitutes and thieves. All it takes is a couple of puffs on a joint and virginal Wanda Johnson (*Mary Lou O'Connor*) eagerly submits to a little passionate necking with Joe, who has all of the charm of a gob of spit, with her boyfriend asleep in a chair not five feet away. Once Joe gets them hooked, they need money to feed their habit and will do anything to get it. Wanda is told that in order to be a member of the gang, she has to service five guys. She's a little hesitant at first, but as soon as she hears that everyone else did it, she's on board. Happily on board.

"I cannot believe what this movie contains for the time period," Mary Lou's daughter remarked. There is a lengthy sequence that explains how to freebase. "It is astonishing the things that they show the people doing, or is it just the fact that my mom is in it that I find it so unbelievable?"

Even in a movie like this, they have to go outdoors every now and then for a little fresh air, but with no money for sound or dubbing, the characters have to communicate during these sequences as best as they can through gestures, like charades. In a car-jacking sequence, we see two members of the girl gang, waiting by the side of the road for a sucker, standing like two zombies, not saying anything to one another the way normal people would. Just waiting, waiting, and waiting. Understandably, they hitch a ride with the first car that pulls over, which isn't nearly soon enough. They climb into the front seat, smiling all the while at this poor fool behind the wheel, but nobody can say anything! So they just sit there, stupidly gazing at each other until another car mercifully pulls up. Two more members of the gang get out, with guns at the ready. The driver can't even say, "Hey! What's the big idea?" Instead, he quietly gets out, they bonk him on the head, and drive off with his car.

Once the girls are back at Joe's place, they are able to speak again, and they have a quite lot to say. And as you sit there, listening to this uninteresting, poorly written, badly acted prattle, you start thinking that maybe the filmmakers were onto something when they cut the sound. Maybe the picture would be better *without* it. As an experiment, you turn the volume off and find that, in fact, it *is* better! Of course, one can't help but wonder, at this stage of the game, if the movie might be better still without the image.

"*Weed today. Shot tomorrow.*"

GIRLS IN THE NIGHT (January, 1953) Universal-International
M Henry Mancini, Herman Stein, *W* Ray Buffum, *P* Albert J. Cohen, *D* Jack Arnold

Jack Arnold directed this depressing yarn of poverty and hopelessness, filmed on location on New York's East Side and in Brooklyn, in the slum of the city where crime and delinquency flourish.

"I made a documentary called **With These Hands** [1950] that was nominated by the Academy, and Universal was looking for directors. **Girls in the Night** was one of their B-pictures. They'd made a picture called **The Naked City** [1948] that did very well for them that was filmed entirely on location, which you always had to fight for because of the cost. They wouldn't have let me shoot on location if **The Naked City** had been a flop. We had some very good people, one girl—I can't remember her name [Jaclynne Greene]—they called her 'Ugly.' She was *very* good."

The film centers on the Haynes family, cocky and tough Chuck (Harvey Lembeck), his beauty-contest winning sister Hannah (Patricia Hardy), their worn-out mother (Glenda Farrell) and their laborer-father (Anthony Ross), all of them longing for a better life. Chuck and his girlfriend Georgia (Joyce Holden) decide to rip-off an old beggar (Paul Burns) who gets sympathy money by pretending to be blind. Irv Kellener (Don Gordon), a two-bit punk, and his shrewd and calculating girlfriend Vera (Jaclynne Greene), beat them to the punch. But the old man catches them in the act and Irv shoots him dead. Irv and Vera have to split before they can find the loot. Chuck and Georgia find the money ($600), but they never see the corpse. It all ends with an exciting chase along the waterfront.

Said Arnold, "The actors had to run across this narrow ledge that was ten or twelve feet high, and I could see that they weren't happy about it, so I did it myself, turned around and said, 'See. Nothing to it.' Some actors think walking up a flight of stairs is a stunt."

The New York Times called it "a hackneyed and colorless street scene," and accused it of going off "on a number of unbelievable side trips from many of which it never returns." The Hollywood Reporter called it "a solid little melodrama," and Motion Picture Herald reported the audience at the sneak preview screening at Lowe's "had a rousing good time all the way." Exhibitor James Hardy thought it was "an excellent picture."

Joyce (The Werewolf) Holden and Harvey (Beach Party) Lembeck.

The Terrifying Truth About the Big City's Delinquent Daughters!

GIRLS ON THE LOOSE (April, 1958) Universal-International
M Irving Gertz, W Alan Friedman, Dorothy Raison, Alan Rivkin, P Harry Rybnick, Richard Kay, D Paul Henreid

The sensational drama of crime-crazy girls, love-hungry girls, trigger-happy girls, girls who will stop at nothing. A story filled with excitement that cuts like a switch-blade knife!

Snappy dialogue from writers Alan Friedman and Dorothy Ralson, plus Mara Corday in the lead role is reason enough to watch this lively little slice of hokum. Corday is Vera Parkinson, a tough-as-nails broad and owner of a nightclub that's a front for her crime capers. The film opens with a heist, saving the audience from having to sit through the usual boring sequences of the criminals planning the heist. Things start to go wrong almost immediately.

Members of Vera's gang include her equally lethal partner, Joyce Barker (Joyce Johanneson), who before the film is over will engage in some literal back-stabbing. Marie Williams (Lita Milan) is a beautician who does a little shoplifting and pocket-picking on the side, and way too much drinking. "Talking to drunks is like talking to

Mara Corday, Lita Milan and Joyce Barker are on the loose and looking for action.

mud," Vera tells her. "It gets you nowhere." And Agnes Clark (Abby Dalton) is the unfortunate inside gal who supplied the information needed to pull off the heist. When the police start questioning the employees, Agnes starts to unravel. "Thinking takes brains," Vera tells her. "Just forget you've got 'em." Everyone decides that Agnes poses too much of a threat so Vera bumps her off, making her death look like a suicide. When asked if she ever hates herself in the morning, Vera blandly replies, "I never wake up in the morning."

Vera's sister Helen (Barbara Bostock), is the star attraction at her nightclub. She sings two songs, "How Do You Learn to Love?" and "I Was a Little Too Lonely," the latter written by Jay Livingston and Ray Evans, the team responsible for "Buttons and Bows," "Saddle the Wind," and "Tammy." Helen doesn't know what Vera is up to at first, but when she finds out, she begins to question her sister's judgement for the first time and their relationship, like all of the relationships in this film, falls apart. She also becomes a threat when she falls for the cop (Peter Mark Richmond) who isn't so sure that Agnes committed suicide.

This was a pick-up for Universal and was directed by Paul Henreid. Once a romantic lead, Henreid moved behind the camera when he fell victim to the blacklist. Not a name one usually associates with these kind of pictures, as star and co-producer of **So Young, So Bad**, and director of **Girls on the Loose** and **Live Fast, Die Young**, Henreid earned himself a place at the table.

"If you ever say that again, if you even think it, I'll ram these scissors right through you, you thick, ugly slob."

GIRLS TOWN (October, 1959) Metro-Goldwyn-Mayer

M Van Alexander, *W* Richard Hardy Andrews, Robert Smith, *P* Albert Zugsmith, *D* Charles F. Haas

Drippy Mel Torme as a slimy blackmailer, a bunch of nuns, and 28-year old Mamie Van Doren playing a *juvenile* delinquent in Albert Zugsmith's version of **Boys Town**. What more could a body ask for?

Mamie is in Girls Town, falsely convicted of murdering Harold Lloyd, Jr. There were those who suspected her motive had something to do with the song he sang in **Frankenstein's Daughter** but, in fact, Lloyd's death was an accident. He was trying to rape Mamie's sister, Elinor Donahue, when he lost his balance and fell over the side of a cliff. Hot-rodder Mel Torme saw the whole thing. First he blackmails Elinor into helping him with some robberies, then plans to take her across the border to sell to white slavers. He gets his comeuppance from Gloria Talbott when Mamie and the girls arrive in time to thwart Mel's plans.

Minister Domenico Magri, at the insistence of Italy's Committee for the Theatrical Review of the Ministry of Cultural Heritage and Activities, ordered the removal of a scene of Mamie singing in the shower that they found "offensive to decency." Zugsmith had flown to Italy to show the final cut of the film to Cardinal Spellman. His Holiness disapproved of Mamie's bare shoulders. "But your grace," Zugsmith argued, "even bad girls take showers."

Margaret Hayes, Mamie Van Doren and Paul Anka.

In addition to Mamie's song, "Hey, Mama," Cathy Crosby sings "I Love You," and The Platters perform "Wish It Were Me," their sequence staged to conceal the absence of lead singer Tony Williams who had left the group for a solo career.

"I had a 17-year old named Paul Anka in **Girls Town**, and in two years he had made a half million in in records, and he has been booked in the Palladium in London for $15,000 a week, and his record "Lonely Boy" is now number one," bragged Zugsmith. In addition to "Lonely Boy," Anka sings "Girls Town," "A Time to Cry," and "Ave Maria". He was only 15 when his song to his 18-year old babysitter, "Diana," hit the top of the charts.

Charles Chaplin, Jr, Gigi Perreau, Jim Mitchum (son of Bob), Ray Anthony, Jody Fair, Dick Contino, gossip columnist Sheila Graham and Woo Woo Grabowsky (here simply billed as Grabowsky) round out the cast.

"[A] blatantly crude and vulgar film," complained the critic for *Variety*. "There is a patina of fake piety spread over some of the proceedings by putting part of the action at an institution run by Catholic nuns. This won't fool the prurient-minded, although it could easily be offensive to Catholics." Exhibitor Paul Gomoche wished he could have one like it every two weeks. "Mamie Van Doren is a good draw here."

"*Pray earnestly, Sister, before you poke her in the kisser.*"

Molly Bee.

GOING STEADY (February, 1958)
Columbia
W Bud Grossman, P Sam Katzman, D Fred F. Sears

Molly Bee sings "Going Steady With a Dream" behind the credits, setting the tone for what turns out to be a very gentle comedy about teenage marriage, the polar opposite of AIP's **Diary of a High School Bride**.

Molly and Alan Reed, Jr., are a pair of high school sweethearts from Pasadena, California, who go to Las Vegas, Nevada for a school basketball game. It wasn't easy for Molly to get permission from her father, Bill Goodwin, a conservative, old-fashioned guy. "You know what kids are likely to do when they get together at their age," he tells his wife, Irene Hervey. "I have nothing against the boy personally, except that he's an idiot, of course, but I just think we should break up the relationship before it gets serious." He gives in after some friendly persuasion from his wife. "What could possibly happen at a basketball game?" she asks.

After the game, Molly and Alan get married, and decide to keep their marriage a secret from everyone until after they graduate, everyone but Kenny Miller and Susan Easter that is. Susan gives Kenny that look that more than suggests she expects a proposal soon. "Don't look at me like that," he tells her. "I'm only seventeen. I haven't gotten over my acne yet."

Molly decides to tell her mom, knowing she's going to have her work cut out for her, trying to think of a way to sell this marriage to her dear old dad. When Irene finally decides to spill it, Goodwin scoffs. "That is a feeble attempt at humor if ever I heard one." Once he understands that she isn't kidding, he goes through the roof. "*Now* you know what can happen at a basketball game!" he roars. He thinks he's going to have the marriage annulled when Molly announces that she's pregnant. "I won't have it!" he says flatly. Irene reminds him that *he* won't have to.

Boxoffice called it a "pleasing teenage romance," which it is, but *Motion Picture Herald* said it was "slow-paced," and that's true, too. But it's cute, and a welcome relief from all of the films where teenage pregnancy is treated like the plague. There's plenty of reality inside of this candy-coated little film. Said exhibitor S. T. Jackson, "Don't miss playing it."

"*You're as old fashioned as outdoor plumbing. To put it bluntly, you're a big square.*"

GO, JOHNNY, GO! (June, 1959) Valiant Films
M Leon Klatzkin, W Gary Alexander, P Hal Roach Jr., Alan Freed, D Paul Landres

Alan Freed tells Chuck Berry the story of singer Johnny Melody (Jimmy Clanton) as the two men watch him perform. In a flashback we learn all about Johnny, an orphan with ambition who almost ended up in jail instead of on a stage singing rock and roll. His story is told between blocks of musical numbers.

Clanton had a major hit before he made this picture, with a song he'd written called "Just a Dream," and shortly after this movie, he had a minor hit called "Go, Jimmy, Go." His last big hit was in 1962—"Venus in Blue Jeans." Here he sings "Angel Face," "Once Again," "My Love is Strong," "Now the Day is Over," "It Takes a Long, Long Time," "Ship on a Stormy Sea," and "You Done Me Wrong" with Sandy Stewart. Stewart also sings "Playmates" and "Heavenly Father." Chuck Berry sings "Johnny B. Goode," "Memphis Tennessee" and "Little Queenie."

Berry and Freed had a contentious relationship. The D.J. had to be bribed with a music credit before he'd play Berry's first record, "Maybellene," on his radio show. Once, during a drunken moment at a party, Freed promised to give Berry back his

Chuck Berry, Sandy Stewart and Alan Freed

share of the credit, but he never did. It took Berry over a decade to set things right again. "It was during the filming of *Go, Johnny Go!*" said Berry, "that I realized what a heavy drinker Alan was."

Another member of this impressive line-up is Jackie Wilson, once introduced by the bumbling Ed Sullivan as a young man out of Detroit. Said Sullivan, "I suppose there's no performer of his race who is as well beloved by his own people and by record fans everywhere." Wilson sang his all-time best-selling record that night, "Lonely Teardrops." He was singing it again in 1975 when a stroke left him in a heap on the stage. The audience, thinking it was part of the act, applauded.

Ritchie Valens, the first Chicano rock star, makes his one and only screen appearance here, singing "Oh! My Head!" He was killed shortly after this picture in the now famous plane crash that killed The Big Bopper and Buddy Holly. Other singers include Eddie Cochran ("Teenage Heaven"), The Cadillacs ("Jay Walker," "Please Jr. Johnson"), Jo Ann Campbell, ("Mama, Can I Go Out"), and The Flamingos ("Jump Children").

The befuddled critic for the *Los Angeles Times* complained that the "dreadfully noisy production" had 19 musical numbers that left "very little time for story." The *Los Angeles Examiner* was also unimpressed. "The main thing the picture points up is the loudness and sameness to the r&r beat." Exhibitor George Jonchowski had a different take. "What a crowd pleaser—A honey of a show. The teens loved it and business was above average."

"How does a guy get a break, Julie?"

GUN GIRLS (1957) Astor
M Josef Zimanich, *P* Edward Frank, *W-D* Robert C. Dertano

Energy-draining entertainment from writer-director Robert C. Dertano, is not quite as good as his earlier *Girl Gang*, which wasn't quite as good as a case of the clap. The film is halfway over before the *girls* (who are a little long in the tooth by the way) even get their hands on a gun.

The two girls in question, Dora (Jacqueline Park) and Teddy (Jeanne Ferguson), are both on parole. With her parents in the room, Teddy gets a long lecture from her parole officer, and while her parents assure him that she'll do everything that he says, we can see by her expression that it's going in one ear and out the other. Dora's boyfriend Jimmy (Calvin Booth), who happens to be the son of her parole officer, is worried about her relationship with Teddy and begs her to stop seeing her. He has no idea that the two are involved in a series of robberies. They sell their stolen goods to Joe the fence (Timothy Farrell). Every time we see Joe, he's necking with a new lady, and to use a line from the film, he's "got as much appeal as a stopped up sink." Joe is the one who sells them the gun.

As they discuss their plans to cheat Joe out of his share of a payroll job, Dora and Teddy suddenly stop talking and slowly, *very slowly* change their blouses so that we can get a *long* look at them in their undergarments. Apparently these two ladies had been taxed beyond their ability to perform two tasks at the same time.

"You must think I'm a cheap floozy."

THE HEADLESS GHOST (September, 1959) American International
M Gerard Schumann, *W* Aben Kandel and Herman Cohen, *P* Herman Cohen, *D* Peter Graham Scott

Two American exchange students (Richard Lyon and David Rose) team up with a Danish dish (Liliane Sottane) to take a tour of Ambrose Castle. They remain behind after the others leave, for research purposes. The castle, they discover, is like a watering hole for ghosts, among them the Fourth Earl of Ambrose (Clive Revill), who lost his head 600 years ago and would like to have it back. "He can't show his face," one of the ghosts quips, 'because he doesn't know where it is."

Proving that two heads aren't necessarily better than no head, Aben Kandel and Herman Cohen can boast that they challenged the law of averages and created a comedy without a single laugh in it. True, it's only 61 minutes long but, still, one must admit, it's quite an achievement.

Richard Lyon, Liliane Sottane and David Rose.

Cohen was still in post-production on *Horrors of the Black Museum*, when he got an urgent call from Jim Nicholson. Nicholson had booked **Black Museum** into a couple of major theatre chains, and if they had another picture they could own the whole program. Cohen was up to the task. Aben Kandel quickly wrote a script and Peter Graham Scott had the thankless job of directing it. "It was a curious ghost story, but I wasn't very happy with it," he remarked. It's easily his worst film. Just writing about it is fatiguing. "Pretty dismal," said the *New York Times*, and Cohen felt the same way, but the critic for *Motion Picture Herald*, most likely under the influence of a sizeable bribe or some very powerful drugs, called it a "fast-stepping, spirited horror attraction filmed with brisk attention to technical details in England."

"Why don't we get outta here? I can't stand this anymore!"

HIGH SCHOOL BIG SHOT (June, 1958) The Filmgroup
M Gerald Fried, P Stanley Bickman, W-D Joel Rapp

Surprisingly good film, with excellent performances from Tom Pittman and Malcolm Atterbury. The scenes between these two are the heart and soul of the movie and director Paul Rapp was fortunate to have found two actors who could pull it off. The same cannot be said of femme fatale Virginia (**Riot in Juvenile Prison**) Aldridge who is just shy of being good.

Aldridge is Betty Alexander, the prettiest girl in school. She's going to flunk out of English unless she can get Marvin Grant (Pittman), despised by his classmates for being so bright, to write her term paper. She's a clever girl. When she sees her boyfriend, Vince Rumbo (Howard Veit) roughing Marvin up, she steps in and runs

Vince off. "Aren't you afraid he'll be mad?" Marvin asks. "What do I care," she replies. "The world's full of guys like him. You're special." Marvin tells his father that he's got a date with Betty, and the old man's taken aback. "Hey! She's the best looking chick in the whole school, ain't she? What in the world is she goin' out with you for?" This from a guy who can't hold a job and who is about to borrow money from his son.

Alice's plan backfires. The teacher (Peter Leeds) knows she couldn't possibly have written the paper and, furthermore, he knows who did. He withdraws his support for a scholarship that he was working on for Tom and gives Alice the F that she deserves. Now, she has no use for Tom. "Oh, wow," he muses. "You were just using me." But he still loves her and gets involved with some unsavory characters, hoping to steal enough money to make Alice want him.

Rapp never allows his film to lapse into melodrama. It is very well directed and stands head and shoulders above most of its contemporaries. He made several films for Roger Corman, and was introduced to the producer-director as a comedy writer. Corman told him that he rarely made comedies. "Not intentionally anyway," Rapp added.

You call that a kiss? Now, this is what I call a kiss.

HIGH SCHOOL CONFIDENTAL (June, 1958) Metro-Goldwyn-Mayer

M Albert Glasser, W Robert Blees, Lewis Meltzer, P Albert Zugsmith, D Jack Arnold

*M-G-M presents **High School Confidential**, a shattering drama about the rock and roll world of today's teenagers! Not since **Blackboard Jungle** has the shocking picture of these untamed teens been so violently revealed. **High School Confidential** shows you the truth about their torrid temptations! Their violence, speed and ruthless terror! A rocking, hopping, shocking picture of the dangerous truth you never dreamed existed.*

Albert Zugsmith claimed that this exposé of drug use in our high schools was "true-to-life," but anyone who has seen his **Sex Kittens Go to College** (1960) or **Confessions of an Opium Eater** (1962) knows that the producer doesn't live in the same world that the rest of us do. Happily, **HSC** is an absolute delight, sometimes surrealistic, often ridiculous, and *almost* always entertaining.

"I don't make movies without a moral," Zugsmith bragged, "but you can't make a point for good unless you expose the evil!" *Variety* noted that he exploited "to the fullest every facet of this evil situation." And yet, nowhere in the advertising does it say what this "evil" is. Anticipating trouble over the depiction of young people taking drugs, Zugsmith called a press conference, to assure the reporters that **HSC** was in the same crusading spirit of his earlier **Slaughter on 10th Avenue** (1957), a decent rip-off of the Oscar-winning **On the Waterfront** (1954). Zugsmith noted that unlike **Blackboard Jungle**, his film had a clear-cut, moral lesson.

"I am doing my job when I point out the dangers, and the message is inherent in every word of dialogue and every action of movement of the story, and it never stops, and you have to be stupid not to get it."

Writers Lewis (**The Man With the Golden Arm**) Meltzer and Robert (**The Black Scorpion**) Blees talked with some marijuana addicts before they wrote their script. They obviously didn't learn much. Thanks to actor Mel Welles, their script is riddled with jive talk.

"There's a long bit with John Drew Barrymore giving a history lesson in the classroom," said Welles. "I wrote all of that. I was also the technical advisor on that picture. I showed the actors how to roll a joint and explained the effects of marijuana, but the producer wasn't much interested in being accurate."

The kids in the movie think Barrymore's tale of Christopher Columbus in jive talk is hysterical. The kids in the audience I was with made a mad dash for the snack bar. It is the film's only weak moment. One critic, who couldn't make heads or tails of the new language, felt the film should have had English subtitles. Zugsmith did the next best thing. He compiled a list of words and phrases, called it a "DIGtionary" and used it as a promotional gimmick. I am sorry to report that M-G-M saw fit to release "Christopher Columbus Digs the Jive" on a single, with "High School Drag" on the flipside.

The exact nature of 17-year old Kathleen Briggs' contribution to the film wasn't stated in the newspaper account concerning her $9000 lawsuit against Zugsmith. As payment for the *material* she supplied, she was supposed to have been sent on tour with the film as an actress. $750 a week for 12 weeks. Promises. Promises.

Energetic Russ Tamblyn plays undercover cop Mike Wilson, using the name Tony Baker, out to find the scoundrel (Jackie Coogan) pushing drugs to the high school kids. The actor was in England, finishing his starring role in George Pal's **tom thumb** (1958), bracing himself for a two-year hitch in the Army, when he was informed that his military service had been postponed for a couple of weeks

Mamie Van Doren thinks her nephew, Russ Tamblyn, might be a good bonk.

so that he could make this picture. Returning to the states, he was met at the airport by Zugsmith, who took him M-G-M's wardrobe department, then to a hotel in Brentwood, where the producer gave him a copy of the script and told him to report for work the following day.

"It was the first time I'd seen the script," Tamblyn recalled. "After I read it, I said to myself, 'Oh, man, what a piece of crap!' I called my agent and told him I didn't want to do it. He told me the studio would suspend me if I didn't. That was that. I'd been nominated for my role in **Peyton Place** (1957), and when I attended the ceremony, I sat there thinking: Here I was in this big, big movie, and I'm doing this thing with Mamie Van Doren. I couldn't believe it."

In the pecking order of blond bombshells, Van Doren comes in third place, behind Marilyn Monroe and Jayne Mansfield. "Hollywood never appreciated my talent," she would often complain, but Albert Zugsmith sure did. He and Mamie made six or seven pictures together. "Zuggy's pictures were ahead of their time," she remarked. God only knows when we'll catch up with **The Private Lives of Adam and Eve**. **HSC** on the other hand, was right on schedule.

Mamie plays Tamblyn's Aunt Gwen, a character that could well have come from outer space. She doesn't know that Tony is a cop, and apparently doesn't know that his real name is Mike. One thing is clear. She would love to get the boy between the sheets. "Looking for excitement?" she asks Tony, on his way out the door. Taking a bite of an apple, she gives him a wanton smile. "I worry, thinking of you coming up against those young, tight sweaters."

Dr. Stewart Knox, then chairman of the narcotics committee of the Los Angeles County Medical Association, grimly opens the picture with a question for the audience: "How many parents are awake to the temptations facing their children? I do not mean petty infringements. I refer to the terribly dangerous traffic which this films exposes. This story takes place in America, but could happen anywhere, which is why police throughout the world have special divisions in close international cooperation to deal with this modern problem. **High School Confidential** will shock you and, I hope, alert you."

Whatever hope the film may have had of being taken seriously is immediately dashed when out of nowhere, singer Jerry Lee Lewis appears in a flatbed truck, madly pumping his piano, passing through a residential neighborhood in the early morning hours, singing the film's title song. Tony/Mike drives past him on the way to school. Lewis finishes the song and is never seen again. It's truly surrealistic. And wonderful.

Let's pause for a moment to have a look at Lewis and his career, which had taken a dramatic nosedive a few months before he agreed to appear in this movie. He was in England, on a concert tour, and his song, "Breathless," looked to be on its way to being his third big hit, when he made the mistake of telling some reporters that the gum-chewing 13-year old girl he was travelling with, his cousin Myra Gale Brown, was actually his wife. He was booed off of the stage and sent packing. DJs refused to play his records and the sales on "Breathless" dropped dramatically. Lewis found himself playing county fairs and sleazy bars, but was never humbled by the experience. "If you don't like what I'm doing, you can kiss my ass!" he would often say to what he called "unappreciative audiences." He once had to be dragged off of a stage when, after thirty straight minutes, he wouldn't stop singing "Over the Rainbow." Observing all of the fuss and bother, one Southern gentleman remarked, "We don't know what all of the fuss was about. That kind of thing goes on down here all of the time." Myra divorced Lewis after 13 years of being beaten and cuffed into submission. She was his third wife. His fourth wife didn't last a month. His fifth wife died under mysterious circumstances. Lewis's son, Steve Allen Lewis, drown in a swimming pool. Lewis earned the nickname "The Killer" by accidentally shooting his bass player with a .357 Magnum. Small wonder that when The Killer showed up one night at Elvis Presley's home, all tanked up and brandishing a .38 derringer, Elvis told the guard at the front gate to tell Lewis he didn't want to be disturbed. "Get on that damn house phone and call him!" Lewis screamed at the guard. "Who the hell does that sonofabitch think he is? *Doesn't want to be disturbed.* He ain't no damn better'n anybody else!" The Killer was escorted to the local hoosegow.

Meanwhile, back at Santa Bello High School, Tony makes good his boast that by the end of the crummy day, the whole crummy school would know who he was. First he snakes a guy out of a parking space, then makes a pass at Joan Staple (Diane Jergens), the first good-looking girl he sees. "Hi ya, sexy," he swaggers. "You look real cultured. Let's cut out to some drag 'n' eat pad." Later, in the locker room, three characters think they'll put Tony in his place. He chases them off with his switch-blade knife. He whistles when he gets a look at his progressive history teacher, Arlene Williams (Jan Sterling), and ends the day by putting his feet on the principal's desk. A few loose remarks about "looking to graze on some grass" eventually leads Tony to the top drug pusher, Mister A, the owner of a nightclub and part-time piano player.

Zugsmith was one of the filmmakers who did an end run around the ban on nudity by shooting alternate takes on sequences for the less Puritanical foreign market. In the "Continental" version of **HSC**, Jan Sterling is seen in a see-through nightie during her brief phone conversation in her bedroom. In another scene with Tamblyn and Diane Jergens, a young woman (possibly Jody Fair) is shown going through withdrawals. In the Continental version she's naked.

"Zugsmith wanted an out-an-out exploitation picture, a straight-preachy, message film—and if I could put a little nudity in it that would be great!" said director Jack Arnold. "I got along very well with Zugsmith. I just didn't agree with him on everything, but he didn't insist, which was a pleasure. If he didn't like what I did I would just say, 'Well, I like it,'—he'd leave me alone."

"[The] film's crowning absurdity," wrote the critic for The Monthly Film Bulletin, "is its official-sounding homily on the evils of high school drug-taking, delivered over a final carefree sequence showing Tony's alcoholic, nymphomaniac Aunt Gwen necking in the back seat of a car, while Tony sits in front with two blondes—one a schoolgirl described as having recently abandoned 'the weed' for 'ordinary' cigarettes; the other a progressive school-mistress."

HSC was a big money-maker for M-G-M and producer Zugsmith, splitting the profits fifty-fifty. **Platinum High School**, **College Confidential**, and **Sex Kittens Go to College** (all 1960) were soon to follow.

"We did way above average on this picture on a mid-week," said Illinois exhibitor Charles E. Smith. "One of the best Wednesday night crowds I've had in a long time," said James Hardy. But there's always a spoil sport in every crowd. "It seems to me we have had enough of this kind of picture," groused F. L. Murray. "It was not a good drawing card here."

"You got thirty-two teeth, buster. You wanna try for none?"

HIGH SCHOOL HELLCATS (June, 1958) American International
M Ronald Stein, W Mark and Jan Lowell, P Charles "Buddy" Rogers, D Edward Bernds

Listen up! You wanna be a member of The Hellcats? Well, for starters, you'd better not snitch. The Hellcats don't like rats and they don't like show-offs or teacher's pets. Ever stolen anything? You'll learn. If you *have* to pass a test, keep it at the

Jana Lund is Connie, the leader of The Hellcats.

D level. Okay, now you're ready for a belt of booze. And maybe a cigarette.

Joyce Martin (Yvonne Lime) feels like an outcast in her own home so she joins The Hellcats, hoping the make a new "family." In short order, she learns there are a new set of rules to follow that aren't any better than the ones laid down by her parents. She has to steal something as part of her initiation into the club, but when nobody's looking, she leaves the money behind to pay for it.

Campy, melodramatic fun, lets the viewer know right out of the gate that they're going to get what they paid for. Bad girls smoking cigarettes. Switchblade knives. Fistfights. Fast cars. Parents and teachers with their heads in the sand. It's all here. In spades. With wonderful Jana Lund as Connie Ross, the leader of The Hellcats. And Yvonne Lime is as innocent and sweet as Jana is savvy and sultry. Having the two of them in the same film is a stroke of casting genius.

Don Shelton, in a Johnny-one note performance as Joyce's father, is hysterical. He's cranky in every scene and poor Joyce can't do anything to please him. "She's always so slow," he grouses to his wife (Viola Harris). "The way she's always dressed. Those tight sweaters and too much lipstick." And she's a good kid. There isn't a nasty or dishonest bone in her body. The deal-breaker is when Joyce comes out of her room in a slip. "How many times have I told you not to run around like that?!" her dad barks. "But, Dad," she says, but before she can finish, he slaps her. The father's obsession with his daughter's blossoming womanhood suggests something a little darker than I care to explore. These sequences with him are precious, but since they're all basically the same sequence, one would have sufficed, preferably this last one with the slap, when Dad finally has to admit that he's been unfair, and doesn't know what to do. His wife blandly tells him, "You created the problem. You cope with it."

Mike Landers (Brett Halsey) is the one that Joyce ultimately turns to for advice. He works in the coffee shop where the kids hang out, still in school himself, working on an electrical engineering degree. (The background music for these coffee shop sequences is lifted from *Attack of the 50ft Woman*.) Halsey and Lime make a handsome couple and they look like they like each other. But he's a little domineering, too. No matter which way Joyce turns, someone is always telling her what to do.

Harrison's Reports called it "a fairly good program picture," but it was *The Hollywood Reporter* who commented on the audience's reaction to the picture. "I found this teenaged audience so enthusiastically and vociferously on the side of virtue that I left the theatre comfortably reassured concerning the next generation and more than a little inspired." Exhibitor Harry Hawkinson was also "inspired," by the money he made. "The folks at American International have a recipe for teenage pictures that very seldom fails for us."

"She liked you better than me. But I fixed her. And now I'm going to fix you."

HORRORS OF THE BLACK MUSEUM (September, 1959) American International

M Gerard Schurmann, W Aben Kandel, Herman Cohen, P Herman Cohen, D Arthur Crabtree

29-year old Graham Curnow is teen-aged Rick, an innocent lad corrupted and controlled by his psychotic employer, Edmund Bancroft, played to the hilt by Michael Gough. Bancroft makes his living writing novels about the gruesome murders that Rick commits under his influence. Gough's scene chewing performance saves this sadistic exercise from being a bloody bore.

There must have been six or seven of us watching this picture one night, and about three-quarters of the way into the film, Gough had us all in stitches. He was chewing out poor Rick for bringing "a woman" into their sacred and secret black museum. "I tell you no woman can hold her tongue," he snarled. "They're a vicious, unreliable breed." Suddenly, there was this angry close-up of Gough, his face distorted by rage and as rubbery as any cartoon character, and we all cracked up. We laughed so hard we couldn't hear what he said. So we backed it up and ran it again. It was no better the second time, because we all knew what was coming and started laughing in anticipation. So we ran it again. And again. Each time seemed to be funnier than the time before. On the ninth or tenth try, we *finally* managed to hold our laughter just long enough to hear the line. And we broke up again because we couldn't understand what he was saying. "The first time she wants to feel her strength, the first time you quarrel, she can start a..." The rest of the line was lost on us. Five or six more tries didn't help. With our bellies aching, we had to give up and move on. Well, after doing some exhaustive research on his own, I am happy to report that one member of the group finally deciphered the message: "...she can start a toboggan that can crush us."

The movie is only as good as its last, gruesome murder and it never succeeds in topping the surprise and shock of the first one. As a woman (Dorinda Stevens) attempts to adjust the focus on the binoculars she has just received in the mail, two needles poke her eyes out.

Victim two is Bancroft's mistress, played by June Cunningham. Like Jayne Mansfield, Cunningham played the lead in *Will Success Spoil Rock Hunter* on stage. "My ambition is films," she said at the time. "Dumb-blonde parts, of course; nice unsophisticated and curvy." She humiliates Bancroft when he won't give her the money she wants. Rick lops her head off with a portable guillotine.

Beatrice Varley is victim three. She sold Bancroft the binoculars used to kill the first victim. She recognized the mark she put on them from the picture in the newspaper. She foolishly attempts to blackmail a man who she knows is a murderer. Bancroft stabs her neck with a pair of ice tongs.

The doctor (Gerald Anderson) treating Bancroft for his high blood pressure is victim four. Putting two and two together, the doctor realizes that after each murder, Bancroft's blood pressure goes off the charts. He comes to Bancroft's home to give him the opportunity to turn himself over to the police. Bancroft electrocutes him and has Rick dip his body into a vat of acid.

Victim five, of course, is Angela (Shirley Ann Field), Rick's girlfriend. She's seen the museum. Rick takes her to an amusement park and by the time they emerge from the tunnel of love, he has transformed into a wrinkled, green-faced monster. (Bancroft injected him with Dr. Jekyll's formula!) Rick stabs her to death, then does what anyone would do who was trying to disappear into the crowd and make good their escape, he climbs to the top of a Ferris wheel support and waits for the police to gun him down.

The story is unpleasant enough without taking into account the "murky" relationship between Bancroft and Rick. They would appear to be a whole lot closer than we'd care to think. Herman Cohen was surprised when someone told him

Graham Curnow didn't care for the Tunnel of Love and takes it out on poor Shirley Ann Field.

that the homosexual implications in the sequence that had us all in stitches that night, were quite obvious. As it turns out, Curnow was gay and had known it since he was eight. "I used to sit at the bedroom window just to watch one of the boys go by because he was so good looking." He went to a psychiatrist in the hope of making sense out his feelings, but he knew he'd gone to the wrong guy when the doctor said reproachfully, "Do you realize that's against the law?" Curnow looked at him, got up, and on his way out the door said, "Fuck you."

HOTBM was AIP's most expensive film to date, with a good score by Gerard Schurmann and ho-hum direction by Arthur Crabtree, in color and CinemaScope and Hypno-Vista, a revolutionary new screen miracle that actually put the viewer into the movie! "**Feel** the chilling fog! The acid vat of death! The hand reaching for your wallet!" What was HypnoVista? It was, quite simply, a 13 minute, boring lecture by some hypnotherapist about the power of suggestion.

The critics were not pleased. "Unpleasant and ridiculous," said Variety. The Los Angeles Examiner complained that the story was told "without style, dramatic suspense or understandable motivation." "Michael Gough," said the Hollywood Reporter, "is the type of obvious villain who, in a realistic story, would be the first man collared by any precinct captain." Harold J. Smith assured his fellow exhibitors that if their small town was like his small town, "they will talk this one up, because it is something different in the line of horror movies." Charles Burton thought it was "the worst piece of nonsense" he'd ever seen, "an insult to the intelligence and, worst of all, is a bore."

You can't resist it!

*HOT CAR GIRL (July, 1958) Allied Artists
M Cal Tjader, W Leo Gordon, P Gene Corman, D Bernard Kowalski

Good girl June Kenney falls for bad boy Richard Bakalyan and things quickly go from bad to worse. Bakalyan is a thief. His partners in crime—John Brinkley and his girl, Sheila McKay. They steals cars and sell them to junk dealer and fence, Bruno Ve Sota. Before the film is over, Bakalyan graduates from thief to murderer.

"I had the lead in that picture," Bakalyan happily told me. "And I thought it was a pretty good picture. I liked the girl—June Kenney. I thought we played well off each other."

Bakalyan gets tired of listening to Kenney beating on his ears about "going straight," and just so she understands that she's expendable, he flirts with the wonderful Jana Lund who he engages in a drag race that ends when her car smacks into a motorcycle cop and kills him. Afraid that she'll implicate him in the race, Bakalyan kills her, then takes it on the lam with Kenney.

"We shot the big showdown in Bronson quarry," Bakalyan recalled. "If you were around long enough, you ended up in Bronson quarry. It was Bernie Kowalski's first movie."

Bakalyan is trapped in the cave (those who know Bronson caves have to pretend there aren't three other exits), and when he won't come out, the police shoot tear gas at him. He comes out shooting and is quickly gunned down. The cops are about to take Kenney to jail as an accomplice, when one of the cops finds a note in Bakalyan's pocket exonerating her.

Said Bakalyan, "When I play a heavy, I do not try to play him heroic unless the script calls for it. If he's a low life, I try to portray him as the best, blackest low life. To make heroes out of irresponsible people is a disservice to the community and to self."

"As the records will reveal," said *Boxoffice*, "motion pictures about teenagers—particularly those with problems that lead them to behavior reminiscent of Al Capone in his hey-day—are currently sure-fire boxoffice." *Motion Picture Herald* called it "hard-hitting" and "realistic," and singled out Bakalyan as someone special. But it was June Kenney who was shipped off to Lubbock, Texas, to promote the picture. James Fillmore, an actor featured in **The Cry-Baby Killer**, went with her. During intermission, she sang and he accompanied her on the piano.

She's hell on wheels! Fired up for any thrill!

HOT ROD GANG aka FURY UNLEASHED (June, 1958) American International

M Ronald Stein, W-P Lou Rusoff, D Lew Landers

"Swallow your pride and play this and **High School Hellcats**," advised exhibitor Jim Fraser. "You won't gain any prestige, but you can't bank that." He should have added, "Just don't watch it."

Crummy comedy from producer-writer Lou Rusoff (Sam Arkoff's brother-in-law). "He wrote, constructively, some very good screenplays," claimed Ronald Stein, the film's musical director. He had to admit, however, that when it came to writing dialog for teenagers, Rusoff was out of his element. The film's director, Lew Landers, would often complain about how little time he was given to make a picture. "They don't want them good, they just want to get it out."

No better example could you find to illustrate his point than **Hot Rod Gang**, starring John Ashley as John Abernathy the Third, set to inherit the family fortune if he'll only behave himself. He is a perfect gentleman in front of his two aunts (Helen Spring and Dorothy Newman) but away from the house he races cars and sings rock and roll.

"I was offered a part on Matinee Theatre," Ashley recalled. "It was a good, dramatic part and Janis Paige was the star. AIP wanted me to do **Hot Rod Gang**, and

Gene Vincent, Jody Fair and John Ashley.

I asked for a postponement because I really wanted to do this show. I thought it might help pull me out of the B movies. Sam [Arkoff] wouldn't let me do it. He had me under contract and that was that as far as he was concerned. But I thought, 'What the hell. This is my big chance.' So I was going to do the show anyway and Sam got an injunction to stop me. I never really forgave him for that. He could have let me do that show and still had me in his movie."

Ashley has three songs in the film, "Believe Me" "Hit and Run Lover" and an upbeat version of "Annie Laurie." His efforts, energetic though they may be, are overshadowed by Gene Vincent and the Blue Caps. Like Ashley, Vincent was one of the many singers influenced by Elvis Presley, signed by Capital Records during the company's search for an Elvis sound-alike. The song that did the trick for him was "Be-Bop-a-Lula," inspired by the Little Lulu cartoon character. He and the boys sing "Dancin' to the Bop," "Baby Blue," and "Dance in the Street."

Monthly Film Bulletin called it "the tritest entrant" in the teen market. "The comedy misfires woefully, the performances are overstated to the point of caricature, and the general level is decidedly moronic." Said *The Hollywood Reporter*, "The youthful spectators, when I was present, greeted Ashley's tortured and orgiastic attempts to do an Elvis Presley with hoots of ridicule." Harold Bell, an exhibitor in Quebec, simply said, "Same as all the rest—GOOD."

Well, that's that. Shall we dance?

HOT ROD GIRL (July, 1956) American International
M Alexander Courage, W John McGreevey, P Norman Herman, D Leslie Martinson

Listless, very conservative yarn about one cop's efforts to get the kids off of the street and onto a legal drag strip, where they can blow off steam and exercise their need for speed without putting everyone else in jeopardy. He gets Jeff Northrop (John Smith), the leader of a pack of hot-rodders, to help him. It's not a bad film. It just not a very good one.

Lori Nelson and Mark Andrews.

Things are going well until Bronc (Mark Andrews) blows into town, all full of himself in a black leather jacket, looking way too old to be hanging out with a bunch of teenagers. He is the monkey in the wrench, a narcissistic ass who causes trouble for the sake of causing it. He hits on Jeff's girl, Lisa (Lori Nelson), alienates everyone, and challenges Flat Top (Frank Gorshin in his film debut) to a chicken race. Later, he successfully runs Jeff and Lisa off of the road, and accidentally kills a little boy on a bicycle in the process. With no witnesses, Bronc takes off, leaving Jeff to take the blame.

Harry Hawkinson reported "the best business for several months," and Olin Evans reported that it "out grossed anything we have shown lately." Harold Bell thought it was "the best one we have played yet of this type." Said the *Los Angeles Examiner*, "As a thriller, it holds up fine," but *Boxoffice* didn't agree, calling it "woefully weak" in all departments. Lori Nelson had little to say about it other than she wasn't happy about being in it.

Living with her is like driving with your brakes on.

HOT ROD RUMBLE (June, 1958) Allied Artists
M Alexander Courage, *S* Meyer Dolinsky, *P* Norman T. Herman, *D* Leslie H. Martinson

Big Arny Crawford (Richard Hartunian in his only film appearance) walks into "The Shack," a hangout for The Road Devils, and the temperature in the room drops twenty degrees. All he wants to do is talk to Terri Warren (Leigh Snowden). She used to be his girl and he wants her back. Arny isn't the only one who wants her. Obviously, the guy she's with (Larry Dolgin), wants her, and so does Arny's so-called best friend, Ray Johnson (Wright King). While he's waiting, one young lady all but climbs into Arny's lap, with her date sitting at another table. "I don't want anybody two-timing me," Arny tells her, "and I ain't two-timing anybody else." Terri tells Arnie she'll talk with him after Hank takes her home. Terri and Arny belong together. They're both straight shooters.

Terri and Hank *finally* leave the diner and Ray follows them. Hank sees Ray's car in his rear mirror and assumes that it's Arny. Ray runs them off of the road, Hank is killed and Terri is badly injured. She thinks Arny did it and so does everyone else. Ray happily lets Arny take the blame. Some of the Road Devils give Arny a beating and sabotage his car. He works round the clock to get it back in shape. He wants to win the $1500 prize money in a big winner-take-all race.

Ray makes the mistake of driving Terri to the race. As she gets out of his car, she finds the earring she lost the night of the crash, and knows the truth. With Arny in the hands of the police, Terri jumps into his car and wins the race. She forces Ray to confess, then drives off with Arny and the prize money.

"A small picture, but it still did the business," said exhibitors Mickey and Penney Harris. *Boxoffice* called it a "film of real story power for the teenage and slightly older segment of motion picture patronage," and *Motion Picture Herald* said it was "one of the better imports."

That creep so much as opens his mouth, I'll flatten him.

The teenage werewolf, Gary Clarke, producer Herman Cohen, and the teenage Frankenstein, Gary Conway.

HOW TO MAKE A MONSTER (July, 1958) American International
M Paul Dunlap, *W* Kenneth Langtry, *P* Herman Cohen, *D* Herbert L. Strock

Two teenaged actors, Gary Clarke and Gary Conway, under the influence of mad make-up artist Robert H. Harris, kill the new executives (Eddie Marr and Paul Maxwell) who have taken over American International. The boys are made to look like monsters before they commit the murders, and have no memory of their crimes. Harris uses a hypnotic foundation cream that paralyzes their will. "It will have the same effect chemically as a surgical prefrontal lobotomy," he tells his moronic assistant, Paul Brinegar. Harris makes himself up to look like a monster to kill a snoopy security guard (Dennis Cross). Can't say if he needed the foundation cream.

Eddie Marr is the first to go. He's in the screening room, watching dailies of Werewolf vs. Frankenstein, when he is attacked by Gary Clarke as the teenage werewolf. "Take it easy, will ya?" Marr said to Clarke during the rehearsal. "This is a new suit!" Just before they were ready to roll film, producer Herman Cohen took Clarke aside. "This is his last day," he said, referring to Marr. "I want this to be a good shot." It was pretty clear what Cohen wanted Clarke to do, which was not give a hoot about Marr's suit. "They gave me some fizzy stuff," Clarke said, "that makes you look like you're foaming at the mouth. It wasn't supposed to stain his suit."

Amusing satire of AIP and the film business, is also unintentionally funny. Highlight of the film is a glimpse of what we can expect from the new regime, a musical number featuring John Ashley singing, "You Gotta Have Ee-ooo," flanked by a dozen dancing dolls, all hopelessly out of synch.

The last reel of the movie is in color, so the posters could read: See the Ghastly Ghouls in Flaming Color! Harris invites the two young actors to his home to show them his Chamber of Horrors. He tells them he wants add their heads on the wall, only for real. Naturally, they don't cotton to the idea and beat a hasty treat, knocking over a candelabra that sets the place on fire.

"We had a special effects man named Charlie Duncan," director Herbert Strock grinned. "Drunken Duncan we called him. He set the place on fire before we were ready. I shoved all of the actors onto the set and grabbed the cameraman and told him to start filming. I got behind the other camera and we ran the actors through the scene before the place burned to the ground."

Several of the heads had been made to be burned, but the showcase items were all of the monsters that Paul Blaisdell had made for the company's previous horror movies. Some of them were badly damaged or destroyed. The somewhat charred remains of the She-Creature and the Saucer-Man were mounted above the fireplace in Blaisdell's Topanga Canyon home. By this time, Blaisdell and his agent, Forrest J Ackerman (the editor of James Warren's Famous Monsters of Filmland), weren't speaking to each other. Ackerman had dropped the ball on a crucial negotiation for Blaisdell. AIP president Jim Nicholson had always assured the prop and monster-maker that he would grow with the company, which made it a little easier for him to work for so little money. Nicholson had a contract drawn up that would have given Blaisdell a life-time income. Ackerman let it get lost in the shuffle. Months went by. By the time he found it, Nicholson had changed his mind. Blaisdell didn't leave the business. It left him.

How to Make a Monster was the third and final film Herb Strock directed for Cohen. "I found Herman demanding, intractable, determined, and intense, much like the stereotypical director portrayed in Hollywood films," Strock wrote in his autobiography. "He had to be the sole leader of whatever he was working on, and his ego was not small. Since he believed that whatever appeared in the script must be right, it was very difficult to make him see major flaws in the screenplay. Although he lacked many of the qualities that make a good producer, he had those necessary for getting a picture off the ground."

Over the years, AIP has been mistakenly referred to as a studio. It was a distribution company. AIP rented space at other people's studios. Cohen had to make a sign that read American International Pictures to hang over the gate at Ziv studio. "In fact," Cohen laughed, "they left the sign up long after the picture was over, so Jim and Sam would bring people to Ziv all the time, as though it was their studio!"

Variety said, "The script has some sharp dialog and occasionally pungent Hollywood Talk. ('That's the way the footage cuts') although these aspects will be largely lost on the audiences this picture will attract." *Mirror News* found it "better than its jivey title might indicate." The *Los Angeles Examiner* called it "a torpid tale without even the so-called horror which is supposed to attract adolescents."

"It's got to be the greatest fight that's ever been on the screen, and I've got to get it in one take."

I WAS A TEENAGE FRANKENSTEIN aka TEENAGE FRANKEN-STEIN (November, 1957) American International

M Paul Dunlap, *W* Aben Kandel, Herman Cohen, *P* Herman Cohen, *D* Herbert L. Strock

Flabby, tongue-in-cheek Frankenstein, with Whit Bissell as the demented doctor, determined to create an obedient, teen-aged boy who won't mind doing a little killing for him. "It wasn't very good really," said Bissell, "It was done in a hurry, which is pretty obvious when you see it." Gary Conway is his creation, his face horribly disfigured in a fatal auto accident. Though it's never mentioned, he must have had his brain wiped clean, for when he's revived, it's as if he's just been born. He knows nothing, like a lump of clay that the nutty professor intends to mold, control and dominate. Conway was working as a bouncer when Herman Cohen asked him if he wanted to play the monster in his Frankenstein movie. "I said sure," the actor remarked. "It was better than what I was doing."

A particularly bizarre sequence has Dr. Frankenstein and his creation, driving through lover's lane, looking for a better-looking face, like one might select a new tie. "It was a lousy script," said director Herbert Strock. "I tried to give it something with the lighting. Little touches here and there."

In the end, the boy turns on his master, and as the police rush in, he backs into a control panel and electrocutes himself. As the sparks fly, the film suddenly switches from black and white to color. "At the time," said the producer, "I thought that was quite inventive. We couldn't afford to make the picture in color, so I came up with that idea, and I talked Jim Nicholson into letting me spend a few extra bucks."

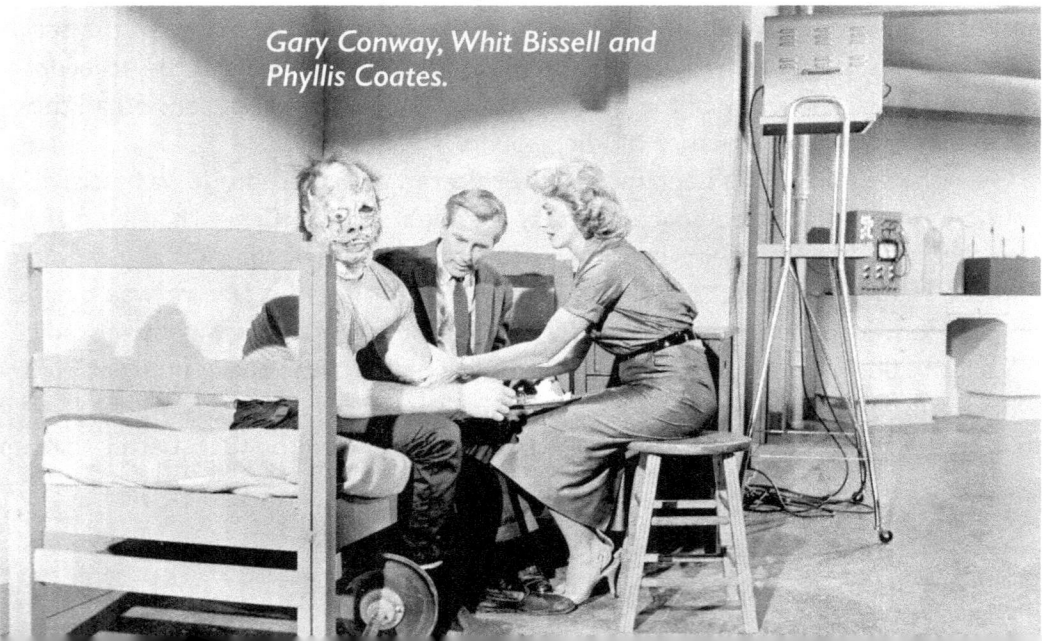

Gary Conway, Whit Bissell and Phyllis Coates.

"Defies all semblances of believability," said *Boxoffice*. *The Hollywood Reporter*, apparently in a humorous frame of mind, said that the movie was "intelligently and imaginatively done." Arkansas exhibitor Victor Weber couldn't believe it packed his theatre. "Sometimes," he said, "I think I would be smart to book what I think would not do business, and I might make more money, as I did on this one."

"The things that one once thought were ridiculous become cult classics," mused Conway. "They take on a certain aura, while the films that people thought were so wonderful at the time turn out not to be wonderful."

"Speak! You've got a civil tongue in your head, I know you have, because I sewed it back myself."

I WAS A TEENAGE WEREWOLF (1957) American International
M Paul Dunlap, W Aben Kandel, Herman Cohen, P Herman Cohen, D Gene Fowler, Jr.

Having just made **Crime of Passion** (1957) with Barbara Stanwyck and Sterling Hayden, Herman Cohen didn't think *I Was a Teenage Werewolf* indicated that his career was headed in the right direction. But his more prestigious picture had been a boxoffice flop and his pal, Jim Nicholson, was having a lot of luck with movies aimed at the kids. So Aben Kandel wrote this werewolf picture, using the pseudonym Ralph Thornton. (Cohen always claimed that they collaborated on these scripts but I'm willing to bet Kandel did all of the writing.) *"You're not going to put your name on it, are you?"* Cohen's friends would ask, and the more he thought about it, he wondered if maybe Ralph Thornton should get the producer's credit as well. "Then all of a sudden, Jack Benny, Bob Hope and various other comedians got ahold of the title and they started making fun of it," Cohen recalled. "Well, when *Time* and *Look* and *Life* started calling for the producer, I decided that the producer was going to be Herman Cohen."

The title was brilliant, stolen from a piece of satire in *Dig* magazine, read by my brother and me, as well as Jim Nicholson's three daughters. "That movie was a success, first of all, because of the great title," said actress Cindy Robbins, "but I think Michael Landon was the only actor I know who could pull off playing a werewolf and do it so convincingly that it wasn't corny. The movie was corny, let's face it. He gave such a fabulous performance. In the hands of anyone else, it could have been a real bomb."

Gene Fowler, Jr., was a film editor who wanted to be a director, but when he read the script, he thought it was crap and didn't think he should do it. His wife Marge, also a film editor, and a very successful one, scoffed. "What's the difference? Nobody'll see it anyway." Behind Cohen's back, Fowler rewrote the script. "In the dialog I wrote, I tried to give the characters dimension, to show where they came from, instead of just moving them around and having them say obligatory lines," said

Fowler. The fact that **Teenage Werewolf** stands head and shoulders above any film in Cohen's horror canon suggests that Fowler had a lot to do with it, and why he never worked for Cohen again. Herb Strock, who directed three films for Cohen, said the producer thought his scripts were written in cement.

Michael Landon is Tony Rivers, a troubled kid with a chip on his shoulder who is always getting into fights. A sympathetic policeman (Barney Phillips) suggests that he seek psychiatric help. "No head shrinker for me!" Tony says dismissively. His widowed father (Malcolm Atterbury), responding to a call from the school about Tony's most recent fight, gently tries to convince his son that no matter how he feels, he has to learn to get along, which sometimes means doing things the other fella's way. He's a good guy. His night job leaves him little time to spend with Tony, but you don't need a lot of time to show someone that you care. We never do find out what's eating Tony. It isn't until he goes out of control at a Halloween party and savagely beats one of his friends (Kenny Miller), and sees the horrified reaction of his friends that he realizes he needs help.

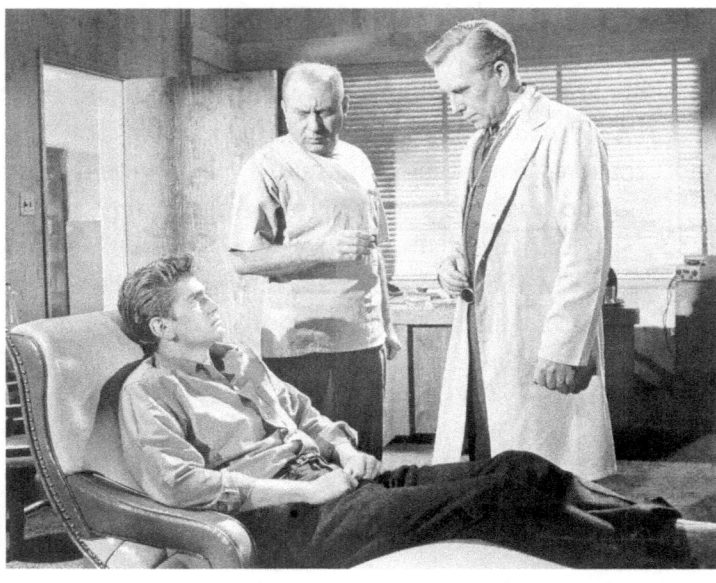

Michael Landon is the troubled teen, Whit Bissell is the even more troubled psychiatrist, and Joseph Mell is his reluctant accomplice.

"We had a stuntman who walked us through that," said Miller, "neither one of us being stunt people, but I got too close and Michael got too close, and he knocked the *shit* out of me. I mean, he really knocked me across that room. It was a great take but unfortunately somebody moved in front of the camera because they realized that Michael really hit me, and it ruined the shot."

Before Miller gets decked, he sings "Eeny Meeny Miney Mo," and does a little dance with Cindy Robbins, so in a way, he had it coming. The song was written by Jerry Blaine who expected to sing it. (Cohen let him sing another of his songs in his remake of **Teenage Werewolf** that same year.) Robbins and Miller knew each other from having worked together on **Dino**. And Robbins went to school with Yvonne Lime, the film's leading lady, and was childhood friends with Dawn Richard, the werewolf's second victim. It was a tight group.

Tony's psychiatrist (Whit Bissell) turns out to be stark-raving mad. "The only hope for the human race is to hurl it back into its primitive dawn," he tells his sniveling assistant, "to start all over again." With drugs and hypnosis, Brandon slowly takes Tony back in time. "Remember how it felt to run over the hills in the moonlight?" he murmurs. "Remember how wonderful it was when you sprang suddenly and you dug in with our fangs—the soft throat, the gush of warm blood? Yes, I want you to remember. You must remember!"

Actor Michael Rougas is Tony's first victim, on his way home from the clubhouse, taking a short-cut through the woods. The sequence had to be shot twice, adding another day to the seven day schedule. Cohen wanted the werewolf kept off camera, that at some point, the camera would become the werewolf. Fowler had Landon in the sequence. It has to be said that, in this instance, Cohen's way was better.

Dawn Richard is attacked in the school gymnasium by werewolf Michael Landon.

Playboy playmate Dawn Richard is Tony's next victim. She's working out on the parallel bars in the school gymnasium when Tony's animal instincts are triggered. Hanging by her legs, she sees the werewolf approaching, upside down. "[When] I see the werewolf, I drop off head first. I did it so hard that I think I frightened [the crew] because they ran over asking if I was okay. I was sure sore the next day," Richard remarked, though she had nothing on Michael Landon, who had to jump over a stack of folded chairs to get to her, and didn't quite make it, landing right in the middle of them instead. "He cried out in pain and limped around for a few minutes, then we went back to filming. The next day, he came in and showed us his black-and-blue legs. They were really bad."

Time magazine called it a new low in lowbrow cinema, "the marriage of the undead and the underdone." *The Los Angeles Times* said "the picture comes apart like a wet tissue." "Shallow entertainment," declared *The Motion Picture Herald*. The exhibitors told a different story. "It was an all-around good job of making a picture on very little cash," observed Victor Weber. Mickey and Penny Harris reported that it did a nice business for them, "partly due to a good date and...eye-catching paper and good trailers."

Kenny Miller landed a role in Cecil B. DeMille's **The Buccaneer** (1958) and was passing by the commissary on the Paramount lot when he heard someone call his name. "Kenny! Hey, Kenny!" He turned around and there was Elvis Presley, taking a break from **King Creole**. He recognized Kenny from **Teenage Werewolf**, which was one of Presley's favorite pictures. Alan Clough, Presley's personal pilot, told Miller that Presley often ran the film. "He also told me that Elvis even knew all the words to 'Eeny Meeny Miney Mo,' and I'm sure he could sing it a lot better than I did!"

"This boy is a free police case. We're probably saving him from the gas chamber."

Note: Thanks to Don Vaughan for his anniversary coverage of **I Was a Teenage Werewolf** in the Oct-Dec. 2007 edition of *Filmfax* magazine.

INVASION OF THE SAUCER-MEN aka INVASION OF THE HELL-CREATURES (June, 1957) American International

M Ronald Stein, W Robert J. Gurney Jr., and Al Martin, P James H. Nicholson and Robert J. Gurney Jr., D Edward L. Cahn

Bonehead comedy, based on Paul Fairman's short story, "The Cosmic Frame," has the distinction of being the first science fiction film to have a teen-aged hero, and the first to bring to life a popular image from the sci-fi pulps of the thirties and forties, the little green man from Mars. Paul Blaisdell made the Martians with huge heads and bug eyes, which is not the way they're described in Fairman's story, but it was closer to what the public had in mind.

Bob Burns, collector extraordinaire, worked with Blaisdell on a lot of these pictures and has said that this movie started out as a straight science-fiction picture, the

Steve Terrell and Gloria Castillo have run over a little Martian.

way it was advertised. *Creeping horror from the depths of time and space!* But half way through the shoot, Jim Nicholson and director Eddie Cahn decided it would play better as a comedy. The writer and co-producer, Robert J. Gurney insisted that his script was *always* a comedy. If Burns' story is true, it means that nobody knew Gurney's script was supposed to be funny. That's the funniest thing about the movie.

Steve Terrell is Johnny Carter, the teen-aged hero of the piece, and Gloria Castillo is his fiancé, Joan Hayden. The two had planned to elope, but on their way through lover's lane they accidentally run over

The Martians damage Steve Terrell's car to frame him for hit-and-run murder.

a little Martian. They rush off to get the sheriff. During their absence, an opportunistic drifter named Joe Gruen (Frank Gorshin) happens on the dead Martian and sees dollar signs. Before he can cart the little fellow away, he is attacked by the Martians who kill him by pumping him full of alcohol, delivered through the needles in their fingertips. It wouldn't have been a lethal dose if he hadn't already been plastered. The Martians dent Johnny's fender and put Gruen's body beneath the car. By the time John and Joan return with the sheriff, "the cosmic frame" is in place, and Johnny is arrested for manslaughter.

The Martians have an eyeball on the back of their hands, and one of the film's best moments has a severed Martian hand on the floor of Johnny's car, crawling up the back of the passenger's seat, where sits the unsuspecting Joan. The kids at the Saturday matinee went nuts. And when a bull attacked one of the Martians and stabs one of his big bug eyes with his horn, everybody went "Eeeeeeewww!" But what I don't remember was a whole lot of laughter going on. It's low-brow, witless comedy Gurney dishes out, and the kids weren't buying it. In other hands the picture could have been a very funny black comedy.

"The moments of burlesque of horror melodrama traditions, whether intentional or not, are at least curious," wrote the critic for *Monthly Film Bulletin*. *Boxoffice* found it "weak in all departments." *Variety's* charged that "poor use of attempted comedy" in a haphazard yarn made the film's "69-minute running time seem twice as long." "The crowd seemed to enjoy it," said exhibitor Victor Weber, and for S.T. Jackson "it did more business than any I've played in a long time." Harlan Rankin called it mediocre entertainment. "If people have other places to go, they won't stop for this picture."

"I expected to be frightened on my wedding night, but nothing like this!"

JAILHOUSE ROCK (November, 1957) Metro-Goldwyn-Mayer
M Jeff Alexander, W Guy Trosper, P Pandro S. Berman, D Richard Thorpe

Elvis Presley's third film, another version of the singer's own rise to stardom, but unlike his previous film, **Loving You**, which was a gussied-up in VistaVision and Technicolor, this time Presley's not naïve and frightened, he's vicious and greedy, and the movie is in black and white Scope. It was one of the few times Presley was able to explore the darker side of his image.

Vince Everett (Presley) is a construction worker with a short-fuse. He gets into a fight, accidentally kills a man, and is thrown in jail. His cellmate is a washed-up country-western singer named Hunk Houghton (Mickey Shaughnessy). Hunk teaches Vince to play the guitar and once he hears Vince sing, Hunk convinces him to join a show they're putting on, which is going to be broadcast from coast to coast. The prison is swamped with fan letters, all for Vince. Hunk hides the letters and makes it seem like a favor when he asks Vince to become an equal partner in his act. Once Vince is released from prison, he embarks on a singing career. He gets some pointers from Peggy Van Alden (Judy Tyler), an employee with a record company. She becomes professionally and romantically involved with him. They start their own record company and Vince becomes rich and famous as a singer and a movie star. He's in the middle

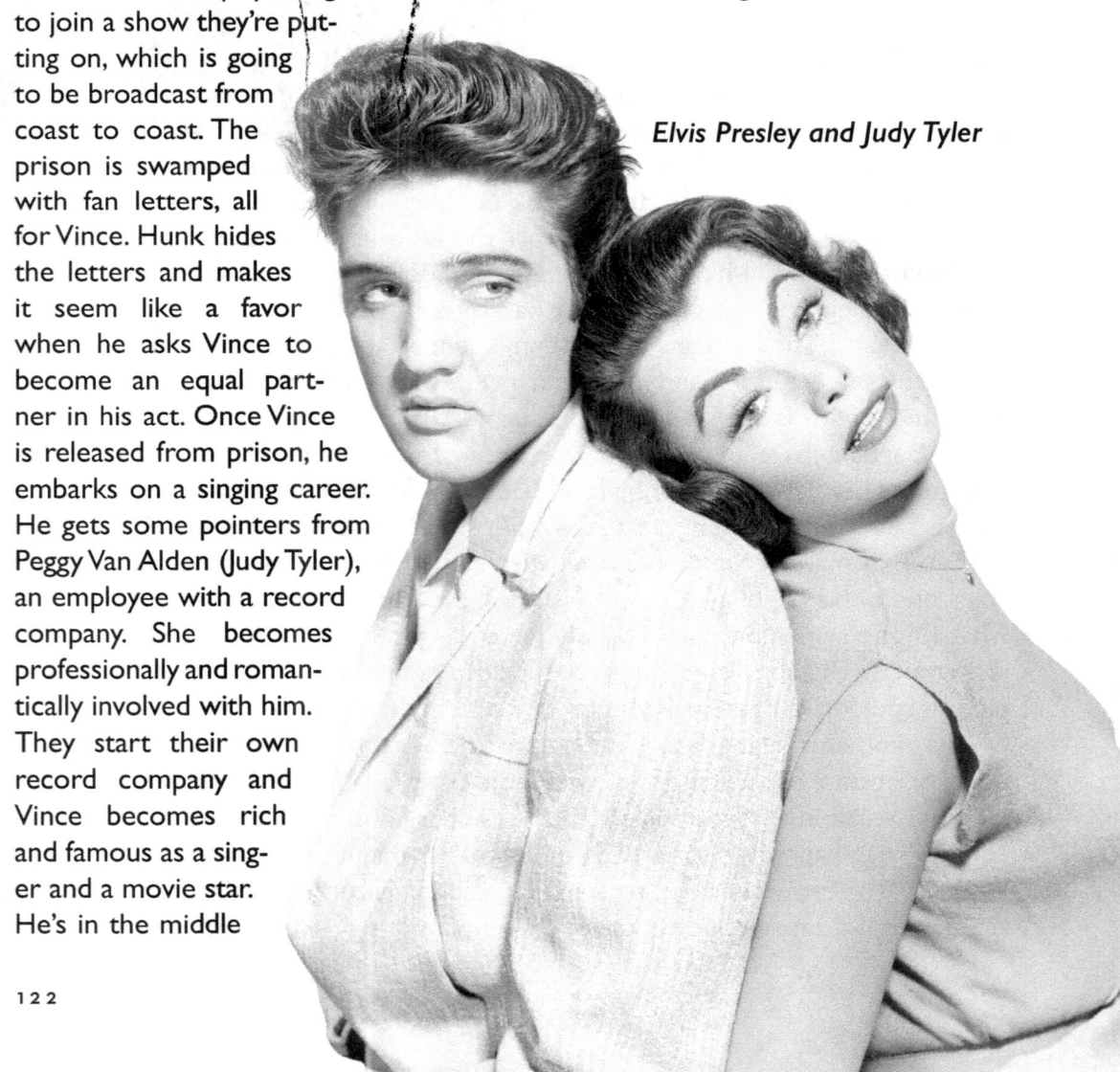

Elvis Presley and Judy Tyler

of a love scene with Laury Jackson (Anne Neyland) when the director, not satisfied, yells cut. Vince waves him off and continues with the kiss. Presley and Neyland had an off screen affair as he was wrapping up his relationship with Yvonne Lime. Neyland was fairly bitter when they broke up, calling Presley a joke. In a more charitable moment, she remarked: "I think he's at a stage now where he's just given up trying to make himself a little more normal life."

Hunk, finally set free, tries to make Vince honor the contract he signed, but Hunk discovers he's washed up and his contract with Vince won't stand up in court. Vince keeps him on as a high-paid flunky, and he has it coming. But Peggy doesn't. Vince treats her like a flunky, too. It all comes to a head when Peggy refuses to sell their record company and Vince tells her that she has no choice. He has the controlling interest. "Trampin' on me is one thing, sonny," Hunk remarks. "Hurtin' a little girl like Peggy is another. Comes a time you gotta take a hand in things. I'm gonna beat hell outta you."

Elvis sings 6 songs—"Jailhouse Rock," "Treat Me Nice," "(You're So Square) Baby I Don't Care," "I Want to Be Free," "Young and Beautiful," "Don't Leave Me Now"—just enough to fill an EP. The first four songs on the list were written by one of the hottest song writing teams of all time, Jerry Leiber and Mike Stoller, two names my brother Steve and I became very familiar with. They wrote dozens of hits for Presley, The Coasters and The Drifters, to name just a few. "When you wrote a song for Presley," Stoller recalled, "you wrote it on spec, because his name on a record was money in the bank. Jerry and I were supposed to write four songs for **Jailhouse Rock** but we were goofing around, enjoying our stay in New York. So this guy shows up and asks to see the songs which we don't have. He walks across the room, locks the door and says 'Nobody leaves until I see those songs.' He wasn't kidding."

The "Jailhouse Rock" number is a standout, and remains the most elaborate and creative staging in the singer's screen history. Elvis and Alex Romero worked on the choreography together, while Gene Kelly watched from the wings. He even applauded when they were done. But Elvis wasn't so sure.

"He was staying at the Beverly Wilshire at the time and I wanted to meet him," said actor Russ Tamblyn. "He was worried about this big dance number, so we practiced a few moves and he liked what we were doing."

The brilliant Bob Fosse liked the number so much he paid homage to it in his parody of the Roxie Hart trial, **Chicago** (1975), and yet in his review for **Jailhouse Rock**, the critic for the *Monthly Film Bulletin* thought the number was "very much over-staged." No matter what Elvis did, there were some people who just couldn't admit that he was doing it right.

Presley couldn't have been happier when he ran into Nicholas Ray in the M-G-M commissary. Ray had directed James Dean in **Rebel Without a Cause**, and Dean was Presley's idol, so Presley got down on his knees and recited huge chunks of the dialog. Said Ray, "Elvis must have seen **Rebel** a dozen times by then and remembered every one of Jimmy's lines."

Variety found ***Jailhouse Rock*** "packed with the type of material Presley's followers go for," but the critic for *Cue* found Presley's singing style obnoxious and overtly obscene, the story distasteful, "ugly in its telling, performance, and presentation." *Time's* reaction was particularly vicious. "For movie-goers who may not care for that personality, Presley himself offers in the film a word of consolation: 'Don't worry,' he says. 'I'll grow on you.' If he does it will be quite a depressing job to scrape him off."

"I now have the answer to the question, how to keep the theatres open," said exhibitor Victor Weber. "Just get ten more like Elvis Presley. With rain, high waters, flu and every other kind of thing to put the hex on business, it still did way above average…It's just amazing how everyone goes for Presley, even the small kids below school age. And the colored people came in large numbers." S. T. Jackson "thought Elvis Presley had lost a little of his popularity but *Jailhouse Rock* did the best business of his three pictures." And writing from Northern Rhodesia, Dave Klein reported that one critic's adverse reaction to the picture helped to fill his house. "The critic said of it that it was like the writing on a toilet wall. The papers here for weeks were full of contempt and fury at his remarks, and all this helped at the boxoffice." Velva Otts thought it was amusing that the kids "like to brag how many times they've seen it." "Some of the teenagers came three times to see Elvis. I can't see what they see in him—but I don't care as long as they keep coming," said L.T. Hawkins.

Written by Guy Trosper from a story by blacklisted writer Ned Young, and listlessly directed by Richard Thorpe, it is a fairly accurate assessment of the cutthroat music business, and the performances, including Elvis's, are good, especially Shaughnessy, who was always much better when he wasn't trying to be funny.

"*Those aren't tactics, baby. It's just the beast in me.*"

JAMBOREE aka DISC JOCKEY JAMOREE (May, 1957) Warner Bros.
M Otis Blackwell, W Leonard Kantor, P Max J. Rosenberg, Milton Subotsky, D Roy Lockwood

The kids got their money's worth from producers Max J. Rosenberg and Milton Subotsky. Like their previous film, ***Rock, Rock, Rock***, this one is almost wall-to-wall music. The plot interferes with the music only long enough for a visit to the snack bar.

> "Film is dated in concept, reminiscent of the early days of musical films when producers slapped a group of singing acts together, but it's okay for the jukebox trade."—*Variety*.

"The Fat Man" was the first rock and roll record to sell a million copies and here's the man who sang it, Antoine "Fats" Domino, Jr.

There are almost as many disc jockeys in the film as there are songs, a clever gimmick since each DJ was certain to plug the picture on his show. In addition to Dick Clark, whose *American Bandstand* TV show was about to go nation-wide, there's Joe Smith (WVDA, Boston), Joe Finan (KWY, Cleveland), Keith Sandy (CKEY, Toronto), Zenas Sears (WAOK, Atlanta), Barry Kaye (WJAS, Pittsburgh), Sandy Singer (WTCN, Minneapolis), Ray Perkins (KIMN, Denver), Gerry Myers (CKOY, Ottawa), Jocko Henderson (WOV, New York), Ed Bonner (KXOX, St. Louis), Robin Seymour (WKMH, Detroit), Dick Whittinghill (KMPC, Hollywood—often seen on Jack Webb's Dragnet TV show), Howard Miller (WIND), Chicago), Werner Goetze (Bayerische Rundfunk, Munich), Chris Howard (West Deutsche Rundfunk, Cologne), Alan Freed (WINS, New York), Jack Payne (BBC, London), and Jack Jackson (not to be confused with Jet Jackson, ATV, London).

"[Not] very well-made, [it] still did a terrific business."—Victor Weber, exhibitor.

The plot concerns two singers (Paul Carr and Freda Holloway) who fall in love at an audition and become a successful team. Their greedy managers (Kay Medford and Robert Pastene) convince them to strike out on their own, a move that threatens their romance.

"I enjoyed it except for the two who played the leading roles. They could have stayed home."—Harold Bell, exhibitor.

Most of the performers opted to sing a new song, instead of one of their hit records, in the hope of making a new hit record. One of the exceptions was Jerry Lee Lewis, who was a last-minute addition to the lineup. His appearance on Steve

Carl ("Blue Suede Shoes") Perkins.

Allen's Sunday night TV show had made Lewis into an overnight success, to use a meaningless phrase. He was signed for this picture the following month. He sings one of his biggest hits, "Great Balls of Fire," a song given to Lewis by the movie's musical director, Otis Blackwell.

> "Jerry Lee Lewis is particularly amusing as he stares mindlessly tinkering at a piano and periodically lets out a yelp of anguish."—*Hollywood Citizen News*.

Buddy Knox sings "Hula Love," a minor hit, inspired by the Metropolitan Opera Quartet's "My Hula Hula Love." His biggest hit was "I'm Sticking with You," written by Knox and his friend Jimmy Bowen, whose biggest hit was "Party Doll," another Knox/Bowen collaboration.

> "…has the advantage of some good natural dialog and some fine performances which most other films in this genre have lacked."—*Motion Picture Herald*.

Other performers include Count Basie, ("Jamboree" and "One O'Clock Jump"), Fats Domino ("Wait and See"), Joe Williams ("I Don't like You No More"), Connie Francis ("For Children of All Ages" and "Siempre"), Carl Perkins ("Glad All Over"), and Rocco and His Saints, featuring Frankie Avalon ("Teacher's Pet").

> "…the singers are as undistinguished as the plot. Exceptions include Joe Williams and Fats Domino—genuine blues singers worthy of better company—and Count Basie's immaculate band."—*Monthly Film Bulletin*.

It's well worth a look.

THE JAMES DEAN STORY (January, 1957) Warner Bros.
M Leith Stevens, W Stewart Stern, P-D George W. George, Robert Altman

Black and white documentary of the actor's brief life, from his boyhood on a farm in Fairmount, Indiana, to his salad days in New York and his struggle for recognition, and finally his triumph in Hollywood. There are interviews with the aunt and uncle who raised him, and other people who actually knew him, unlike all of the actors who would later claim relationships with Dean who barely knew him, this film may be more factual and trustworthy than all of the flapdoodle about the actor that followed. The narration was written by Stewart Stern for Marlon Brando (one of Dean's idols), but it was Martin Gabel who delivered it. The movie received very little ad space in the newspapers when it came to Los Angeles, in support of the sci-fi thriller, **The Black Scorpion** (1957). I haven't seen it since, so there is little else that I can say about it. It seemed overloaded with black and white stills and somber narration and music. I left before it was over, and in those days, I'd sit through almost anything.

"Plenty of walk-outs," exhibitor Mel Daniels reported from Oklahoma.

JOY RIDE (November, 1958) Allied Artists
M Marlin Skiles, W Christopher Knopf, P Ben Schwalb, D Edward Bernds

Compelling story of a middle-aged, middle class couple, Miles (Regis Toomey) and Grace (Ann Doran), terrorized by four punks. It begins with them admiring his T-Bird, not really doing anything but looking. When Miles asks them to leave, three of them scatter back to their car, and the girls who are waiting for them, but one boy, Paul (Rad Fulton) holds his ground. "This kid looked dangerous, the way he was lookin' at me," Miles tells the police. "There were girls in the car. They used words I never even knew when I was their age." Captain Barrett (Roy Engel) says his hands

Regis Toomey forces Brad Fulton to drive at a reckless speed to teach him a lesson.

are tied. "A couple of kids looked at your car and called you a few names." He tells Miles to forget about it. Miles is willing but Paul becomes obsessed with taking a ride in that T-bird, to the point that he and the boys tear the couple's home apart, looking for Grace's spare car key. When Miles comes home she's still hysterical. "The ride ain't the most important thing anymore," Miles tells the others when they want to give up. "It's scarin' that old guy." Miles agrees to give the boys the car, then turns the tables by pulling a gun. The other three take off, leaving Paul alone in the car with Miles. "You said you wanted a ride in my car. You're gonna get one." He forces the punk to drive as fast as he can. "You got no right to do this," Paul whines, as frightened as he can be. Once he's made his point, Miles orders Paul to head for the police station. It's at this point, you should simply turn the picture off.

Writer Christopher Knopf creates a totally believable middle-class nightmare, and director Edward Bernds is lucky to have Regis Toomey in the lead to help sell it. Toomey has always been a good, supporting player, which is why he's so perfect for this story. He looks like who he's supposed to be. If the film had been made at a higher level, a bigger-name actor would have been in the part, and it wouldn't have been as interesting. Charles Bronson helped turn **Death Wish** (1974) into a franchise, but the picture would have been better with someone like Toomey in his stead, the way the character was described in the novel. It may not have been as profitable, but that's a separate issue.

In an era where women traditionally stood cowering in a corner while their men fought the battle, Ann Doran steps way over the line and becomes ridiculous and annoying. Still, if you cut the last six or seven minutes, when the film collapses into a heap of sermonizing, you have a pretty good slice of entertainment here.

"*You couldn't afford the kind of protection you want.*"

JUKE BOX RHYTHM (April, 1959) Columbia
M Arthur Morton, W Mary P. McCall, Earl Baldwin, P Sam Katzman, D Arthur Dreifuss

Jack Jones didn't know when he agreed to make this harmless Sam Katzman musical that he would be signing with Capital Records soon and would have his first hit record—"This Could Be the Start of Something Big"—before the year was up. In this show he sings "The Freeze" and "Make Room for Joy." His co-star, Jo Morrow, sings "Let's Fall in Love."

"It was a poor man's **Roman Holiday** [1953]," Morrow remarked. "They had already signed another girl to play the princess, but I went on an interview for it anyway—again, I was being forced on the director. [Morrow was referring to the role she played in **Gidget**, against the wishes of the producer and the director, because some big shot at Columbia was trying to decide if he wanted to put her under contract, and was using these movies as a sort of screen test.] Well, I did a reading for them and the director [Arthur Dreifuss] told Sam Katzman, 'Gosh, she's so right. She's so perfect for this.' Well, they paid off Lisa Gaye and put me in it instead!"

Morrow is the Princess who flies to New York City to shop for her coronation wardrobe. In her hotel room she hears music coming from another floor. She makes her way to the room with the party, and is listening outside the door when she is pulled into the room by Riff Manton (Jones), a singer whose father, George, is a Broadway producer looking for backing for his new play, "Juke Box Jamboree." Riff has no idea who she is. He just wants to dance with her. A romance blossoms and the princess buys her wardrobe from novice designer Balenko (Hans Conried), with the understanding that the benefit he will reap from the publicity is worth the cost of backing Papa Manton's play.

It has to be said that some of the musical interludes are elaborately staged for a low budget picture. Nevertheless, there ain't much rhythm coming from this ol' jukebox, other than Johnnie Otis doing his hit record, "Willie and the Hand Jive." The Earl Grant Trio perform "I Feel It Right Here" and "Last Night." And The Treniers sing "Get Out of the Car."

"This picture smells—but so did 90 per cent of the other rock 'n' roll pictures. Unlike the others, though, this one did no business at all," said exhibitor L.R. DuBose. Not so for L.C. Brazil, Jr. "Need more of these," said he. "Contrived but acceptable," said *Variety*, "overflows with energy" lied *Film Daily*, and *Boxoffice* played it safe by saying that the teenagers "should come out in droves." Most interesting of all, considering how often these musicals were criticized for having thin plots, was the complaint from the *Motion Picture Herald* that the script was "too complicated and wordy" for a rock and roll movie.

It's a rock 'n' royal romance!

JUVENILE JUNGLE (March, 1958) Republic Pictures
M Gerald Roberts, W Arthur T. Horman, P Sidney Picker, D William Whitney

Republic Pictures president Herbert J. Yates was taken aback when AIP's **Hot Rod Girl** and **Girls in Prison**, two black and white, low budget pictures, made more money in one week than Republic's **Lisbon** and **Dakota Incident** (1956), both in color with major players. Republic spent $1,663,245 on their package while AIP held the line at $206,000. The first week in Los Angeles, Republic made a respectable $81,000. A week later, playing the same theatres, AIP grossed $104,329, then a week later, **The She Creature** and **It Conquered the World**, made for $109,000, yielded a very respectable $102,812 in its first week. There was no getting around it. Yates had been making pictures for the wrong audience. Jerry Roberts, the head of the music department, suggested they make a couple of movies with a lot of rock and roll music. With his empire crumbling around him, Yates told director William Whitney and producer Sidney Picker to get to work. **Young and Wild** and **Juvenile Jungle** had a combined negative cost of $226,820.

Smooth talking Corey Allen, who gives the most interesting performance in the picture, blows into town and takes over a gang of punks. He intends to romance, then kidnap Anne Whitfield to get the payroll money from her father's safe. "There's a ready-made ransom in that safe every Friday afternoon," he tells the gang. But his plan goes awry when he falls in love with his mark.

Other members of the cast include William Schallert, Leon Tyler, Richard Bakalyan and Yvette Vickers, who has quite a lot of screen time and is featured on the poster, yet receives no screen credit. The film has its moments, and looks more like a real movie than anything AIP had to offer, but not nearly as fun as its companion feature.

A girl delinquent...a jet-propelled gang...out for fast kicks!

KING CREOLE (July, 1958) Paramount

M Walter Scharf, W Herbert Baker, Michael Vincente Gazzo, P Hal B. Wallis, D Michael Curtiz.

First rate melodrama set in New Orleans, with gorgeous, black and white photography by Russell Harlan that the *New York Times* described as "beguilingly drenched with atmosphere." This was the kind of role Elvis had been hoping for, a chance to give James Dean a run for his money. And Elvis was getting better with each picture. Michael Curtiz was impressed with him and believed Elvis would be a *great* actor one day. This was his fourth (and favorite) film, the second for producer Hal Wallis, who hereafter would take the singer away from his edgy persona and turn him into a lightweight Howard Keel. Presley's induction into the army, a few days after this picture wrapped, would have a drastic effect on his screen image and his choice of music. Wallis, Uncle Sam and Tom Parker successfully amputated the rock from Presley's roll.

Elvis plays Danny Fisher, a troubled kid who lives with his sister (Jan Shepard) and his father (Dean Jagger) in the French Quarter in New Orleans. The death of their mother has left their father a broken man, unable to hold a job. Tired of being broke, Danny drops out of a school, gets a job as a busboy at The Blue Shade, a nightclub owned by gangster Maxie Fields (Walter Matthau), and briefly joins a gang of thieves, led by Shark (Vic Morrow), who works for Maxie. During their robbery of a Five and Dime, Danny meets Nellie (Dolores Hart), a good girl, and a romance develops. He invites her to a "party" which turns out to be him and a hotel room. Nellie isn't that kind of a girl, but if that's what she has to be, she will. Danny takes her home. He is also attracted to Ronnie (Carolyn Jones), Maxie's mistress. In no time at all, Danny is in over his head, and indirectly responsible for the beating of his father.

Between takes, Jones and Presley would sit at the piano and sing old ballads. "He'd sing harmony with that beautiful baritone of his," she told Ray Bennett. "He also played piano quite well."

Toward the end of the film, Maxie shoots Ronnie just before he takes a bullet and ends up in the mud. "It was good that I was supposed to be dying in the film because I felt like I was, and I think I looked like it, too," Jones said. She had a temperature of 103 that would eventually put her out of commission for two weeks. Elvis was supposed to kiss her and she was afraid she'd make him sick and asked if there wasn't some way they could get around it. "That's all right," he told her. "Maybe it'll get me out of the army." With that, they really went at it.

Dolores Hart, Elvis Presley and Carolyn Jones. I'm sorry to report that Hart, a very gifted actress, left the business in 1963 to become a nun.

Elvis Presley and Carolyn Jones.

Hal Wallis bought Harold Robbins novel, *A Stone for Danny Fisher*, about a boxer in New York, for James Dean. Once Elvis was on board, screenwriter Herbert Baker and Michael Vincente Gazzo switched locales and made Danny a singer. Things were set in place and ready to go when Elvis received his draft notice. Paramount's production chief, Y. Frank Freeman told Uncle Sam it was going to cost the studio over $300,000 if they shut down production, and was able to get a postponement. Tom Parker claimed that Presley's time in the Army cost the government half a million in taxes, plus the $78 a month the singer would draw as a private.

Elvis sings 11 songs in this one, many of them with a Dixieland flavor. The main title song, "Danny," was replaced with an instrumental version of "King Creole." An instrumental version of "Danny" can be heard briefly toward the end of the film, when Elvis sings "As Long as I Have You." "Danny" eventually became a minor hit for Conway Twitty, the title changed to "Lonely Blue Boy." "Hard Headed Woman" was the only hit song from the film, released in advance to promote the picture. It was a major disappointment that Elvis didn't sing it in the movie. There's an establishing shot of the club, and the song can faintly be heard from the inside as it comes to an end. Other songs include "Lover Doll," "Trouble," "Young Dreams," Crawfish," "Dixieland Rock," "Don't Ask Me Why" and "Steadfast, Loyal and True."

The *Los Angeles Times* called Elvis "the surprise of the day," and many critics had to grudgingly admit that he delivered a "sympathetic" and "believable" performance." The critic for *Citizen News*, who'd always cut Elvis some slack, praised his "virility and natural dramatic ability." "Hardly offers a challenge to Marlon Brando," chimed *Motion Picture Herald*, and *Monthly Film Bulletin* called **King Creole** "the most unattractive Presley vehicle so far."

"Presley always does a standout business and this was no exception," said Iowa exhibitor Harold Smith. Fellow Iowa exhibitor M.W. Long complained that it was "the poorest Presley picture to date" and his theatre was empty. Yet Sam Elrod said Elvis always "holds his own in Iowa."

"When they swing at you, Pop, it's not enough to duck, you gotta swing back."

Julius La Rosa would eventually become a disc jockey.

LET'S ROCK! aka KEEP IT COOL (June, 1958) Columbia
M Tony Pastor, *W* Hal Hackady, *P-D* Harry Foster

Casting a crooner like Julius La Rosa in a film called **Let's Rock** seems like an oxymoron to me. It was an attempt by the producer to broaden his audience base. La Rosa had a gig on Arthur Godfrey's radio and TV show. (An anonymous writer for *Boxoffice* thought he'd be "a cinch for movies—if he wants 'em.") When the singer had the nerve to hire his own manager, and wanted to handle his own business affairs, something that Godfrey insisted on doing as a way of keeping his talent from straying too far afield, Godfrey fired him on the air and told the press he'd done it because La Rosa had lost his humility, unaware of the irony of his remark. The incident gave La Rosa's career a boost and resulted in his own TV show. Introducing the Everly Brothers on his program one night, he seemed very uncomfortable as he tried to joke with them, and came off looking like a real square. When he learned that Don and Phil were younger than his socks, he lamely told the audience that Pat Boone was old enough to be their father. Not getting the laugh he expected, La Rosa wisely left the stage.

In this picture, La Rosa's career as a pop singer has hit a slump. His manager (Conrad Janis) says, "When are you gonna come to the party? Rock and roll's been around a long time. It's gonna be around a lot longer." La Rosa sings "Crazy Crazy Party" and becomes a successful rock and roller, almost making it a science-fiction picture.

"Even if La Rosa could act, and by now it should be sufficiently established that he can't, **Let's Rock!** would still be difficult to endure."—*Los Angeles Times*.

Danny Rapp, Dave White, Frank Maffei and Joe Terranova. Dick Clarke suggested they change the title of "Do the Bop" to "At the Hop."

The big drawing card here is Danny and the Juniors singing "At the Hop," one of the most popular songs of the decade. Other performers include Della Reese ("Lonelyville"), The Royal Teens ("Short Shorts"), Paul Anka ("I'll Be Waiting There for You"), Roy Hamilton ("Here Comes Love"), The Tyrones ("Blast Off"), and Wink Martindale ("All Love Broke Loose").

"Ouch! Where did they dig up this clinker? And what an assortment of oddballs all assembled in one picture. Fair teenage crowd the first night, but had an $8.35 total the second night."—exhibitor Frank Sabin.

Boxoffice managed to single out the film's greatest asset. "Joi Harmon, in a small but potent role as a cheap pickup girl, burns up the celluloid in the short time she is on the screen and should garner her share of interest from the male viewers."

Let's rock with Joi Harmon instead of Julius La Rosa. What do you say?

LIFE BEGINS AT 17 (July, 1958) Columbia
M Henry Russell, *W* Richard Baer, *P* Sam Katzman, *D* Arthur Dreifuss

Sam Katzman is not a name that one associates with quality merchandise, and coupled with director Arthur Dreifuss doesn't offer much hope either, so it is with some trepidation that I say that (relying on a very old memory) this is an okay movie, written by Richard Baer, who would become a very successful television writer, mostly for sitcoms. This is his only feature film.

I don't recall many laughs in **Life Begins at 17**, at least not the intentional kind. I just remember that it held my attention because it touched on matters not often addressed in these films, with some measure of restraint. Carol Peck, played by Luana Anders, who would later star in Francis Ford Coppola's first feature, **Dementia 13** (1963), is nothing like the wicked character she played in that film. Here she's a fragile little thing, living in the shadow of her beautiful sister, Elaine

Luana Anders and Mark Damon.

(Dorothy Johnson). When Carol wins a local beauty contest, Elaine has to win the title of Miss Indianapolis. Russ Lippincott (Mark Damon) tells all his buddies that he intends to date her, but Elaine gives him the brush off. It isn't until he starts dating Carol, which he only does to be closer to Elaine, that Elaine shows any interest. She starts to move in but needs none of her wily ways since Russ wanted her all along. "All the time I was dating Carol, I was falling for you." Yep. Elaine is a selfish creep. And he's a jerk. He will later suffer the consequences when Carol's old boyfriend (Edd Bernds) delivers a haymaker to his jaw.

"Richard Baer's screenplay is inventive and well-plotted," said *The Hollywood Reporter*. "Story Flaws Mar **Life Begins at 17**" was the headline on *Daily Variety*. *Boxoffice* believed the kids would like it, "but most of their elders may be unable to suppress a few yawns."

"What are my stockings doing here?!"

Dorothy Johnson and Edd Byrnes

Jay Jostyn and Normal Eberhardt.

LIVE FAST, DIE YOUNG (1958)
Universal-International
M Irving Gertz, W Allen Rivkin, Ib Melchior, P Harry Rybnick and Gordon Kay, D Paul Henreid

The sin-streaked story of the runaway teenage girls of today's beat generation! The motion picture that takes you into the broken homes, the skid-row bars, the penthouse girl-traps on the one-way highway to trouble!

Norma Eberhardt has had enough of her crummy life and her abusive father (Gordon Jones), and runs off to find a better life in the big city. She makes some quick money rolling drunks, and gets involved with Michael Connors and Troy Donahue, who sell their high-ticket, stolen merchandise to anyone looking for a bargain. They're planning to steal a package of diamonds worth $150,000, being shipped to the post office by registered mail. Norma and Troy have no trouble getting part-time jobs in the post office during the Christmas deluge.

"The film tapped into what the kids were feeling—that society sucked and they were rebelling against it," Eberhardt remarked.

Back at the homestead, Norma's sister, Mary Murphy is taking another tongue lashing from their worthless father. "You're a tramp, like your sister," he barks. "Like your mother!" This coming from a guy who has been living off of his daughter since his wife wisely ran off with a traveling salesman. Fed up with working six days a week as a waitress, fending off customers with too many hands, only to be treated like a tramp at home, and havin her father's friends try to rape her, Mary leaves to find her sister, who she is certain will get into trouble.

Michael Connors and Mary Murphy.

"[Working] with Norma Eberhardt was a pleasure," said Mary Murphy. "She was very congenial, and I knew her before we did the picture. We lived at the Studio Club for Women."

Motion Picture Herald described Eberhardt's performance as being "like an 18-year old imitating Mae West and Marilyn Monroe at the same time," and while there's some truth in what they say, she's fun in the picture. The critic found Murphy to be "sweet but insipid." *Boxoffice* accused the script of going off on more tangents "than an imperfect ballistic missile." Exhibitors Mickey and Penny Harris called it "rough and tough and one we were embarrassed to be showing."

Will not disappoint.

"Nothing's against anything until you're caught."

LOVE ME TENDER (November, 1956) 20th Century-Fox
M Ken Darby, W Robert Buckner, P David Weisbart, D Robert D. Webb

Routine western, originally titled *The Reno Brothers*, marks the screen debut of Elvis Presley. Worried that Presley's popularity might be short-lived, the studio put him in a supporting role as Clint, the youngest Reno brother, though they had little cause for concern. His first RCA album was the biggest selling record in the company's history before it was even pressed. "Love Me Tender" went to the top of the charts, pushing Presley's two-sided hit, "Hound Dog" and "Don't Be Cruel," into the number two slot, the first time the same singer held both positions until The Beatles came along a decade later. There was no question that Elvis could sell records. But could he sell movies? The amount of fan mail generated before the film went into production convinced the studio heads to change the title of the film to **Love Me Tender** and to give Elvis more screen time. Elvis told a group of reporters that as far as he knew, he wouldn't be singing in the film, and he really didn't want to. He didn't think he could build a career on singing alone. "Look at Frank Sinatra. Until he added acting to singing he found himself slipping downhill."

The four songs Elvis sings—"Love Me Tender," "Poor Boy, "Let Me," and "We're Gonna Move," are credited to Vera Matson, the wife of Fox's musical director Ken Darby, who actually wrote them. Not wanting to split the residuals, Darby refused to use Elvis's musicians—Scotty Moore, Bill Black and D.J. Fontana—in favor of his own Ken Darby Trio. The songs aren't very good.

David Weisbart was assigned to produce the picture, coming off **Rebel Without a Cause**, and Robert D. Webb, no stranger to westerns, was set to direct. Studio contract players Richard Egan and Debra Paget were given the leads. Egan didn't want to do the picture, having only recently moved from supporting to featured player roles, knowing that he'd be taking a back seat to Elvis, yet he got more fan mail after appearing in the film than any other actor on Fox's payroll. He's Vance Reno, reported dead during the Civil War, who comes home to find his girl

Elvis Presley and Deborah Paget.

(Paget) married to his brother Clint. It was a marriage of convenience and Cathy is still in love with Vance. His presence, Vance fears, can only bring heartbreak to them all. He's set to leave when he's jailed for robbing a Union train. At the time of the robbery, Vance didn't know the war had ended. His partners in crime bust him out of jail so he can take them to the money. Vance wants to give it back but he's the only one. The others tell Clint that Vance is planning to run away with Cathy. Clint wounds Vance then is killed trying to save his life. The movie ends with the ghostly image of Presley, singing lyrics to "Love Me Tender" that weren't on the hit single: *When at last my dreams come true, darling this I know. Happiness will follow you, everywhere you go.*

Exhibitor W.A. Windschitl expressed his hope that they'd keep Presley alive in future films. He was all set to lock up his theatre when he found ten young girls still sobbing in the auditorium. They were back the following night to sob some more. "The bigger joke," said Windschitl, "was on the married man who walked out ahead of his wife and who was getting a big kick out of the criers, until he turned around to find his own wife red-eyed too."

Debra Paget had mixed emotions about meeting Elvis. She'd heard a lot of bad things about him, none of which she found to be true. She liked him. She liked him a lot. She was impressed with his professionalism and his ability to quickly learn the mechanics of film acting. "He called from El Paso and asked me to marry him," Paget recalled. "My mother and daddy were not for me getting involved. I probably would have married him."

Motion Picture Daily called it "a first-class western," suggesting that Elvis could hold his own without "his now infamous bumps and grinds." *Modern Screen* said his acting was "as good as anyone else's." "When not too intent on his acting," said the *Hollywood Reporter*, "Presley has a good screen appearance."

Jealousy and confusion soured the profits made by some of the exhibitors who just couldn't relate to Elvis or his fans. "What's this Elvis got that I haven't got or that I couldn't twist out of shape?" asked one perplexed fellow as he counted his biggest take in years. "What we can't understand," said Walton Oakerson, "is how Elvis sold sweets when he looks like he's been eating sour pickles."

It didn't take Presley long to get comfortable with the camera or the critics to get comfortable with him. David Weisbart made three more films with him, three of Presley's best— **Flaming Star** (1960), **Follow That Dream** and **Kid Galahad** (both 1962). These were the kinds of films Presley wanted to make, but his manager, Tom Parker, wanted to make the musicals because of the additional money to be made from the soundtracks.

"*Go on, say it, Cathy. Say I'm lying. Say he weren't your lover!*"

LOVING YOU (July, 1957) Paramount

M Walter Scharf, W Herbert Baker, Hal Kanter, P Hal B. Wallis, D Hal Kanter

Loving Elvis would have been a more apt title for this pretty, Technicolor, VistaVision package, designed to sell Elvis Presley to Middle America. The screenplay by director Hal Kanter and Herbert Baker, based on Agnes Thompson's short story, "A Call from Mitch Miller," is a dandified version of the singer's own rise to stardom, and the controversy caused by rock and roll music. As Deke Rivers, Presley is a simple country boy, promoted by a ruthless woman fighting for her life. She'll do whatever it takes to put Deke over, and when Deke finds out about some of the shenanigans she's pulled, he's ready to call it quits. The woman forces him to face some hard facts about the music business and himself. "You've got fifteen minutes to get on that stage and find out if you've even got a future," she tells him.

Wallis had intended to play it safe with Presley, by giving him a supporting role in **The Rainmaker** (1956), much the same way Fox had treated him. Then Presley's first film, **Love Me Tender**, started packing them in and everyone with half a brain knew that leads Richard Egan and Debra Paget had nothing to do with it. "This kid is dynamite," Kanter told Wallis. "He hurtles off the screen and grabs you by the throat." That was enough for Wallis who made two kinds of movies—"prestige pictures" which were always a gamble, and the "bread and butter" pictures, the ones he could count on to pay the bills, like the Dean Martin and Jerry Lewis comedies. Martin and Lewis had gone their separate ways. Wallis needed a replacement, and as he would later say, "Elvis is money in the bank."

Three exhibitors in Arkansas felt the same way. "You know, they make a lot of fun of Elvis," said Victor Weber,

Elvis Presley and Dolores Hart.

"but, brother, he's doing okay—a little better than okay, as far as I see." Terry Axley happily announced, "SRO during its run here!" "Had good business despite every kind of competition known to man," Audrey Thompson marveled.

Variety engaged in a little wishful thinking when they declared that the rock and roll craze had hit its peak, but felt "that a sizable part of the citizenry will welcome Presley back for his second screen appearance, nevertheless." *Time* smugly suggested that to "be true to its own brand of ballyhoo, the film would have to show Elvis—modest and shy fellow that he is—rejecting all offers to lend himself to Hollywood commercialism." *Boxoffice* laid it on the line. "No matter what an exhibitors' personal opinion may be of Elvis Presley, he can't afford to pass this one up."

Lizabeth Scott plays the determined promoter, her last film for Wallis who'd had her under contract for years, as was Wendell Corey who plays the country western singer who doesn't know that he's washed up. Delightful Dolores Hart (who wouldn't fall in love with her?) plays Elvis's main squeeze, but it's the always welcome Jana Lund who gives Elvis his first screen kiss. Elvis had the good sense to take Jana to **The Ten Commandments** instead of the actress he was supposed to take.

Elvis sings "Mean Woman Blues," "Got a Lot o' Livin' to Do," "Lonesome Cowboy," "Hot Dog," "Party," "Loving You" and "(Let Me Be Your) Teddy Bear." The last two songs were released on a single that became yet another two-sided hit for the singer.

Loving You gives the viewer the opportunity to see Elvis in his prime, at the top of his form, slim and sexy, and full of energy. He's positively electrifying. And the picture's okay.

"*Well, you ain't bad, sideburns.*"

*MAD AT THE WORLD (December, 1955) Filmmakers Releasing Organization
M Leith Stevens, P Collier Young, W-D Harry Essex

When young people become angry and violent, it affects the whole community-your town and mine. Anger breeds anger, until finally, it sweeps over all age groups. Here now, is the story of how one police department in a great American city, fought to bring this destructive human fire under control!

Sam and Anne Bennett (Keefe Brasselle and Cathy O'Connell) are a happily married, lower middle class couple whose baby is critically injured after being hit by a bottle, thrown by a gang of joy-riding hoodlums (Stanley Clements, Paul Dubov, Joe Turkel) known as The Wolf Pack. Tom Lynn (Frank Lovejoy) is the cop assigned to the case, and he's working it, but not fast enough to suit Sam. He goes searching for the punks on his own, in the rougher sections of town, and in a moment of unbridled rage in his quest for vengeance, uses an innocent witness like a punching bag. Sam learns where The Wolf Pack hangs out from a lonely, hip-talking waitress (Karen Sharpe), much to his regret. The boys give him a pretty good working over and are about to incinerate him when the cops show up.

The critical reaction to this film was unusually harsh, even from the trade publications, with the exception of the most forgiving of the trade magazines, *Motion Picture Herald* who called it "effective and generally entertaining." It was Sam's violence they reacted to. He was supposed to the hero. The irony is, this is the only film of its kind *endorsed* by none other than Senator Estes Kefauver. He's the one giving that little lecture quoted at the beginning. Why you old faker, you.

MISTER ROCK AND ROLL (April, 1957) Paramount

Mus Lionel Hampton, *W* James Blumgarten, *P* Ralph Serpe, Howard B Kreitsek, *D* Charles Dubin

Crammed with music, this independently made film won't disappoint, unless you're looking for something other than the music. It is yet another tale of Fearless Freed and his quest to prove that rock and roll music is not a harmful influence. While Teddy Randazzo recalls how the D.J. discovered him, Freed's out raising money for medical research.

On the program: La Vern Baker ("Love Me Right," "Humpty Dumpty"), Brook Benton ("If Only I Had Known," "Your Love Alone"), Chuck Berry ("La Juanda," "Oh Baby Doll"), Shaye Cogan "Pathway to Sin," "Get Acquainted Waltz"), Al Fisher and Lou Marks ("Sing Song Siren"), Lionel Hampton ("Mister Rock and Roll," "Hey Poppa Rock," "Hello Folks," "Drum Hi!," "Star Rocket"), Ferlin Husky ("This Moment of Love," "Make Me Love Again"), Frankie Lymon and The Teenagers ("Fortunate Fella," "Love Put Me Out of My Head"), Clyde McPhatter ("Rock and Cry," "You'll Be There"), The Moonglows ("Barcelona Rock," "Confess It to Your Heart"), Lois O'Brien (It's Simply Harvest" Teddy Randazzo ("I Was the Last One to Know," "I'll Stop Anything I'm Doing," "Kiddio," "Perfect for Love"), Little Richard ("Lucille).

This sequence with Screamin' Jay Hawkins was cut.

Said the snooty reviewer from the *Los Angeles Times*, "Evidently working from the presumption that if you've got a bad thing don't let it go away, Paramount studio—of all concerns—has perpetuated still another of those rock and roll films." *Variety* said it had "the artistic impact of an animated jukebox" while the presumptuous *Hollywood Citizen News* predicted the kids would snicker at the antics of some of their favorite singers. Ever hopeful, the *New York Times* suggested that "with the rock 'n' roll apparently wobbling toward the end of the line, where do we go from here?"

"This was a picture they really went for," said exhibitor Charles E. Smith. "Plenty of rock that helped theaters roll into the ticket window," D.W. Trisko happily reported. Sam Holberg called it a "very good rock and roll picture in black and white, with no story to mention."

The big story of the musical sensation that's swept the nation...told by the King of Rock and roll himself!

MONSTER ON THE CAMPUS aka MONSTER IN THE NIGHT aka STRANGER ON THE CAMPUS aka THE TENURED TERROR (December, 1958) Universal-International
W David Duncan, P Joseph Gershenson, D Jack Arnold

The blood from a coelacanth, a survivor of the Devonian period that was treated with radiation, turns a friendly dog into a vicious throwback, a dragonfly into something the size of a poodle, and Dr. Donald Blake into a prehistoric man. Lively, sometimes shocking, sometimes silly science fiction from writer David Duncan, made for the bottom half of a double feature.

"Jack Arnold directed it," said the film's star, Arthur Franz. "He was more like a traffic cop. If you hit your marks and said your lines you moved on. I don't think it was his choice to make the picture, but that was just an impression."

He was right. Universal had a policy of pairing one of their contract stars with one of their contract directors. Audie Murphy had Jesse Hibbs. Rock Hudson had Douglas Sirk. And Jack Arnold, who had been the studio's go-to guy for sci-fi, was pulled off of **The Monolith Monsters** to work with Jeff Chandler in a series of A-pictures. **MOTC** was a step down for Arnold. He couldn't have been happy about it.

Still, the picture is a lot of fun in its own screwball way, with a terrific performance by Franz, moody Russell Metty photography, and the sloppiest music mix in the studio's history. And the film was produced by Joseph Gershenson, the head of the music department! What do you think he was trying to tell us?

The picture opens with college student Jimmy Flanders (Troy Donahue) and his dog, arriving at the University with the coelacanth, packaged in a large crate, in the back of his van. As Blake examines the fish, bloody water drips into the gutter. The

German Shepard laps it up and becomes a snarling throwback with huge fangs. The animal is caged. Overnight, the fangs are gone and he's back to normal. Blake accidentally cuts his hand putting the fish away and becomes ill. Molly Reardon (Helen Westcott), a fellow teacher, drives him home. He suffers a blackout and when he wakes up, his place has been trashed and Molly is hanging by her hair, from a tree in the backyard, dead from fright. At first the police think Blake's the murderer, but strange handprints left behind suggest there was someone else involved, and a cop (Ross Elliott) is assigned to keep an eye on Blake, believing he was the one the killer was after.

Jimmy and his girlfriend, Sylvia (Nancy Walters) come to get his dog back and hear a strange tapping at the window. Blake opens the blinds and there is a giant dragonfly trying to get in. Blake opens the window, uses the fish for bait and stabs the dragonfly. Blood from the knife drips into Blake's pipe and he suffers another blackout. Like before, when he wakes up, his clothes are torn and this time it's the bodyguard who's dead, and the dragonfly is nothing but a stain on Blake's desk.

The police don't seem to making much progress in catching the killer, so Blake starts an investigation of his own, unaware that he's the man he's looking for. When he learns that the coelacanth was treated with gamma rays to preserve it, he's certain that its blood caused the dog and the dragonfly to revert to their original selves. Holding a vile of blood, Blake tells his colleagues, "I say that if you were injected with this, you'd revert to a primitive anthropoid, physically as well and mentally." Everyone, including his fiancé Madeline (Joanna Moore), thinks he's gone off the deep end until Jimmy and Sylvia break their promise and tell her about the giant dragonfly.

Variety called it "a pretty fair shocker," while *The Hollywood Reporter* said, "Franz gives gentlemanly and scholastic values few boogey tales possess." *Monthly Film Bulletin* thought writer Duncan had loaded his story with so much "hypothetical" laboratory research, "that one finds it difficult to challenge the credulity of the fantastic story."

"*Sometimes, Professor Blake frightens me.*"

MOTORCYLE GANG aka FURY UNLEASHED (October, 1957) American International
M Albert Glasser, W Lou Rusoff, P Alex Gordon, D Edward L. Cahn

Guys and gals living with no tomorrow. **Motorcycle Gang** *with an all-star cast of excitement. See an actual motorcycle chicken race. It makes the hot-rod game look like a Sunday drive in the park. See the world's champion stunt rider. See a deadly follow-the-leader race and a motorcycle duel with death to the loser!*

John Ashley and Steve Terrell return as villain and hero respectively in a remake of **Dragstrip Girl**, originally titled **Motorcycle Girl**, written, produced and

John Ashley and his gang.

directed by the same people, with Ashley returning home after spending fifteen months in jail for a hit and run, for which he blames Terrell. Terrell is on probation and doesn't want any trouble. Aggravating the situation is Anne Neyland, a terrible tease who enjoys provoking the boys into bad behavior while a sympathetic cop (Russ Bender) tries to keep them in line.

Much of the picture was shot at Iverson's Ranch near Chatsworth, in the hills and roads in and around Hollywood and Griffith Park. Top competitive rider Blair Bernbaum doubled several of the actors in the film, while famed flat track star Dude Griswell did most of the fast and dangerous spills. Lucille Merker doubled the ladies.

Production on this film was delayed when John Ashley received his draft notice. It was completed during his two-week furlough following his basic training at Fort Ord. "I felt like I was Tony Curtis or something," Ashley remarked. "One of the first things they do, of course, is give you a Yul Brynner haircut. I explained the situation to a second lieutenant who let me start growing my hair out. But

Believe it or not, Anne Neyland didn't know anything about riding a motorcycle and yet, she insisted that she could do this stunt.

there was this one drill sergeant who was out to get me, and he used a full field inspection as an excuse to march me and several others to the barber shop. I saw this guy delivering newspapers and I called him over, handed him a couple of bucks, and traded my fatigue jacket for his sack of papers, which I quickly threw over my shoulder. He took my place in line. When the rest of the group did a column right, I executed a left flank, and returned to the barracks with my hair intact."

This could either be Chaplin Studios or Raleigh Studios. Or not.

Variety said the picture "kicks up a cloud of dust as soon as it hits the screen, and the haze thickens, never letting enough story break through to lift pic out of the rough-and-rumble class." The Hollywood Reporter agreed that it was short on plot "and what there is does not always ring exactly true." Boxoffice thought the film "should draw a better than average response from teenage crowd, albeit there is little interest for anyone outside this age category." Which was fine with Victor Weber, who booked the picture with **Sorority Girl**. "The teenagers came in large numbers. The guys went for 'Gang' and the gals went for 'Girl' and so everyone was happy." Commenting

Anne Neyland and friend.

on all of the smart-mouth, *The Los Angeles Examiner* said the dialog sounded more "like it came from the author than the mouths of the actors."

"Burning rubber is my one big vice."

NO TIME TO BE YOUNG aka THE YOUNG REBELS aka CRYBABY COLLEGE PUKES (August, 1957) Columbia
W John McPartland, *P* Wallace MacDonald, *D* David Lowell Rich

Buddy Root (Robert Vaughn) has a big fat chip on his shoulder and a big fat problem. He should have spent more time on his studies and less time with the widow Doris (Dorothy Green), because now he's flunked out, and eligible for the draft. Life south of the border sounds preferable to a two year stint in the military, but Buddy needs money. His two buddies, Bob (Roger Smith) and Stu (Tom Pittman) need money, too. Bob is in love with his boss's daughter, Gloria (Merry Anders), but guys who bag groceries for a living don't exactly run her motor. Stu (Tom Pittman) needs money to impress his new father-in-law (Ralph Clanton). It seems the boy has been lying to his wife Tina (Kathleen Nolan), and her pop about the money he'll be making as soon as he finishes the novel that he isn't writing. Buddy thinks that robbing the market where Bob works is the answer to all of their problems. At first, they're against the idea but then Tina finds out that Stu's broke and leaves him, and Bob's carelessness puts Gloria in the hospital. Now everyone *really* needs money. Naturally, the robbery doesn't run as smoothly as the three masked banditos expected, and one of the clerks ends up dead, shot by Buddy.

Your reward, should you stick with this dreary tale of nitwits on parade, will come shortly after the robbery. The police have nabbed everyone but Buddy, and he's got all of the money stuffed into his jacket. He ducks into a dance hall to catch his breath and the cops show up. Hoping to blend in with the crowd on the dance floor, Buddy asks a young lady to dance. Now, I know that what follows would have been funny to me no matter who was playing Buddy, but Robert Vaughn made it that much more delicious. Don't get me wrong. I like him. And he may be a very good dancer. But there was something about the sight of Vaughn, who always seems like he's above it all, cutting a rug on the dance floor that proved to be more than I could have hoped for. I was already laughing *before* the money started falling out of his jacket. Because Vaughn really gets into this moment. It's as if his character has forgotten the police are after him. He's forgotten the reason he's on the dance floor. The money keeps flying and he keeps on wildly dancing until he notices that all eyes are on him. These are the little moments that I live for, and while I can't recommend this film to anyone, this bit of business with Vaughn made it worthwhile for me. However, make no mistake. The film is no credit to anyone involved.

"I got a price on fat guys calling me a punk."

ONE WAY TICKET TO HELL aka TEENAGE DEVIL DOLLS (December, 1955)

No. No. No. No. No! Do NOT watch this piece of propaganda, masquerading as entertainment! It is the brainchild of one Bamlet Lawrence Price, his master thesis for his film class at UCLA. "He was obsessed with his film projects," said Anne Francis, married to Price at the time. She gave him $4,000 to complete the thing and because she was who she was, the film received a lot more attention than it would have. It is a pseudo-documentary, mostly narrated, and will tax the patience of the most forgiving viewer.

ON THE LOOSE aka THIS RESTLESS AGE (September, 1951) RKO
M Leigh Harline, W Dale Eunson, Katherine Albert, P Collier Young, D Charles Lederer

Parental neglect leads to suicide in this cautionary tale from The Filmmakers, a production company formed by husband and wife Ida Lupino and Collier Young. They set the bar a little higher than their low budget contemporaries, tackling controversial subjects as realistically as possible. "I suppose we were the New Wave at the time," said Lupino, the *only* female director in Hollywood at the time. **The Hitch-Hiker** (1953) and **The Bigamist** (1953) are stand-outs, and are often part of any discussion about The Filmmakers, but **On the Loose** never gets so much as a mention. It was not a success at the boxoffice or with the critics. Frankly, it's not very good.

Marilyn Hendrickson, a senior at Hollywood High School where some of the movie takes place, was hired to pepper the script with idioms. Lupino narrated it. Joan Evans (the daughter of the screenwriters) is Jill, the neglected daughter of Frank and Alice Bradley (Melvin Douglas and Lynn Bari). She is recovering from a suicide attempt when the film opens. In flashbacks, we learn how she got there.

Expecting a celebration on her birthday, Jill comes home to find a cake and note from her parents explaining that they had plans for the evening that didn't include her. She goes for a drive with her boyfriend Larry Lindsay (Robert Arthur), and gets a lecture about staying out late when she returns.

On her next outing with Larry, they get drunk and make out, and declare their undying love for each other, but that's the end of their relationship. Larry's mother catches him passed out on the couch and forbids him to see "that tramp." Jill attempts to tell her mother how torn up she is, but her mother is only half listening, and simply tells her to forget about Larry and date other boys. Jill takes her advice and though her dates are innocent, she gets an unsavory reputation. Her friends shun her. And when she gets into a fight defending her honor, she's hauled into the principal's office and gets slapped by her father.

After all is said and done, the best you can say on the film's behalf is that it's full length.

Teenage girl with age old ideas!

THE PARTY CRASHERS (December, 1958) Paramount
W Bernard Gerard, Dan Lundberg, P William Alland, D Bernard Gerard

Looking at the very dull party around her, Barbara Nickerson (Connie Stevens) tells her boyfriend, Josh Bickford (Bobby Driscoll in his final screen appearance), "I'm bored." You will be too, for a while, but rest assured that this little gem finally pays off, though it doesn't even sound like it's going to be any good. **The Party Crashers**. Big wow. You throw the bums out or, if they get combative, have the cops do it for you. Not much promise in that scenario. Here's two hot titles Paramount might want to consider as a double feature: **The Beer Drinkers** and **Teenage Waitress**.

Barbara tells Josh that she wants to leave but changes her mind when Twig Webster (Mark Damon) and his gang crash the party. Her blood races as she watches Twig make fun of the host (Gene Persson) when he asks Twig to leave. As bottles are tossed and broken, Twig engages in a mock bullfight, and falls against Josh. Josh pushes him away and Twig, already off balance, hits the floor. He goes after Josh, and once they start fighting, everybody starts fighting. Later, after he's walked her home, Barbara gives Josh the cold shoulder. "I don't know why you're mad at me. I didn't

Mark (Young and Dangerous) Damon found steady employment in Europe for a decade, then came home and became a very successful producer.

start the fight," he reminds her. "That's crazy," she mutters. "It was a little bit sick if you ask me," he remarks. She scoffs. "It was different." He's shocked. "Does that make it good?" There's a sparkle in her eyes when she purrs, "He's like an animal." Josh agrees. "He *is* like an animal." Only when he says it, it's an accusation. "Don't knock it," she snaps, and walks off.

The screenplay flip-flops back and forth between the teenagers and their parents. The Nickersons (Cathy Lewis and Onslow Stevens) are reasonable people and so are the Bickfords (Francis Farmer in her last film, and Denver Pyle). The Websters, however, are a different story. Twig's dad is a drunk. His wife, Hazel, understandably, spends a lot of time away from home. Through innuendo, Webster accuses her of having an affair but won't come right out and say it. This is a daily routine the couple engage in. Twig has heard it many times. We get to hear it a few times as well, until the drunken sot finally, at her repeated insistence, comes right out and calls her a tramp. She beats him into submission with her purse. This delightful meltdown is almost immediately followed by another highlight.

Twig comes home, despondent and emotionally drained. He isn't in the door three seconds when his father tells him about this big party he's heard about. "Every *decent* kid in town'll probably be there. Maybe if you'd learn to act like a gentleman, they'd invite you." Twig hasn't heard about the party and has no interest in it. He tells his father that several times, but his father insists that he can't wait to crash it, and warns him that if he does, he'll lose his allowance. It's at this point that the sequence becomes like a vaudeville routine. As the conversation continues, in bits and pieces, and in spite of Twig insisting that he doesn't want to hear about the party, his father tells him everything that he needs to know about it—the time, the address, the people who'll be attending, and maybe the caterer's name for all I know. I was laughing so hard I can't honestly tell you what he was saying. Damon had become Lou Costello; his father Sidney Fields.

As it turns out, Twig should have listened to his old man. He and the gang find themselves prisoners of some drunken adults who might be gangsters for all we know. Some of them look like gangsters. They lock the doors and it looks as if they intend to have their way with the young ladies. While Josh creates a diversion, Twig looks for another way out. Down a long hallway he sees a man coming out of one of the rooms, looking like he's been well serviced. Twig looks in the room and finds his mother, sitting in front of a mirror, fixing her makeup. Good grief! His dad was right! She *is* a tramp!

Connie Stevens told Mike Fitzgerald that she got the surprise of her life while she was working on this picture. "I was sitting at a table, having my makeup applied," she explained, "when I noticed, in the mirror, this good looking guy come up behind me. 'You're Gary Gray!' I said enthusiastically, and he admitted he was. 'You don't know it, but I was president of the Gary Gray Fan Club back in New York.' Can you imagine it? In such a short time I was actually 'starring' in a movie, and my long-ago crush was in it with me."

"*I just want to have a little fun and you make a federal case out of it.*"

*THE REBEL SET (December, 1959) Allied Artists
W Bernard Gerard and Louis Vittes, P Earle Lyon, D Gene Fowler, Jr.

Caper movie with a beatnik backdrop, this is Hollywood's version of "beatsville," and bears little resemblance to the real thing. It's doubtful that anyone involved with this project ever saw the inside of a beatnik hangout, or ever even talked to a beatnik.

The principal players: John Mapes (Gregg Palmer), an actor down on his luck, and his wife Jeanne (Kathleen Crowley); Ray Miller (John Lupton), a writer looking for a publisher; George Leland (Don Sullivan), the son of movie star Rita Leland (Collette Lyons). These three gentlemen, all patrons of Mr. T's beatnik coffee house, become involved in an armored car robbery, master-minded by Mr. T (Ed Platt in a ridiculous beard). The plan: Take the train from Los Angeles to New York, and pull the heist during a four hour stopover in Chicago. For a change, everything goes smoothly. It's after the robbery that things go terribly wrong.

The drifters, the hipsters and the hot sisters!

REBEL WITHOUT A CAUSE
(October, 1955) Warner Bros.
M Leonard Rosenman, W Stewart Stern, P David Weisbart, D Nicholas Ray

In late March of 1955, amid apprehension among Warner Bros. executives, the cameras started rolling on a little black and white movie, **Rebel Without a Cause**, starring James Dean, an intense young method actor who had just made his film debut in the studio's botched adaptation of John Steinbeck's beautiful novel, **East of Eden** (1954). Dean had been struggling for years to make a name for himself, and finally took James Whitmore's advice and moved to New York to study acting at the Actor's Studio. "He told me I didn't know the difference between acting as a job and acting as a difficult art," said Dean.

Sal Mineo and James Dean.

Rebel was ten days into production when the front office threatened to pull the plug. Ray offered to purchase the rights and continue on his own. He had to make the picture now. He was consumed by it. "The thing that interested me in **Rebel** was doing something that would counteract **The Wild One**," he said. 'I went out and hung around with kids in Los Angeles before making the movie. Some of them call themselves 'wild ones.' They wore leather jackets; go out looking for somebody to rough up a little. These aren't poor kids, you know. Lots of them have money, grow up and become pillars of the community. Boy, they scared me."

After looking at the rushes, the studio changed its mind and told Ray to keep going. Two days later, in a surprise show of faith in the project, Ray was summoned to the front office and told to throw out everything he'd done and start over, in color and CinemaScope. This new found enthusiasm came from **East of Eden** which was proving to be a financial and critical success, with Dean becoming the talk of the town. Coupled with the fact that **Blackboard Jungle** was making money hand over fist, to have their new "star" in anything but a respectable "A" movie was simply out of the question.

Dean's co-star, 16-year old Natalie Wood, was elated. She had fought hard to get the part. Though she'd already made a place for herself in film history by playing the super serious little girl in the holiday classic, **Miracle on 34th Street** (1947), parts for teenagers were few and far between. Her domineering mother kept her looking like a little girl and that was the way she was seen by almost everyone in Hollywood. The parts she played usually required her to wear pigtails. She wept when she read the script. "I felt exactly the way the girl did in the picture toward her parents," she said. "It was about a high school girl rebelling, and it was very close to home. It was really about my own life." Knowing well the ways of Hollywood (she'd already been raped by an actor twenty years her senior), the young actress was willing to do *whatever* it took to get the part. It didn't take long before she and the 43-year old Ray were lovers, but even that wasn't enough. Ray still had reservations. He was even thinking of Jayne Mansfield for the role, another actress he was sleeping wih. It wasn't until Wood got stinking drunk with Dennis Hopper and her friend Jackie Perry, and got into a horrible accident, that Ray gave in. They were driving down Laurel Canyon Boulevard on a rainy night, headed for Googie's restaurant, a hangout for struggling young actors, when Hopper accidentally hit the brake and slid into oncoming traffic. Thrown from the car, Wood was a mess when she was taken to the hospital, but instead of calling her parents, Wood insisted the hospital call Nick Ray. She was lying in her hospital bed when Ray walked in. She grabbed him, pulled him close and whispered in his ear, "They called me a goddamn juvenile delinquent. Now do I get the part?" Ray told the doctors, "Take good care of this young lady. She's the star of my next movie."

Dr. Robert M. Lindner wrote a book called *Rebel Without a Cause*, a case history of the psychologically disturbed young juveniles that Lindner treated at a federal penitentiary. The studio bought the book for Marlon Brando then let it sit. When Ray told Lew Wasserman that he was interested in making a movie about juvenile delinquency, Wasserman suggested Lindner's book, but Ray had his own ideas, and kept only the book's title.

Ray wanted Clifford Odets, a personal friend of his, to write the screenplay but the studio insisted on Leon Uris, the author of a very successful novel, *Battle Cry*, which the studio was making into a movie. After two screenplays, Uris still had no understanding of what Ray was after. Ray turned to Irving Schulman, author of *The Amboy Dukes*, the first great modern novel about juvenile delinquency. He was the one who finally gave the story some structure (such as it is) and was responsible for changing Ray's "blind run" to the now famous "chickie run." A blind run (the original title of Ray's treatment) is when two drivers start at opposite ends of a tunnel and speed toward each other. A chickie run is when two drivers speed toward the edge of a cliff. In both cases, the first one to jump out of the car is the loser. Schulman had a lot to do with what viewers saw on the screen, but he couldn't stand working with Ray and left the project before it was finished. He turned what he wrote into a novel called *Children of the Dark*. Leonard Rosenman, who would eventually score **Rebel Without a Cause**, suggested Stewart Stern, a young writer who knew Dean. Stern turned out to be a Godsend. He and Ray spoke the same language. It was Stern and Ray who finally defined the characters.

Sal Mineo, James Dean and Natalie Wood.

William Hopper slaps his daughter when she asks for a little affection.

And it was Stern's idea to have the story take place in a single day and night. Said he, "The purpose of the film was to tell the story of a generation growing up-in one night. That's why I consider it mystic, because it was a night journey."

Credit also must go to a gang leader and actor named Ray Mazzola, who told Stern and Ray when the script didn't ring true, and supplied them with the language the kids were actually using.

In the original black and white footage, the movie opened with a typical, middle class man, returning home late at night, loaded with presents for his family. He is accosted by Buzz (Corey Allan), the leader of a group of toughs, who worked him over. He drops his packages and runs for his life. A few seconds later, a completely snockered Jim Stark (Dean) staggers by and sees one of the toys the man dropped, a mechanical monkey, and lies down on the pavement next to it as the sound of police sirens gain volume. The color version begins with Jim's entrance, leaving no explanation for the toy monkey or a later reference to "that beating on 12th street."

After the credits roll, Jim is taken to the police station's juvenile division, where the two other principal characters, Judy (Wood) and Plato (Sal Mineo) await their fates. Judy is there for wandering the streets after curfew. Plato shot some puppies. It is during this sequence that the dividing line between the teenagers and the adults is firmly drawn.

It was Ray's intention to show the parents as their kids see them. Intentional or not, the result is the kind of two-dimensional characters one would find in an AIP film. They don't *verge* on caricature, they are caricatures. Jim's father (Jim Backus) is totally impotent, dominated by his shrew of a wife (Ann Doran). When he shows up wearing an apron, it's simply too much. Judy's mother (Rochelle Hudson) gives her little in the way of guidance beyond a few platitudes about growing up. Her father (William Hopper) not only won't give her any affection, he slaps her face when she tries to hug him. Plato has been completely abandoned by his parents to the care of their housekeeper (Marietta Canty), to whom they send generous checks while they're off pursuing a life that doesn't include Plato.

The one exception is Ray Framek (Edward Platt), an officer at juvenile hall who is tough enough to demand Jim's respect, yet compassionate enough to convince Jim that he cares. He is the perfect father figure. (Not as good as Atticus Finch but who is?) He gets Jim to open up: "If I didn't have one day when I didn't have to feel all confused, and didn't have to feel that I was ashamed of everything…if I felt I belonged somewhere, you know." Framek *does* know. He tells Jim, "If the kettle starts boiling again, will you come and see me before you get yourself in a jam. It's easier sometimes than talking with your parents. Any time. Day or night." But Framek is out on a case when Jim needs him the most.

The teenagers are forced to protect themselves, hiding behind a guise of tough indifference. Even Plato, who wears his pain and vulnerability like a coat, rejects Jim's offer of a jacket to keep him warm. Judy puts Jim down when all that he's trying to do is introduce himself, calling him a "real yo-yo" and a "new disease." She tells him, "I go with the kids." Much later in the film, she says, "You shouldn't believe what I say when I'm with the rest of the kids. Nobody is sincere." Buzz slashes Jim's tires and challenges him to a chickie run. Just before the race, Judy lets her guard down and asks Plato, who worships Jim, what he knows about him. She's obviously attracted to him, which Buzz sensed from the beginning. As he and Jim stare at the edge of the cliff they'll be racing toward, Buzz says, "That's the edge. That's the end." He takes a puff from Jim's cigarette and says, "Know something? I like you. You know that?" Jim innocently asks, "Why do we do this?" Buzz shrugs. "Well, you gotta do something now, don't you?" Like Marlon Brando's disjointed voice over in **The Wild One**, Buzz's rationale for this rite of passage expresses everything while explaining nothing.

I was 10 years old when I saw this film in 1958, when it was re-released with **East of Eden**. I liked it much better then than I do now, but I remember it was the first time that I had heard young people expressing feelings that I felt, that sense of alienation and wanting to belong so much that it hurt. I think that's why the film was a success, and why it was so important to so many young people. Dean's affected and jittery performance served him well. Whether he would have been the world's greatest actor had he lived is open to speculation. According to Dennis Hopper, Dean believed that he had Brando in one hand and Monty Cliff in the other. He was unique, and sometimes I thought he was great and sometimes I thought he

James Dean and Natalie Wood.

was ridiculous, exactly the way I feel about the film. I got into the biggest argument I ever had with my buddy Randy Robertson over this film. He thought the movie was gold and Dean a God. It started by my suggesting that no matter how talented Dean may have been, it always takes a piece of luck to be successful. What followed was one of the most bizarre conversations that I've ever been engaged in. We could not agree on anything. I'd say something that I had, until that moment, thought was beyond question and he'd challenge it. After three hours, I decided I was going to put a stop to it. Looking out the window at the night sky, I said, "Will you at least agree that it's night right now?" Randy cocked his head in that arrogant manner than William Buckley often employed and remarked, "Some people might call it night." I was speechless. And it was obvious that we could go on talking for three more hours and it would be more of the same. I was remarkably calm, but very firm when I said to him, "Get the hell out of here before I strangle you to death."

The New York Times called it "a picture to make your hair stand on end" and Dean's performance "a clumsy display." The New York Herald Tribune found the writing and acting "inept" and the direction "sluggish." The Hollywood Reporter complained it was "a superficial treatment of a vital problem" that had been brilliantly staged. As an honest drama, said the New York Daily News, "the film just doesn't measure up." Variety found it "fairly exciting, suspenseful and provocative, if also occasionally far-fetched."

"It has everything my patrons ask for, drama, action and suspense in liberal doses," said exhibitor Fred I. Murray. A. Madrid and Sam Holmberg both strongly recommended the film. The only complaint Harold Bell had with it was "the parents that should have seen it were not in the theatre." Said H. D. McCloughan, "This made me slightly ill, but it did very well, even though it had played three times before in this area."

"You're tearing me apart!"

REFORM SCHOOL GIRL (August, 1957) American International
M Ronald Stein, P Robert J. Gurney, Samuel Z. Arkoff, W-D Edward Bernds

As the credits role, Donna Price (Gloria Castillo) is in her undergarments, getting ready for a date. Though she dresses behind a partition, she doesn't realize that her Uncle Horvath (Jack Kruschen) can see her reflection in the mirror. He sits in his chair, in a wife-beater undershirt, unshaven, pretending to read the newspaper while he ogles her. Ronald Stein's sleazy, melancholy score perfectly captures the mood of what has to be one of the all-time great main title sequences. The audience breathes a collective sigh of relief, believing they've been spared what could have been a most unpleasant scene, when Donna's awful Aunt Rita (Claire Carleton) comes home from work. She looks at Donna with disgust. "You're a smart one, running around with a bunch of no-goods." After a few more choice words

Gloria Castillo.

she retires to the bedroom. A horn honks for Donna, and that's when her Uncle makes his move. He grabs her shoulders. "Stay here. We could have a ball. Tell 'em to beat it."

Unfortunately, Rita was right. Donna's date is a "no good" named Vince (Edward Byrnes). He shows up in a stolen car and when the police attempt to pull him over for speeding, he leads them on a merry chase that ends when he clobbers a pedestrian. Being the stand-up guy that he is, he flees the scene, leaving Donna to take the rap. In court, Rita assures the judge that Donna is just no good, "always making plays for my husband." She's sent to a reformatory. As the police continue to investigate the accident, Vince worries that Donna will turn him in, and attempts, with the help of some of the inmates, to kill her.

Edd Byrnes and Ralph Reed.

Reform School Girl is both engaging and silly at the same time, saved from completely collapsing into satire by some very good performances, with Castillo holding her own all of the way. Others in the cast include Ross Ford as the psychiatrist who believes in Donna, and Ralph Reed who is in love with her, fan favorite Yvette Vickers, Luana Anders and Sally Kellerman in her film debut.

"I made two films for AIP," Bernds told me.

"***Reform School Girl*** and ***High School Hellcats***. I wasn't aware that I broke any new ground. I did a little research for the one. I visited a couple of reformatories and asked a lot of questions. I had profit participations in both pictures, but I never saw a dime until they sold the pictures to television. They needed my signature for that deal, so they offered to buy me out, at a fraction of what they owed me. Sam Arkoff told me that I could take them to court, but it would take years to settle, so I took the money."

One year later, Edd Byrnes became one of the best-known actors on television, as the super cool Kookie on the ***77 Sunset Strip*** TV series. A minor character at first, an avalanche of fan mail put him up front and center, a real threat to leads Efrem Zimbalist Jr. and Roger Moore. "Kookie, Kookie, Lend Me Your Comb" became a hit record. AIP re-released ***Reform School Girl*** with Byrnes' face all over the poster, on a double bill with ***Dragstrip Girl*** whose leading lady, Fay Spain, had landed a meaty role in ***God's Little Acre*** (1958).

"[Asserts] strong strain on plausibility picturing the girl's reformatory with less discipline than a well-managed brothel," complained the critic for *Boxoffice*. *Harrison's Reports* felt the picture was "so capably directed and acted that the characters seem genuine." Exhibitor Victor Weber said, "My patrons really went for it and I was surprised by the fact that it is very well made and held interest throughout."

"If there's anything I like better on a hot day, it's a cool chick."

THE RESTLESS YEARS (October, 1958) Universal-International
M Frank Skinner, W Edward Anhalt, P Ross Hunter, D Helmut Kautner

What happens when a girl first feels a woman's need…and a boy first faces a man's desire? ***The Restless Years*** *tells the whole dramatic story, electrifyingly exposes the morals, the mistakes, the shame, the scandal of a town with a 'dirty mind,' when ugly rumors, evil gossip, can make a decent girl a target for the teen-age pack, and turn a tender young romance into a nightmare of disgrace.*

"I know what's on your mind," Polly Fisher (Luana Patten) says to her boyfriend Bruce Mitchell (Jody McCrea), as they watch Melinda Grant (Sandra Dee) gathering flowers. "You think because she illegitimate, she's easy." It seems that every little school kid knows Melinda was born out of wedlock except Melinda. The shame of it has turned her mother, Elizabeth (Teresa Wright), into a frightened recluse, unable to admit that her lover deserted her. Each day she goes to the mailbox, looking for the letter that will never come. It's the only time she leaves the house.

Will Henderson (John Saxon), a newcomer to town, likes Melinda the second he lays eyes on her. His father, Ed (James Whitmore) objects. He has returned to the small town of his childhood, hoping to salvage what's left of his sagging career. Image is everything to him now. He prays no one will see how desperate he is as he tries to worm his way into the business community.

Teresa Wright and Sandra Dee.

But Will knows a good thing when he sees it. He asks Melinda to join him on the hillside, a spot where lovers neck. "People make *love* there," she balks. The next day the two are rolling around, playing like kids, when desire kicks in and Melinda runs off. Will won't be discouraged. When this shy young lady looks in the mirror, she obviously isn't seeing what he sees. He encourages her to try out for the lead in the school play. Her teacher, Miss Robson (Virginia Grey), is delighted. She wanted Melinda from the start, though everyone expected Polly Fisher to get it. She's the daughter of the wealthiest, most influential, and possibly unhappiest people in town (Alan Baxter and Dorothy Green). "The door's open anytime you want to use it," Fisher tells his wife. "Go find yourself another man!"

Polly sees Melinda on the bandstand, changing into her costume to rehearse. Then she sees Will and her little mind starts spinning. At "Parents Night," Polly tries to blackmail Melinda into giving up her part in the play, and when she won't, she races to the stage and spreads the word. "I caught [them] up at the bandstand and she had her dress off!" Will gets into a fight defending Melinda's honor. Later, when they're alone, Melinda tells Will that she's ashamed. "You haven't *done anything*," he reminds her. "But I *wanted to*," she says.

Screenplay by Edward Anhalt, from Patricia Joudry's play, *Teach Me How to Cry*, makes for pretty good melodrama, with Dee in her first leading role, giving the kind of nuanced performance that made her a star. Producer Ross Hunter believed in her before the studio did. He signed Dee to a personal contract and made her believe it was a studio contract, not wanting to undermine her confidence. Hunter loaned her to MGM for a supporting role in **Until They Sail** (1957), with Paul Newman and Jean Simmons. She came back a star. After this picture, the studio immediately paired Dee with Saxon again in **The Reluctant Debutant** (1958).

Saxon and Dee work well together, and it's refreshing not to have their love for each other treated as puppy love. Those teenage years were mighty restless, as I recall. I don't expect they've gotten a whole lot better.

"It is a period piece, with the dressmaker mother of an illegitimate child, and would have been more plausible if it had been played in period," said Variety. "But granting that, it has a feeling of poetry and sensitivity. Dee gives the picture its strongest sense of reality." Said exhibitor M.W. Long, "A teenage picture that the older patrons enjoyed, too."

"It's just as easy to go with a girl from the right side of the tracks as it is the wrong side."

THE RETURN OF DRACULA aka THE CURSE OF DRACULA aka THE FANTASTIC DISAPPEARING MAN (April, 1958) United Artists
M Gerald Fried, W Pat Fielder, P Arthur Levy, Jules Gardner, D Paul Landres

Norma Eberhardt was 29-years old when she played the teen-aged Rachel Mayberry in this film, the same age as the film's writer, Pat Fielder. "I was influenced by the original Bram Stoker story, of course, (the angle about the friendship of the two girls)," said Fielder. "Thornton Wilder's film for Hitchcock, **Shadow of a Doubt** [1943], was my model for the script."

28-year old Ray Stricklyn is Rachel's boyfriend, Tim Hansen. They make a cute couple. As she's getting into his car, Rachel complains about his loutish behavior. "That's not what you said last night," he reminds her. She smiles and playfully hits him. "Shut up." It's a very good moment, something missing from so many of these movies, and an example of what made Fielder's scripts several notches above her contemporaries. Changing Uncle Charlie into Dracula was a clever way to bring The Count into modern day, small-town America.

Rachel and her family are looking forward to the arrival of their Cousin Bellac Gordal, who they have never seen. They meet him at the train station, unware that their cousin has been killed by Dracula (Francis Lederer), who has taken his place, hoping to escape the man who has vowed to hunt him down and kill him, John Merriman (John Wengraf).

Lederer, who claimed that his agent tricked him into doing the picture, is the creepiest vampire since the silent **Nosferatu**, at times turning the charming, middle class home into a tomb. Rachel finds him mysterious and attractive. Tim is a little jealous, and thinks there's something fishy about him. We know it will be the kids, not Merriman, who will have to bring Dracula to his knees, and we know it won't be easy. Director Paul Landres works the showdown for all it's worth. Creepy Gerald Fried score is a big help.

"*There is only one reality, Rachel, and that is death.*"

Richard Tyler and Dorothy Provine.

RIOT IN JUVENILE PRISON (April, 1959) United Artists
M Emil Newman, W Orville H. Hampton, P Robert E. Kent, D Edward L. Cahn

The three titans of mediocre cinema—writer Orville H. Hampton, producer Robert E. Kent, and director Edward L. Cahn—join forces to fashion this by-the-numbers account of reform school reform. It didn't impress this 11-year old when I saw it with **Hercules** back in 1959. It wasn't bad. It just wasn't very good. I must add, however, that I was impressed with Dorothy Provine, who plays Babe in a supporting role. She never looked better.

The Governor sends psychiatrist Paul Furman (Jerome Thor) to the Ditman Hall reformatory to change the way Col. Walton (John Hoyt) does business. Walton makes his position clear. "You can't treat these kids the way you do the kids next door." Furman expects no cooperation from Walton, but he makes it clear that he won't let him stand in his way. The first order of business is to empty The Larkin Home for Girls and bring all of the young ladies to Ditman Hall.

The toughest nut in the place to crack is Eddie Bassett (Scott Marlowe). He and a few of his buddies came very close to making a successful break shortly before Furman arrived. Trapped by a wire fence, they were ordered to surrender. "If they try to use those guns," Walton told guard Quillan (Dick Reeves), "teach them a lesson." Two of teens end up dead. Eddie vows to get even.

In a short time, the inmates are getting better treatment, better food, and a weekly dance. Next, Furman wants to get rid of the armed guards, and have vocational and educational training for the inmates. At one point, Eddie is willing to sacrifice everything that Furman has and will accomplish to satisfy his lust for revenge. Furman wants to know why. Through hypnosis he able to get to the heart of the problem. "It was my eighth birthday all right, but my old man, he did all the celebrating." With his mother too drunk to do anything about it, Eddie's father slapped him across the mouth, knocking two of his teeth out.

If ever a film needed a stronger leading man it's this one. Normally a television actor, this was Jerome Thor's first big screen appearance, after which he returned to television in supporting roles and didn't surface again on the big screen for six years. John Hoyt was a good choice for his nemesis, but Hoyt has nothing to do but rain on Thor's parade. Every scene with him is the same scene. Which is pretty much the problem with the whole movie.

"You don't hate me. That shows you something, doesn't it?"

*ROADRACERS aka ROAD RACERS (March, 1957) American International

M Richard Markowitz, W Ed Lakso, Stanley Kallis, P Stanley Kallis, D Arthur Swerdloff

Joel Lawrence, in his one and only big screen feature, is a 24-year old race driver whose reckless conduct caused the death of another driver, and the boy's father will later do his best to orchestrate a fatal accident for Lawrence.

Banned from American racetracks, Lawrence decides to go to Europe and make a better show of himself. His girlfriend, Marion Collier, promises to wait for him but when he returns, awash in medals and citations, she's fallen for Skip Ward, another racer. Lawrence puts some polish back on his name by racing Ward in the American Grand Prix.

I caught enough of this film that I can say there's some good racing scenes, with nary a rear screen projection shot in the mix. It's the real McCoy, with the camera moving in and out of the action. Stanley Kallis wrote the screenplay. He was the son of Al Kallis, AIP's poster guy. Producer-director Arthur Swerdloff was an Award-winning filmmaker with over 120 documentaries and educational films to his credit. It was filmed at the Paramount Ranch race track.

"You know, Rob didn't kill Billy Johnston. You did."

ROCK ALL NIGHT (1957) American International

M Curly Batson, Buck Ram, W Charles B. Griffith, P-D Roger Corman

Deceptively titled gangster melodrama, rushed into production to take advantage of the availability of The Platters before they went on tour. Tony Williams, Herbert Reed, David Lynch and Alex Hodge began as a quartet. Their manager, Buck Ram, insisted they add Zola Taylor shortly after they signed with Mercury. Disc jockey

Dick Miller.

Bob Salter premiered their first recording, "Only You," in the Seattle area after hearing it on Hunter Hancock's radio show. Hancock's secretary was Tony Williams' wife. Initially, the group had been foisted on Mercury as part of a package deal. The song was originally released on Mercury's purple label, indicating that the record was rhythm and blues, but it was reissued a few months later on Mercury's standard black label. One hit record followed another until 1959, when the four male members of the group were busted for smoking dope and consorting with soiled women. Radio stations refused to play their records, and the group never recovered. When they agreed to appear in **Rock All Night** (their last appearance together), it was for a week's work.

Roger Corman bought a half hour teleplay by David P. Harmon called "The Little Guy," and gave it to Chuck Griffith to expand into an hour, tailored to center around The Platters.

"We had two weeks," said Griffith. "Then, there was a change in their schedule and we could only have them for a day. I had forty-eight hours to re-write the script. I took a pair of scissors and cut the script into pieces. I added about twenty percent additional characters. I pasted what I could use from the original script on the new pages. The Sir Bop character that Mel Welles played, was written for Lord Buckley."

"Dick Buckley was a guy I used to write for," said Welles. "He was an outrageous comedian that talked in hip talk and yet looked like an English Lord. But, as usual, Dick was kind of flakey about his movements and he disappeared. So, I decided to play the part myself. Nobody else could. In those days, nobody else understood hip talk. The only people that ever used any kind of hip words on television were Frank Sinatra and Steve Allen, and they used words like 'dig.' And that was it. So, we're right in the middle of the beat generation and beatniks were the only ones who understood the language, and Roger got very scared that nobody would understand the picture. So I wrote the first dictionary of hip talk—the Hiptionary. There were five million [I don't think so] of those sent out with the picture as a move for everybody to be able to understand not only what *I* said, but there was a lot of hip talk in the picture. If I'd have done that for a major studio, I would get the royalty off that. I didn't even get ten dollars for it."

The Platters.

Mel Welles.

Russell Johnson, Ed Nelson, and Jonathan Haze.

"I'm Sorry" and "He's Mine" are the only two songs The Platters sing. "We had a crane for that," said Griffith. "It was the first time I saw Roger use a crane. They had to move the nightclub tables out of the way so the crane could get into the shot. It was very elaborate."

Other songs include "Rock All Night," "I Wanna Rock Now," and "Rock and Roll Guitar" by The Blockbusters, and subbing for Abby Dalton, Nora Hayes sings "The Great Pretender" and "I Guess I Won't Hang Around Here Anymore." In his first starring role, Dick Miller plays Shorty, a little guy with a big chip on his shoulder. After being thrown out of one nightclub, he wanders into the Cloud Nine where Sir Bop, a small-time, hip-talking agent introduces his newest singing discovery, Julie (Abby Dalton). Nervous as she can be, Julie performs miserably. Everyone tells her it was fine. "No. It wasn't," Shorty snaps, and when everyone protests, Julie says, "No. He's right. I know he's right and so do you. I'd have said so if he hadn't." Shorty is right about everything. Somehow, this acerbic little ball of hate can read everyone like a book.

All of a sudden, Pete (Ed Nelson) rushes in with big news. He was standing in front of a market when he heard shots fired and two guys came running out. Inside, an old couple lay dead. The two guys he saw, Jigger (Russell Johnson) and Joey (Jonathan Haze), are sitting at the bar. Pete makes a run for it and Jigger shoots him in the back, a vivid memory for actor Nelson. Russell Johnson forgot to shoot to one side. Said Nelson, "The wadding went through my sports coat, through my shirt, and into my back. I may still have the scar on the left side of my back. I went to the hospital and they took the wadding out. And, you know what? They didn't use the take where I really got shot, they used the one where I pretended."

To placate the beat cop who finds the door locked, Jigger forces Julie to sing again, so that everything will appear to be normal, and this time she nails it. The bartender (Robin Morse) tells the cop everything's fine but the cop isn't buying it, and soon the place is surrounded. Jigger wants to make a break for it, holding Julie as a hostage. Shorty knows Jigger is a coward. He knows he won't shoot anyone he has to face, so he backs him down. Jigger screams and threatens, which Shorty brings to a close with a backhand across Jigger's face. The cops take Jigger and Joey to jail. Shorty says he thinks he'll take in a movie. "Shorty," Julie says, "think I'd like to see a movie, too."

Dick Miller got himself an agent and took out a full page ad in *Variety*, the cost of which he'd hoped to split with AIP. Taking a quote from the *Variety* review of **Rock All Night**, it read: "Only the performance (very good, especially considering the so-so-production and direction) of Dick Miller in the lead keeps the audience's interest in the film from disintegrating." Nicholson and Arkoff were not amused.

Harrison's Reports called it "an ordinary program picture," and *Variety* agreed, saying it drew "unintended guffaws at its matinee bow here yesterday." *The Hollywood Reporter* thought Griffith's script had "some funny lines and amusing characterizations." Exhibitor Victor Weber was sure "they must have made this picture in one day," but thought it was "better than some that take a month." Stan Farnsworth's audience was "well-pleased," and C.J. Otis doubled it with **Dragstrip Girl** "and the youngsters ate it up," even though they'd seen it before.

"*If he could talk, he'd tell you I ain't got no sense of humor.*"

ROCKABILLY BABY aka MOTHER WAS A STRIPPER (1957) 20TH Century-Fox

M Paul Dunlap, W Will George, William Driskill, P-D William F. Claxton

Excruciating throwback to the Andy Hardy films, is an exercise in unbelievable niceness that quickly becomes grotesque. Every line rings false and flat. It isn't nearly as interesting or entertaining as any given episode of **The Pinky Lee Show**, which was insufferable.

Virginia Field and her two kids are new arrivals in Springfield. Gene Roth is the real estate agent who shows them their new home. He wants them to come for dinner and promises to introduce her to everyone in town who matters. He's as accommodating as he can be. The kids, Judy Busch and Gary Vinson, find the principal of their new school, Douglas Kennedy, just as accommodating as he can be. He falls in love with their mom.

The only sour note is Roth's wife, Irene Ryan. She's just one of those people who always seem to be in a snit about something. She doesn't like Field's plan to have a place for the kids to go and dance and listen to their music, instead of driving thirty miles to the next town to do it. Field meets with resistance from everyone but Ellen Corby, the grand lady of the town who swings the vote in Field's favor. Ryan makes it her business to know everything there is to know about Field. And what does she find? That she used to be a stripper!

Paul Dunlap who has several good soundtracks to his credit, wrote several songs for this picture. Luis Amando sings four of them: "We're On Our Way," "My Calypso Baby" "Is It Love?" and "Why Can't I?" Marlene Willis sings "I'd Rather Be." "Teenage Cutie" was written by Dick Kallman.

"Bright and breezy," said *Variety*. Likewise, *Motion Picture Herald* found it "wholesome and enjoyable." It was "tastefully done" according to *The Hollywood Reporter*. "These Regalscope pictures are real good," said exhibitor B. Berglund. "Did better than we expected," reported Velva Otts. Jim Fraser played it with **Young and Dangerous**. "Everyone liked the combination and it did average business."

Regardless of what they say, this movie is guaranteed to send any self-respecting teenager running for the exit within the first ten minutes.

I don't see anybody asking you to leave. You're not going anyplace.

ROCK AND ROLL REVUE (May, 1955) Studio Films, Inc.

"Soundies" were cheaply made musical shorts produced for jukeboxes and later for television as fillers. Snader Telescriptions produced hundreds of these three minute soundbites, and in 1952 they sold their library to Studio Films, Inc. which had produced over 700 titles of their own. This movie is a collection of some of those titles. Willie Bryant introduces the performers, with a little help from

tap-dancers Coles and Atkins and Little Buck, and comedians "Nipsy" Russell and Mantan Moreland.

The artists: Ruth Brown ("Tears Come Tumbling Down"), The Clovers ("You Cash Ain't Nothing But Trash"), Nat Cole ("The Trouble with You Is Me"), Larry Darnell ("What More Do You Want Me to Do?"), Delta Rhythm Boys ("Take the 'A' Train"), Duke Ellington ("The Mooch"), Martha Davis ("Vip-i-ty Vip-i-ty Vop"), Lionel Hampton ("Beulah's Boogie"), Joe Turner ("Oke-she-moke-she-pop"), Dinah Washington ("Only a Moment Ago").

ROCK AROUND THE CLOCK (March, 1956) Columbia
M Fred Karger, W Robert E. Kent and James B. Gordon, P Sam Katzman, D Fred F. Sears

Promotor Steve Hollis (Johnny Johnston) and his pal, Cornie LaSalle (Henry Slate), are passing through the town of Strawberry Springs, when they hear a strange sound coming from the dance hall. The joint is jumping to a kind of music that neither Hollis nor LaSalle can identify, played by Bill Haley and The Comets. Hollis takes Haley and his Comets to New York, where he hopes to enlist the aid of successful booking agent Corrine Talbott (Alix Talton). But she's in love with Hollis and wants him to work for her. She does everything that she can to sabotage him, but with a little help from real life disc jockey Alan Freed, the music just can't be suppressed. Desperate, and knowing that Hollis is in love with Haley's agent, Lisa Johns (Lisa Gaye), Corrine tells Lisa that she'll help Hollis if Lisa promises not to marry him.

Bill Haley was 13 when he started playing guitar with some local Michigan bands. Five years later he cut his first record and formed his own band, The Saddlemen. Said Haley: "We started out as a country-western group, then added a touch of rhythm and blues. It wasn't something we planned, it just evolved. We got to where we weren't accepted as country-western or rhythm and blues. It was hard to get booking for a while. We were something different, something new. We didn't call it that at the time, but we were playing rock 'n' roll."

Everywhere the picture played, it raked in the money. An exhibitor in Michigan had run it so many times he thought Columbia should let him keep the print and save the shipping cost. Said another enthusiastic exhibitor, "We played [it] once, then played it twice (only a month apart) and likely will play it once again if the youngsters keep pleading. Frankly, the teenagers were so enthusiastic that they got the personnel in the snack bar sort of swaying and rocking, too." From Illinois, L. J. Bennett wrote: "This show sure did have the kids dancing in the aisles, and it did happen on a Thursday night, which really caused a panic, but was enjoyed by all."

One of the reasons the picture was such a big hit was producer Sam Katzman told writer Robert E. Kent not to let the story get in the way of the music. In addition to the title song, Haley sings "Happy Baby," "Rock-a-Beatin' Boogie," "Razzle

Dazzle," "A.B.C. Boogie," "Mambo Rock," "Rudy's Rock," "R-O-C-K," and "See You Later, Alligator. Other performers: Freddie Bell and His Bellboys ("Giddy Up Ding Dong," "We're Gonna Teach You to rock,"), Tony Martinez and His Band ("Codfish and Potatoes," 'Sad and Lonely," "Cuero," "Mambo Capri"), The Platters ("The Great Pretender," "Only You").

"Speaking as an admittedly middle-aged square," wrote the critic from the *Hollywood Reporter*, "I found this off-beat, low budget, black and white musical thoroughly entertaining. In theatres catering to bobbysoxers and hep-cats, it should have the joint really jumping."

"It's rock and roll, brother, and we're rockin' tonight!"

ROCK AROUND THE WORLD aka THE TOMMY STEELE STORY
(1957) American International Pictures
M Lionel Bart, W Norman Hudis, P Herbert Smith, D Gerard Bryant

Touted as England's answer to Elvis Presley, Tommy Steele was an unknown commodity when AIP bought the U.S. rights to this picture, so it was vital to give it a more marketable title. An introduction by American disc jockey Hunter Hancock was added to the front, explaining that rock and roll was becoming an international phenomenon. At the film's climax, Steele thanks his fans by putting on a big show featuring "his friends," mostly older jazz artists and folk-skiffle groups. The film was quite popular in England. Eddie Fisher and Debbie Reynolds attended the premier.

The Los Angeles Times critic announced that he could watch Steele gyrate like an unbalanced top and not feel shame. "Good clean fun" he called it. Said *The Hollywood Reporter*: "[It] remains emphatically British in concept and largely in locale, even if more in the Cockney than the stiff-upper lip tradition." *Variety* complained that the picture looked cheap. "Numbers recorded at a London teenage bash are used through pic in other contexts, but are easily recognizable by distinctive tonal quality and poor lip synch."

"Certainly one of the poorest of this present trend type that I have shown," said Rod Hartman, an exhibitor in Washington. "Doubled with **Reform School Girl**, which was far superior. If you have your choice on these, would certainly suggest you pass this one. Even had some students walk out, which is unusual." Exhibitor Harold Bell was reluctant to play the picture as British pictures didn't do well for him. "But, as this is rock and roll all the way, it's okay." Arkansas exhibitor Victor Weber said it pleased his audience. I'm glad it pleased somebody.

ROCK BABY, ROCK IT! aka HOT ROCKS (October, 1957) A Freebar Release
M Jay Salem, W Murray Douglas Sporup and J. G. Tiger, P J. G. Tiger, D Murray Douglas Sporup

This is probably what one of those backyard musicals that Mickey Rooney and Judy Garland were always promoting would have really looked like. Nobody in this film can act. They don't look like they ever wanted to. But even if they could, you wouldn't want to watch them. They've all gone through a charisma bypass. Fortunately, the movie is nearly wall-to-wall music. Like the Alan Freed films, the music comes in blocks.

The story of the making of this obscure movie comes from Matt Weitz who spoke with Donnie Gililland, one of the guitarists in the film.

A music promotor and low level booking agent named Jack Goldman, who went by the handle J.G. Tiger, put this show together and shot it in a week in Dallas, Texas. Tiger was an imposing figure, a big man with a booming voice and a very long beard, with chunks of garlic tangled in it. "He was such a con man," Gililland remarked. "It was a very rag tag operation." Most everyone worked for free. Still, Tiger kept running out of money and would race to the phone to beg for more. "He would yell and holler. Later, we found out that the phone wasn't even hooked up." The director, Murray Douglas Sporup, wouldn't let him back on the set after the first day.

The plot: Teenagers put on a show to raise money to save their clubhouse from the gangsters who want to buy it. The gangsters (played by the wrestlers who worked at the local Sportatorium) break in, just before the big show, and Johnny Carroll busts his breakaway guitar over a bad guy's skull. The take didn't work so they taped the guitar back together and tried it again. This time, one of the wrestlers forgot to pull his punch, and the kid he hit could be heard cursing on the soundtrack. Said Gililland, "The prop guitar was now mostly tape, but a third take and some editing saved the day."

There's all kinds of music in this show—doo-wop, Dixieland, rhythm and blues. Local TV show celebrities The Belew Twins sing two numbers, "Love Me Baby" and "Lonesome." Other singers include Johnny Carroll and the Hot Rocks ("Rock Baby, Rock It," "Wild, Wild Women," "Crazy Love," and "Rockin' Maybelle"), Don Coats and the Bon-Aires ("Love Never Forgets," "China Star"), Cell Block 7 ("The Saints Come Rockin' In," "Hot Rock"), Roscoe Gordon and the Red Tops ("Chicken in the Rough," "Bop it"), The Five Stars ("Your Love is All I Need," "Hey Juanita"), Preacher Smith and the Deacons ("Eat Your Heart Out," "Roogie Doogie").

"When the movie came out, the reaction was so bad that everybody was pretty ashamed and embarrassed. It was so terrible." Gililland was glad it was raining that day. It gave him an excuse to cover his head. He had to camp out in front of Tiger's for a week to get the fifty dollars he owed him.

With everyone speaking with thick, Texas accents, regional booking was the best the film could hope for. Star Kay Wheeler, who founded the first Elvis Presley Fan Club, was also seen in **Hot Rod Gang** and wrote for *Dig* magazine.

The Livin' End.

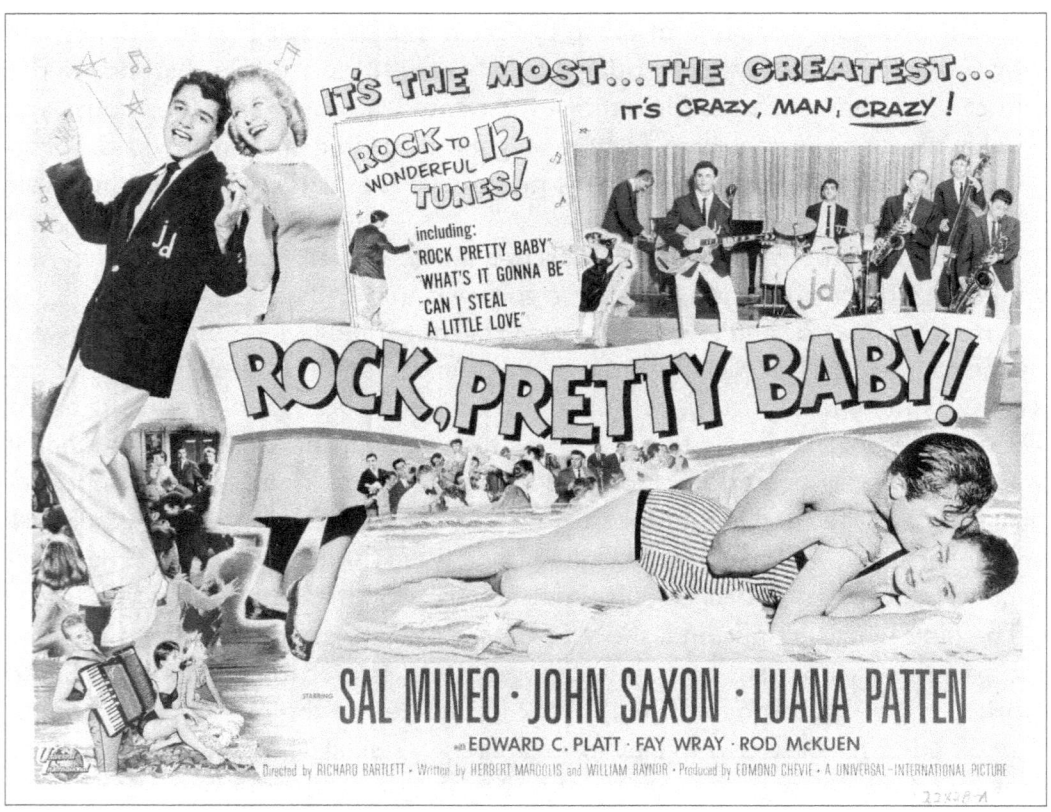

ROCK PRETTY BABY (December, 1956) Universal-International
M Henry Mancini, W Herbert Margolis, William Raynor, P Edmond Chevie, D Richard Bartlett

Wholesome comedy, popular enough to warrant a sequel the following year, but it's afraid to really rock and roll and isn't nearly as funny or as entertaining as any given episode of **Leave It to Beaver**.

Sal Mineo gets top billing but the film belongs to John Saxon. The flood of fan mail that followed his appearance in **The Unguarded Moment** caused the studio to revamp their ad campaign of this picture to take advantage of his rise in popularity, and though I don't know this to be true, it would stand to reason they may have revamped the script to give Saxon a little more screen time.

In **RPB** Saxon is Jimmy Daley, the leader of a rock 'n roll combo. As Angelo Barrato, Sal Mineo is his drummer (who, unbeknownst to them is secretly practicing for his future gig in **The Gene Krupa Story**). Joan Wright (Luana Patten) hears them play and begins arranging songs for the group. They hope to win DJ Johnny Grant's combo contest and the cash prize that goes with it. Jimmy's father (Edward Platt) wants Jimmy to forget this silly notion of his and go to college.

John Saxon and Luana Patten.

"I have a scene with Ed Platt where we have an argument and I trashed a guitar," Saxon recalled. "The director, Dick Bartlett, was very sincere about all of us doing a good job so I really got into this moment. After we did the scene, I heard one of the grips say, 'If I had a kid like that I'd kill him.' So I guess I did okay."

The favorable reaction the film received when it was previewed at the Academy Theatre in Pasadena, California, prompted the studio to do something it had never done before. At another sneak, this time in Encino, they filmed the reactions of the audience instead of having them fill out cards. Sal Mineo was sent to a Florida premiere where fans seeking autographs caused a major traffic jam. In Washburn, South Dakota, the picture was booked during the city's Diamond Jubilee, a three-day carnival that promised the film would being playing to an empty house. It was the best business the theatre had seen in over a year.

I don't know about you but when I think rock and roll, Henry Mancini is not a name that immediately comes to mind. Don't get me wrong. I think the guy's terrific. His main title for **Experiment in Terror** (1962) is one of my favorites. His instrumentals for this movie sound so similar it's difficult to keep track of how many there are. Even the studio's publicity department couldn't seem to decide, their estimates ranging from eight to twelve, depending on which press release you happen to read.

Jimmy Daley and His Ding-a-Lings (actual players unknown) perform "Rock Pretty Baby," "What's It Gonna Be," "Rockabye Lullabye Blues," and "Can I Steal a Little Love." Rod McKuen has two numbers, "Picnic by the Sea" and "Happy is a Boy Named Me." The rest of the music is all Mancini: "Hot Rod," "Big Band Rock 'N' Roll," "Rockin' the Boogie," "Juke Box Rock," "Teen Age Bop," "Dark Blue," "Kool Kid," "The Most," "Young Love" and "Free and Easy." On the Decca soundtrack album, Alan Copeland sings "Rock Pretty Baby," and Hal Dickinson sings "Rockabye Lullabye Blues." And Bill Haley sings "The Saints Rock" which I'm pretty sure isn't in the movie. (Please don't make me watch it again!)

"It'll make adults squirm and probably drive them out of the theatre," predicted *Motion Picture Daily*. The exhausted critic for the *Los Angeles Times* said "it stretches into the longest hour and a half in recent movie history." The *Hollywood Reporter* called it "a well-paced story" with a "tasteful but explicit romance," while the *Motion Picture Herald* inaccurately reported that it jumped "from beginning to end with lots of frantic rock-and-roll."

Luana Patten, John Saxon and director Richard Bartlett.

"Oh, yes," said exhibitor Sam Holmberg, "they came, they saw, they liked every minute of it. A really good story, also. Play it. You can make dough off it if bought middle bracket." W.M. Finley was surprised. "Television didn't seem to hurt this one, as we noticed a good many people present who have television sets." W. L. Stratton reported that it drew "very well to a profit. Nuff said."

It's the most! The greatest! It's crazy, man, crazy!

ROCK, ROCK, ROCK (December, 1956) DCA
M-W Milton Subotsky, *P* Max J. Rosenberg and Milton Subotsky, *D* Will Price

Screen debut of 13-year old Tuesday Weld, and the first collaboration of producers Milton Subotsky and Max J. Rosenberg, who would later attempt to challenge England's Hammer Films with a string of horror films using Hammer's directors and actors, but they never even came close. This picture, written by Subotsky and directed by Will Price, is an unpretentious excuse to bring rock and rollers to the big screen. Rosenberg credited Paul Case with selecting the singers, but it's likely that Alan Freed, who stars in the film as himself, had a hand in it, as many of the performers were straight from the D.J.'s legendary stage shows. The line-up is impressive.

La Vern Baker ("Tra-La-La"), Chuck Berry ("You Can't Catch Me"), The Johnny Burnette Trio ("Lonesome Train"), Jimmy Cavallo and His House Rockers ("The Big Beat," "Rock, Rock, Rock"), Cirino and the Bowties ("Ever Since I Can Remember"), The Flamingos ("Would I Be Crying?"), Connie Francis ("Little Blue Wren," "That' Never Happened to Me"), Frankie Lymon and The Teenagers ("I'm Not a Juvenile Delinquent," "Baby Baby"), The Moonglows ("I Knew From the Start," "Over

Tuesday Weld.

Frankie Lymon, Sherman Garnes, Joe Negroni, Herman Santiago and Jimmy Merchant. Their first big hit was "Why Do Fools Fall in Love," despite cover versions by Gale Storm and The Diamonds.] Lymon left the group after this film for a solo career and had one hit record, "Goody, Goody" before his voice changed and ended his career.

and Over Again"), Teddy Randazzo ("We're Gonna Rock Tonight," "You'll Have the Things Your Heart Needs," "Thanks to You," "Won't You Give Me a Chance?"), "Big" Al Sears ("Right Now"), and Ivy Schulman ("Baby Wants to Rock").

Sandwiched between all of these singers are poorly staged vignettes of Tuesday Weld's efforts to get the money to buy a new dress for the senior prom. It never crosses her mind to work for the money. Instead, she tries to pry it out of her father, who's already given her more than she deserves. She borrows $15 from her best friend to go into the loan business. She figures she'll undercut the banks by charging one percent interest instead of three, believing that one percent of fifteen is fifteen. When her boyfriend hears that she's charging 100 per cent interest, he's angry until he realizes that she's not a crook. She's just plain stupid. Miss Weld, always a welcome addition to any movie, sings a couple of songs, her voice dubbed by Connie Francis.

"Tuesday Weld was a lovely young lady to work with," said Rosenberg. "Sweet and gentle and lovely. All in all, it was a very nice picture."

The critics didn't agree. *Variety* called it "unimpressive," and both *Boxoffice* and *Hollywood Citizen News* said it had the look of a "rush job." The exhibitors told a different story. "Not nearly as good as **Shake, Rattle and Rock**, but why should I complain, with it doing very fine business and pleasing the ones it was intended to please. Fact is, I could use more like it," said S.T. Jackson. Harold Smith couldn't complain either. "Brought the teenagers out in droves, so business was good, but 'no comment' on the picture." Moe Waxman, the manager of a theatre in Philadelphia, got the surprise of his life when his patrons began clapping and stomping to the music. Nearly 400 people started dancing in the aisles and in the lobby. Afraid that things might get out of hand, Waxman placed a frantic call to the police. Thirty policemen, eight patrol cars and two patrol wagons later, the enthusiastic dancers were cleared from the theatre, some of them dancing all the way into the street, while the rest of the audience kept their seats and the rhythm. No one was hurt.

"*Now, nail down the roof gang, because here's a Sugar Baby that can blow it right off.*"

RUMBLE ON THE DOCKS (December, 1956) Columbia
W Lou Morheim, Jack DeWitt, P Sam Katzman, D Fred F. Sears

Based on Frank Paley's 1953 novel, it's *On the Waterfront* (1954) again, this time with James Darren in the Marlon Brando role as Jimmy Smigelski, a decent kid at a turning point in his life. His righteous father (poorly acted by Edgar Barrier) is trying to break the hold that gangster Joe Brindo has on the union. Jimmy looks at the humble way he and his family live and it seems to him that Brindo must have the right idea. "He's got money, hasn't he?" Jimmy tells his friend. "What else is important?"

Brindo loves to talk about himself in the third person, a narcissist of the first order, as played by Michael Granger, seeming very much like the character he played in another Katzman movie, **Creature with the Atom Brain** (1955). I thought he might unleash his atomic-powered zombies on the dock workers during the final showdown, but it turned out that he had something even worse up his sleeve—Timothy Carey.

Was there ever a more bizarre character than Tim Carey? Nobody could possibly appear to be as unbalanced without actually being unbalanced. The first time I saw him was in **Bayou** (1956) where he did this bizarre dance. He did it again in **One-Eyed Jacks** (1961), and again in a movie he wrote-produced-directed and starred in, **The World's Greatest Sinner** (1962). I saw the latter at a private screening a million years ago, arranged by my pal, Bob Greenberg who knew Carey. It was me, Bob, and Tim Carey. I wasn't sure if it was supposed to be funny or not, so I held my laughter for as long as I could, but there came a point when the dam burst. I'm

James Darren and Laurie Carroll.

still not sure exactly what I saw that evening, but I can tell you this. I've never seen anything like it. In one of the most bizarre coincidences I've ever been a party to, I was working at a collection agency as a secretary, and though it was not my responsibility to answer the phone, the one and only time that I did it was Tim Carey. "I'm calling for my wife, Doris Carey." I almost laughed. I didn't know his wife was named Doris, but I recognized his voice. Who else sounds like Tim Carey? He was surprised that I knew who he was. I asked him how much he owed, he told me, and I told him not to worry. "It isn't enough for them to bother with. They'll send you two more letters and that'll be the end of it." Is it any wonder they didn't want me to answer the phones?

"My first movie was a film called **Rumble on the Docks**, which was a low budget film for a gentleman named Sam Katzman, who did all those John Wayne, six day Westerns," James Darren recalled in an interview with Gary James. "But, he did some decent films. Fred Sears was a wonderful director. That really was my first break because I started getting 400-500 letters a month from that film. You're not talking about a major film here. So, that kind of put me on a different level at the studio and they took notice."

Jimmy is a gang member himself, the leader of The Diggers, and eventually does favors for Brindo. The difference between the two is a conscience. And if his hardheaded father could have seen the good in Jimmy, he would never have fallen under the gangster's influence. "Why don't you have me arrested," Jimmy says during a heated argument with his dad. "Then I'd be outta your hair!" Papa kicks him out instead. The boy's mother is on Jimmy's side. "He was right," she tells her husband. "You couldn't break his back, so you're trying to break his spirit." The mother is played by Celia Lovsky, who played the mothers of gangsters so many times her

The Diggers.

portrait appears in the home of gangster Mike Lagana in **The Big Heat** (1953), even though the actress plays no part in the film. She's usually better than she is here. She's overplaying her part as badly as Barrier is, and the two of them together are simply too much to take.

Otherwise, it's okay, and Darren is very good, though I have to say it's a little bit of a stretch to imagine him as a member of any street gang. Unlike Lovsky and Barrier, and Grainger for that matter, he gives an honest performance.

Boxoffice called it "exciting." The *Motion Picture Herald* said it was "fast-moving," and the exhibitors sold plenty of tickets. "The teenage crowd really went for this picture," Jerry Walden reported. Victor Weber had a full house, "even though it had played here once before." Wrestling with his conscience for a moment, considering the possibility that these movies might be making "the delinquents more delinquent," Bob Walker concluded that if this was the kind of entertainment his customers wanted, "Let's keep 'em coming." Katzman, on the other hand, never made another film about juvenile delinquency. "I've got kids," he told the *Los Angeles Mirror*. "One goes to college. I'm trying to bring him up right and I don't think these pictures of messed up youngsters are doing our youth any good."

"Joe Brindo says nothing will happen if they walk off today. You tell 'em that."

Marla English, Mary Ellen Kaye and Gloria Castillo.

RUNAWAY DAUGHTERS (November, 1956) American-International
M Ronald Stein, W Lou Rusoff, P Alex Gordon, D Edward L. Cahn

The parents are the real problem in this picture. Marla English's parents give her everything but love and understanding. Mary Ellen Kaye's dad worries that she'll disgrace the family, the way her mother did. No boyfriends for her. Gloria Castillo's mom is living abroad, working on her third divorce. The three girls run away from home to start a new life in the big city. Adele Jergens gives them a job in the nightclub owned by Gloria's ex-con brother, Lance Fuller. Adele succeeds in keeping two of the girls out of trouble.

When Sam Arkoff heard that producer Alex Gordon had signed Anna Sten for the role of Marla's mother, his head exploded. "I swear to God," said Arkoff, "we thought he was going to the graveyards to cast his pictures."

Actually, Gordon got most of his players from actor-turned-agent Wallace Middleton who, unlike some of the larger agencies, was not afraid to let his clients work in low budget pictures. Anna Sten was one of his clients. Sam Goldwyn had imported her from Russia back in 1933, hoping she would be another Greta Garbo. But the magic wasn't there. It had been a long time between jobs and she was happy to work for a week for $1000. She arrived in a limousine and retired to her dressing room, which her husband had filled with flowers. It was both comical and sad, and it didn't take long for reality to set in. "You gotta talk to her Alex," said Bart Carre, the production manager. "She's found out she has to share her dressing room with Adele. She wants her own dressing room." The actress had some caviar on rye when Gordon walked in and told her the hard facts. "If only he had explained," Sten said graciously. "Why of course. Adele and I will get along just fine." (Gordon managed to place a piece of total flapdoodle in Edwin Schallert's column in the *Los Angeles Times*, claiming that he and Miss Sten were "endeavoring" to secure the rights to **The Tempest** for a remake in England.)

Tom Conway, star of *The Falcon* series, and another client of Middleton's, was chosen to play Sten's husband. Two days into production, at three in the morning, Gordon got a call from Middleton. Conway had suffered a stroke. Gordon went searching through the *Player's Directory* for an actor who would not only be available but be able to learn the lines with so little preparation. Gordon settled on John Litel, an old veteran with plenty of experience on short-schedule films.

"He was right on time," Gordon recalled, "and we hadn't finished shaking hands when he said, 'Let me see the script.' I gave it to him and he said, 'Just give me twenty minutes.' He went into one of the dressing rooms and came out twenty minutes later with his makeup on, and went through the whole day without fluffing a line once."

In spite of the two-day set-back, and running only an hour into overtime, director Cahn was able to bring the thing in on schedule.

Said *The Daily Cinema*, "Familiar atmosphere of revolt with desperate fun, brawls and callous sophistication; good acting and basic sympathy for victims of family upbringing. Recommended adult fair of its kind." *Variety* thought it was "in need of considerable trimming," and *The Hollywood Reporter* thought the resolution was "somewhat melodramatic," but from an adult point of view "good reasoning for the kids to see."

They called her "JAILBAIT!"

RUNNING WILD (1955) Universal-International
W Leo Townsend, P Howard Pine, D Abner Biberman

*"They're too young to be careful, too tough to be afraid, and too smart to get caught. A story wild and violent as the big city jungles, where there's an easy racket for every easy-money hungry punk, and a girl to run wild at his side! Feel the wild rhythm of "Razzle-Dazzle" and other great new rock and roll dance music. Be jilted by the stark, brutal, bare-knuckled fury of **Running Wild**."*

An old woman (Grace Mills) drops a bag of groceries and when a Good Samaritan leaves his car to help her, someone jacks his car and runs him over. The old woman calmly picks up her groceries and walks off, leaving the body in the middle of the street. Later we learn she's Ken Osanger's mother. Ken (Keenan Wynn) runs a car theft ring. He's got his eye on Ralph Burton (William Campbell). Ralph came looking for a mechanic's job and beat feet when a cop pulled in for gas. Ken wants to know more about him. When Ralph shows up at The Cove, Ken's hangout, Ken insists that he dance with his girl, Leta (Kathleen Chase). Leta's job is to pump Ralph for information. "If Osanger wants to know about me, I'll save the next dance for him," he says glibly. He takes Leta back to Ken's table where he is introduced to Vince Pomeroy (John Saxon), who's convinced the two have met.

Ken's right hand boy, Scotty (Jan Merlin), expresses his dislike of Ralph. "A hot rod boy," he remarks. "All mouth. No guts." He attempts to humiliate Ralph and ends up with the contents of a chocolate malt dumped in his lap. The two trade blows until a cop shows up, and hauls Ralph away. He's taken to the police station where we learn that he's an undercover cop, sent to bring Ken Osanger to justice.

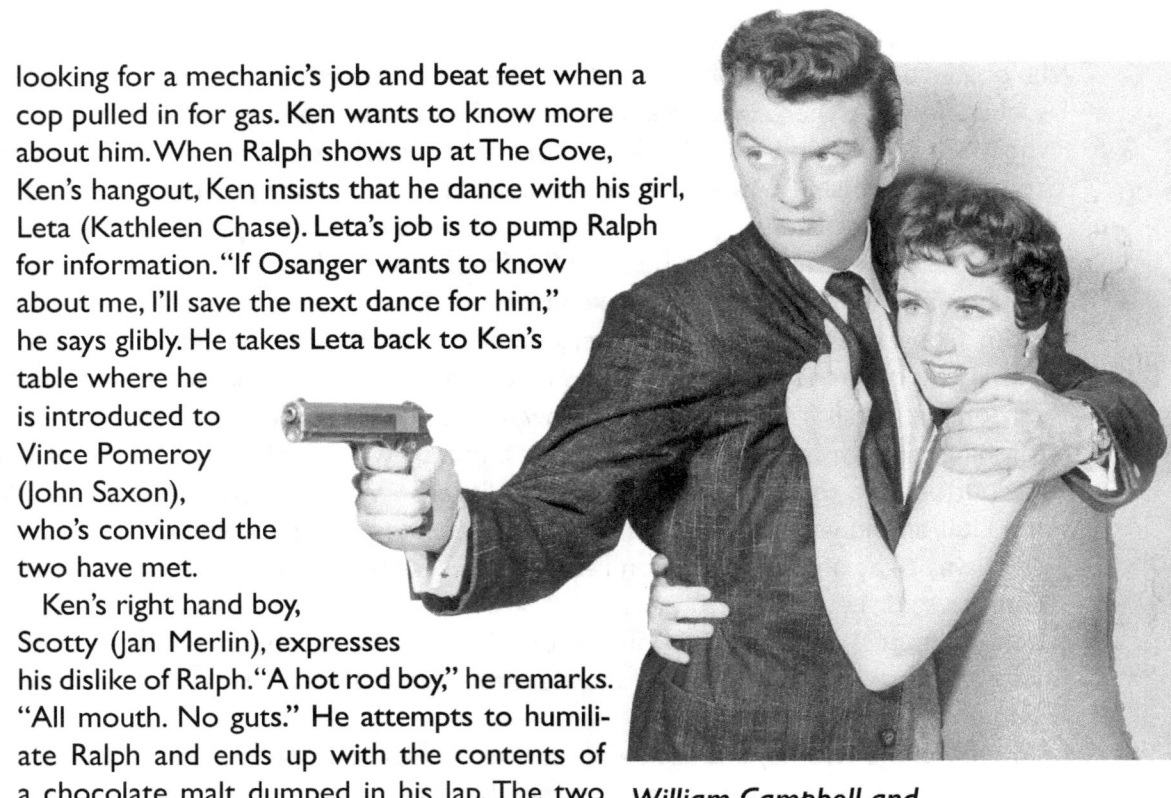

William Campbell and Kathleen Chase.

One of Osanger's men, Vince Pomeroy (John Saxon), recognizes Ralph as being the cop who gave him a speeding ticket a few years back. Pomeroy is frightened and he wants Ralph to meet him at his house, later that night. He has some information that could put Osanger behind bars, but he's dead by the time Ralph gets to him.

Okay crime drama, has a lot of snappy patter and moves along at a nice clip. Jan Merlin, who got his start on TV's **Tom Corbett, Space Cadet** (1950-55), makes a delightful villain. "The heavy is the engine that runs the film," he said. "He leads the rest of the cast on a merry chase until the end, when he generally gets his just desserts."

"A cheap little show about the young kids, which will out gross what is called an upper-attraction," said exhibitor Leo Baker. It drew an above-average crowd for Lloyd Bellefuelle. "Very good mid-week pic for adults as well as teenagers."

"When I want something, I want it now."

SENIOR PROM (December, 1958) Columbia
M Van Alexander, W Hal Hackady, P Harry Rohm, D David Lowell Rich

Jill Corey had come a long way from Avonmore, Pennsylvania. She was 17 when a friend sent Mitch Miller a tape of her singing a Tony Bennett song. Miller paid for

Jill, her sister and mother to fly to New York. She came home with a seven year contract with Columbia Records. Pretty soon she was all over the place, on Dave Garraway's show and Johnny Carson's early variety show, and Ed Sullivan. And then, in a one-two punch, she became a regular on the final season of *Your Hit Parade* and landed the starring role in this picture.

Rich co-ed Corey falls for bandleader/singer Paul Sheridan, but her snobbish mother, Frieda Inescort objects. So does Tom Laughlin, suffering under the delusion that Corey was his girl. Sheridan is scheduled to perform at the prom but Laughlin tells everyone that, with his family's connections, he can book the top acts. Meanwhile, somebody finds an old record Sheridan cut the year before and it climbs to the top of the charts. When Laughlin can't deliver on his promise, now celebrity Sheridan steps in and saves the day.

In keeping with Columbia's new policy of giving the youngsters the kind of music that their moms and dads wanted to hear, we have Louis Prima, Kelley Smith, Mitch Miller, Connie Boswell, Bob Crosby, and Tony Arden and his orchestra. *Motion Picture Herald* called it "relaxing entertainment," which tells you all you need to know. "A teenage picture that they did not like," said exhibitor W.G. Hall.

Big surprise that.

THE SHADOW ON THE WINDOW (March, 1957) Columbia
M George Duning, W Leo Townsend, David P. Harmon, P Jonie Taps D William Asher

Little Petey Atlas (Jerry Mathers) is outside playing when he hears his mother Linda (Betty Garrett) scream. He runs to the window and sees her thrown to the ground while her employer, Canfield (Watson Downs) comes to her defense and gets his skull bashed in. Three punks have come to rob the place. They thought it was going to be easy. Just an old man alone in the middle of nowhere. Who would have thought the old coot would hire a stenographer. Petey beats feet and goes into shock. He's found wandering along the highway by a couple of truckers. It just so happens that his father is Detective Tony Atlas (Philip Carey). He and Linda have been separated and now Petey is the only one who knows where she is.

"We were lucky to have Betty Garrett on that show," said director William Asher. "She was a well-known comedienne but she was a solid, dramatic actress and she really came through for us. The whole picture was on her shoulders."

Joey (Gerald Sarracini), Gil (Corey Allen), and Jess (John Drew Barrymore) are the three young thieves in over their heads. They hold Linda hostage while they try to figure out what to do with her. Jess and Gil want to kill her but Joey won't have it. "Nobody's gonna hurt her," he says emphatically. "We've done enough." Jess turns to Gil, Joey's friend. "The cops got my picture downtown. We let her go and five minutes later she'll pick me out of the mug book and I'm not going to the gas chamber alone. If I gotta go because your buddy over there's got rocks in his head you're gonna go with me. So you better talk to him."

And that is pretty much the conversation for the next forty or fifty minutes. Early on, Linda says to these bumblers, "You've got the money you came for. Why don't you go?" It is an important question that's never really answered.

Things get really tense when Gil goes to get his stepfather's gun. The police arrive and Gil is killed during an exchange of lead. Tony finds Linda's wallet in Gil's pocket. With time running out, Petey is taken to the spot where the truckers found him, in the hope that he'll recognize something. Anything that will lead them to Linda.

Philip Carey, very good in **Pushover** (1954), seems disengaged here. He's remarkably calm for a man whose son is in shock and whose estranged wife (who he still loves) is obviously in jeopardy, maybe even dead. His blasé attitude robs his scenes of any sense of urgency, which the film badly needs. However, even if Carey was firing on all pistons, he couldn't have saved the picture. Only the writers could have done that. They should have watched **The Desperate Hours** a few times. Might have helped.

Till somebody figures out somethin', we're staying right here.

SHAKE, RATTLE AND ROCK! (November, 1956) American International
M Alexander Courage, W Lou Rusoff, P Alex Gordon, D Edward L. Cahn

It's rock and roll vs. the squares in this broad comedy, released on a double bill with **Runaway Daughters**. Mike Connors is the likeable host of a rock 'n roll TV show, patterned after Dick Clarke and his *American Bandstand*. He loves two things—rock and roll and Lisa Gaye. Lisa's parents (Margaret Dumont and Raymond Hatton) are on a campaign to stamp out rock music. Egged on by a small-time hood (Paul Dubov), some of the youngsters engage in some petty vandalism during one of the local dances, and Connors gets into a bind when he won't name names. The kids rally to his side when Connors decides to put rock and roll on trial. With television cameras rolling, Connors interrogates his hipster sidekick (Sterling Holloway) whose "jive talk" responses are accompanied by translated English subtitles. He finally calls himself as a witness, as Woody Allen would do fifteen years later in *Bananas* (1971). To wrap up his case, Connors runs an old film of the kids in the 1920s, wildly dancing to the Charleston. Lisa's mom is one of those frantic dancers, caught with her panties down so to speak. Case closed. Fats arrives in time to sing "I'm in Love Again" and everyone is rockin' as the film fades out.

The collection of old fuddy-duddies in this film, while of no interest to the kids at the time, is quite remarkable, thanks to Alex Gordon's love of the old-timers. Margaret Hamilton, a favorite foil of the Marx Brothers, plays Lisa Gaye's mother, and Raymond Hatton, who can claim to have appeared in more westerns than John Wayne, Randolph Scott and Bill Boyd combined, is her father. Also part of this little conspiracy is Douglas Dumbrille, Clarence Kolb and that wonderful little weasel, Percy Helton.

The big draw here is Fats Domino, his scenes shot in a single day to accommodate his busy schedule. Notice that he's never actually shown in the same scene with the kids, and the kids are never shown dancing to his songs. Instead, they clap to the beat. Had they been shown dancing, the picture could not have played in Texas, where AIP had a very good relationship with Bob O'Donnell, the owner of the largest theatre chain in Texas. Fats sings three songs: "Honey Chile," "I'm in Love Again," and one of his hits, "Ain't That a Shame," often called "Ain't It a Shame," as it was mis-

labeled when the song was originally released. For his services, Fats was paid $1500. A few days prior to the shoot, Domino's agent, Lou Chudd phoned to say the deal was off. 20th Century-Fox had offered to pay Domino $25,000 for *one* song in **The Girl Can't Help It**. Sam Arkoff threatened to get a restraining order unless Chudd agreed to honor the contract.

Of the three other singers in the film, Joe Turner was probably more familiar to the teenagers than either Anita Ray or Tommy Charles. Often called "Big Joe" because he stood 6'2" and weighed 250 pounds, his first big break came when he got a gig with Benny Goodman in 1938, but the people didn't seem to care for Joe's brand of blues. He was back at the Apollo Theatre in Harlem when, in 1951, Ahmet Ertegun, the owner of Atlantic Records, signed him to a contract. Turner's recording

Michael Connors and Lisa Gaye. Said Lisa, "I worked quite often with Michael Connors, when he was known as 'Touch' Connors.' One day, he told my husband, Ben [Ware], 'Ben, I spend as much time with your wife as you do.'"

of "Shake, Rattle and Roll" crossed over the black barrier and has become one of the classics of early rock 'n roll. In this show he sings "Feelin' Happy" and "Lipstick, Powder and Paint." Tommy Charles sings "Sweet Love on My Mind" and Anita Ray belts out "Rockin' on Saturday Night".

Variety thought Edward Cahn's direction kept the action "lively" and that Mike Connors made "a good impression as the deejay." *The Monthly Film Bulletin* complained that the film's conclusions were "arrived at in a singularly unpersuasive manner," and found the musical numbers "surprisingly dull." *The Los Angeles Times* called it a "rather hasty little black and white pudding."

"We played this with **Runaway Daughters** and drew our biggest Sunday and Monday crowd of the year. If you book this when 'Fats' has a record on top, as we did, it cannot miss," said O. M. Shannon, an exhibitor in Portland, Texas.

Say, cats, if you want to dig the most skin-whaling gam, the most in bop stomping and strictly scenic from top to bottom, orb this flick.

SING BOY, SING (May, 1958) 20th Century-Fox

M Lionel Newman, W Claude Binyon from a teleplay by Paul Monash, P-D Henry Ephron

Yet another effort by Fox to promote another teen talent, this thinly disguised version of Elvis Presley's rise to fame—*He came out of the south to sing his way to the*

"I was a millionaire by the time I was 21," mused Tommy Sands. "I was a star of films by the time I was 21. I was an idol by the time I was 21. You can't ever get that back again."

top of the world!— stars Tommy Sands, reprising his role in "The Singing Idol," sans the sideburns he wore on *Kraft Television Theatre* in January of 1957. He plays Virgil Walker, raised by his southern Bible-thumping grandpa (John McIntire) and grandma (Josephine Hutchinson). Grandpa wants the boy to be a preacher, but Virgil is persuaded to join the world of rock and roll by a fast-talking manager (Edmond O'Brien), who makes Virgil famous. But he's lonely in tinsel town, and when grandpa suffers a stroke, Virgil makes a death-bed promise to give up rock for religion. His aunt saves him from this bone-headed decision by convincing the boy that God gave him his singing voice to make people happy.

The filmmakers were savvy enough to hire three of the nation's leading disc jockeys— Art Ford of New York, Bill Randle of Cleveland, and Biff Collie of Houston—to appear in the film, giving it built-in DJ support.

Tommy Sands sings "Bundle of Dreams," "Crazy 'Cause I Love You," "I'm Gonna Walk and Talk with My Lord," "Just a Little Bit More," "People in Love," "Rock of Ages, "Sing Boy Sing," "Soda Pop Pop," "That's All I Want from You," "Your Daddy Wants to Do Right," "Who Baby," and "Would I Love You."

Boy, oh boy, did the critics love Tommy Sands. *Variety* called him "surprisingly sensitive and sincere," while the *Los Angeles Times* was quick to point out that he sang "much more clearly and grammatically than Elvis." *Boxoffice* said he was "a far better actor" than Elvis or Pat Boone. *The Los Angeles Examiner* gushed that it was the kind of a show that would make any audience "plain happy." Getting into the groove, *Film Daily* encouraged the exhibitors to "book this quick daddy-o, 'cause Tommy Sands is very big with hepsters."

Tommy Sands and Lili Gentle, who married Richard Zanuck shortly after this and quit the business.

The exhibitors had a different take on Sands. "Not since we opened have we hit rock bottom like this. Even the teenagers called it square. They were being polite," moaned Dave Klein. Victor Weber complained that too many people had seen the story on TV. "Really, boys, are stories so hard to find that you have to give us this? It did below average business for me, and Sands is, oh, so dead in Kensett."

Sands had one hit record, "Teenage Crush," then hooked up with Walt Disney and sang the title song for **The Parent Trap** (1961) with Annette, and appeared with Annette in **Babes in Toyland** that same year. His marriage to Nancy Sinatra secured him a meaty role in father Frank's **None But the Brave** (1965). Los Angeles Times critic Kevin Thomas made some unkind remark about Sands in his review of the film, and Sands punched him in the nose. Rumor has it that when he divorced Nancy, father Frank made it his business to see that Sands never enjoyed success again.

"From now on, if he wants a close friend, he's gotta hire one."

THE SLASHER aka COSH BOY aka THE TOUGH GUY aka COSH BOY GOES CALYPSO (August, 1953) Lippert Pictures, Inc.
M Lambert Williamson, W Lewis Gilbert, Vernon Harris, P Daniel M. Angel, D Lewis Gilbert

A bleak little essay on teenage gangs who steal purses from little old ladies. *Little old ladies, for crissakes!* One would think these boys would be a laughingstock in the criminal world. 16-year old Roy Walsh (James Kenney) is the leader of one of these gangs, and is the focus of the story. Based on the play "Master Crook" by Bruce Walker, the film is ahead of its time in the way it deals with teenage sex and abortion, and was one of the first films to receive an "X" certificate, restricting it to adult audiences in England, as well as drawing fire from angry critics. In response, the critic for the *Sunday Graphic* remarked: "I don't remember such an outcry when it was played on the London stage. I suppose they assume that theatergoers are far steadier fellows than the film public." In America, it was released without the approval of the MPAA, assuring its obscurity. It's a good show, and deserves some respect.

Before the credits even roll, we see Roy and his nitwit buddy Alfie (Ian Whittaker) in action. And we discover that they're not very good at what they do, because a few minutes after the credits have played out, the two are standing in front of the magistrate who gives them both a year's probation, though it is clear that he doesn't believe Roy's mother (Betty Anne Davis) or Alfie's mother (Hermione Baddeley) when they assure him that they're good boys. The magistrate assumes that it isn't the first time the boys have engaged in criminal activities. It's just the first time they've been caught. And between the two boys, he knows which one is the bigger stinker.

We soon discover that Roy treats his girls pretty much like he treats the little old ladies. He sets his sights on Alfie's sister Rene (Joan Collins). Sorry, she tells him. She's already with someone. "No you're not. You're with me." To prove his point, Roy has the gang give her boyfriend (Michael McKeagh) a beating. This excites her, and before you can say *"You'll be sorry,"* she's pregnant. Like Roy has the time for a brat. He dumps Rene without a second's thought, and couldn't care less when she tries to kill herself.

Hermione Baddeley played Collins' mother, and apparently she was jealous of all of the publicity that Collins seemed to be generating, for they hadn't even been introduced when Baddeley marched up to Collins, and with disdain dripping off of her lips, said, "So! This is the new Jean Simmons! Let me tell you, my dear, Jean has nothing to worry about! You don't have her looks! You don't have her talent! And you certainly don't have half the thing things the papers have been saying about you!" I wish I could report that Collins shoved a blueberry pie in her face.

The film blames parental bungling for youngsters like Roy Walsh, but all of the guidance and discipline in the world wouldn't have made a bit of difference because Roy is a sociopath. Which is why the climax is so silly, in which Roy's new stepfather (Robert Ayres) takes off his belt and gives Roy what's coming to him. The police even let him do it. They've come to arrest Roy for his attempt to rob his stepfather's club and the shooting that resulted from it. The arresting officer sees what the stepdad has in mind and decides to arrest the other boys involved first, and come back in ten minutes. I will confess that watching this sniveling little coward break down in tears is mighty satisfying.

Boxoffice called it an "unrelentingly sordid study of adolescent delinquency in the slums of London," that *Motion Picture Herald* found "completely convincing." *Variety* thought it was "bound to provoke controversy."

The burning question of to-day! Are they getting the punishment they deserve, these bandits of society!

SORORITY GIRL aka CONFESSIONS OF A SORORITY GIRL (October, 1957) American International

M Ronald Stein, W Ed Walters, Leo Lieberman, P-D Roger Corman

June Kenney and Susan Cabot.

Calder Willingham's novel and play, *End as a Man*, about a Southern Military Academy ruled by a sadistic military cadet named Jocko de Paris, is the basis for this remarkably restrained but ultimately disappointing melodrama. Sabra Tanner (Susan Cabot), emotionally crippled by her icy, socialite mother (Fay Baker), uses blackmail and intimidation to rule her sorority sisters. During lunch at a fancy restaurant, her mother tells her, "You were bad the day you were born. It was in your eyes." Sabra icily replies, "I hate you." Her mother shrugs. "What a pity when I love you so much." Feeling alone and unloved, we hear what Sabra cannot say out loud. "I want to hurt everybody. What's wrong with me?"

A pledge named Ellie (Barbara Crane) becomes Sabra's punching bag. She belittles her constantly, and makes her do things a pledge shouldn't have to do, but Ellie does them willingly. Lovingly. She even submits to a periodic spanking with a wooden paddle. In the first draft of the screenplay, Sabra used a belt, (possibly borrowed from Bob from the previous entry). Production Code watchdog Geoffrey Spurlock put a stop to that. In a letter to AIP he wrote:

The sequence in which Sabra administers the vicious whipping to Ellie with the belt is unacceptable for two major reasons, the most important of which is established on Page 64—that Sabra has achieved a perverted sexual satisfaction from administering the beating, and, secondly, the belt that she uses implants in this entire sequence an overtone of sadism and brutality which is unacceptable. We believe the same story point could be established if she were to employ the traditional paddle used in sorority and fraternity initiations and it was indicated that she struck Ellie several times (in all likelihood across the posterior) with this paddle. In any event, any overtones of sex perversion will make this impossible for us to approve this entire sequence.

Spurlock got his paddle, but the sexual implications of Ellie's and Sabra's relationship remain, however slight they may be.

Sabra's roommate, Rita (Barbara Morris), walks in on the aftermath of one of these hazing's and threatens to go to the Dean. That's when Sabra pries open the box that Rita has been so secretive about, the one that contains the letters from her father, written from prison. "What do you think your chances of becoming president of the student body if everyone knew your father was a jailbird?" Sabra asks, effectively shutting Rita's trap. Rita's boyfriend, Mort (Dick Miller), who is also her campaign manager, tells her, "The secret of life is not to become involved." Mort runs the local tavern where everyone hangs out. "Beer and laughs." That's what he's about.

No sooner has Sabra plugged up one hole than another gives way. Her mother cuts off her allowance. She's wondering what she's going to do when Ellie tells her that Tina (June Kenney) is pregnant, needs money, and doesn't know where the

Barbara Morris and Dick Miller, two of the best of the Corman Stock Company Players.

father is. Sabra sees a way to shore up her sagging finances. She convinces Tina, who works as a waitress at Mort's place, to name Mort as the father, unless he forks over some hard cash. Mort tells her to come back after closing time, then tapes their conversation, during which Tina admits that he's not the father. At this point, Tina is ready to commit suicide.

This was one of the sixteen or seventeen movies that Corman made for American International in three short years. Sometimes he would go to them with an idea and sometimes they'd develop a project and bring him in. This was one of AIP's. Their script had to be rewritten very quickly, which may account for its lack of focus.

Said Corman, "Because I was a partner in the film with AIP, I questioned some of the construction costs, but AIP kept the bill. I decided to rent a house and use it for the sorority house and saved a great deal of money." Corman said it took him five or six pictures to learn what someone would learn in film school. Unlike the students, his mistakes are there for all the world to see. He learned a big lesson on this show.

"When I first starting directing, I had no experience with actors," said Corman. "My education had simply not been in that area. I'd come from writing and production. After the first few films, I found that I really needed some training in acting in order to communicate better with the actors. I went to Jeff Corey's acting class and studied with a number of people. The lead in **Sorority Girl** was Susan Cabot, who was a very dedicated method actress from New York. I remember there was an extremely emotional scene she had to play around a swimming pool, with an actress playing her mother. I was going to shoot the scene in a medium shot. And she was brilliant. She was really wonderful. The crew applauded and I went over and congratulated her. Then we set up for the close shot and although she was good, she was never able to reach the level of intensity she had in the medium shot. Of course, what you want is the close shot for the most emotional part of the scene, but I left more of the medium shot than I had planned to. I learned a lesson and that was to let the performers know they needed to save something for the close shot, and not use all of the emotion for the medium shot."

Boxoffice called **Sorority Girl** "a somber, depressing depiction of a sadistic coed," and that's as good a description as any. It also has some of the best performances of any Corman film, especially from Morris, Miller and Cabot. "Susan Cabot displays some bursts of fine acting as the maladjusted student who goes in for paddling, blackmailing and out-and-out hair-pulling," said *Variety*. *Motion Picture Herald* didn't have much good to say about it, other than it was "an admirable example of how best to spread an obviously limited budget." Writing in the *Los Angeles Times*, Dean Gautschy displayed a remarkable grasp of the situation when he said it fell "short of being a picture that the entire family, from dad on down, would enjoy." *The Mir-*

ror News had one word to describe it: "excruciating." Which is a little harsh. It *is* interesting. It's just not engaging.

"I don't need you. I don't need anybody."

SO YOUNG, SO BAD (May, 1950) United Artists
M Robert W. Stringer, W Jean Rouverol, Bernard Vorhaus, P Edward and Harry Danziger, D Bernard Vorhaus

If you enjoyed Hope Emerson in **Caged** (1950), know that she can't hold a candle to Grace Coppin as Mrs. Beuhler in this show. *Every* time Coppin was on camera, I kept hoping that one or all of the young ladies in her care would beat the tar out of her and make her eat the annoying little whistle she keeps blowing. Likewise, Mr. Riggs (Cecil Clovelly), the oily sadist who runs the Elmview Correctional School for Girls. Every time he opens his mouth he might just as well be saying, "You think you hate me now. Just wait." Not since **Brute Force** (1947) has an institution been run with such loving care. The "meditation room" is simply Orwellian speak for solitary confinement. Yes, **So Young, So Bad** is way over the top. And I enjoyed every minute of it.

Paul Henreid (who co-produced the show) plays Dr. John Jason, a psychiatrist. He's also the narrator, singling out four of the young ladies—Loretta, Dolores, Jackie and Jane—and the circumstances that led to their incarceration. Anne Francis, Rosita (Rita) Moreno, Anne Jackson and Enid Rudd make their screen debuts playing these four characters, and they give a good account of themselves, but may I add that Anne Francis and Rita Moreno are drop-dead gorgeous.

Anne Francis, Anne Jackson and Enid Rudd.

Paul Heinreid and Rita Moreno.

Dr. Jason has been foisted on Mr. Riggs, who simply ignores all of his recommendations. "Believe me," Riggs tells him, "your whole approach is impractical." And the woman working with Jason, Ruth Levering (Catherine McLeod) more or less agrees with Riggs, until she falls in love with Jason and comes to realize that she's been co-opted into a system that is now a part of the problem. "You're in a spot," Loretta tells her. "You're beginning to feel like a woman, but you don't know how to act like one." Ruth slaps her. Loretta smiles. "Hey! You're human after all."

The conditions in this institution are so horrific, one expects to find Bela Lugosi or Boris Karloff in charge. Discipline is the order of the day and the only consideration. When Riggs feels like he's losing his hold, he orders the walls of the barracks to be stripped of all decorations. Personal items like mementoes or toys or whatever are thrown into a bag, to be burned in an outside barrel. Jane has been keeping a pet rabbit. Beuhler drops it on the ground and squashes it with her foot. It all comes to a head when Beuhler cuts Dolores's hair just before the dance that Jason had to blackmail Riggs into letting him throw. Dolores hangs herself. The young ladies rebel and Beuhler turns a firehose on them.

The *New York Times* blasted the movie, calling it "so clumsily made and acted—that it is downright embarrassing to watch." Says them. "Had a capacity crowd and bought this one right, so I made myself some money on it," said exhibitor Howard C. Bayer.

Against the advice of his friends and financial advisors, Paul Henreid put his own money into this thing and happily reported that he made more money on this picture than any other title in his inventory.

"I like a lot of guys, for a little while."

*SPEED CRAZY (June, 1959) Allied Artists

M Richard La Salle, W Richard Bernstein, George Walters, P Richard Bernstein, D William Hole, Jr.

European sports cars ultimately seemed more appealing than the good old fashioned hot-rod, but a guy would have to bag a lot of groceries or flip a lot of burgers before he could even think about putting a down payment on a car like that. He'd be an old man by then. So you can't really blame Brett Halsey for robbing a gas station and shooting the attendant. It wasn't his fault that his car was so expensive.

Leaving the corpse behind, Halsey jumps into his super-duper deluxe little set of wheels and burns rubber, headed for a big racing event in another town. He isn't there long before Jacqueline Ravell catches his eye. He makes his move and she rejects him. He pulls a knife and she lets him have his way. A real Casanova. And he hopes to make Yvonne Lime his next conquest. But Yvonne has a boyfriend. Charles Wilcox. Halsey figures he'll make quick work of him during the big race. The event is well underway when the cops show up. They've traced a tire print left at the gas station to Halsey's car, and now everyone realizes that Chuck is at the mercy of a cold-blooded killer!

Brett Halsey.

"I remember having to stand, pretending to cheer at a race," said Jackie Joseph, making her film debut. "I also remember the first scene I did was a master shot. You could be in college forever (which you usually are), and at that time no one told you what a mark was, what overlapping was... You didn't know what a master shot was, over-the-shoulder or close-ups. Well, we did the master and I went home. I didn't know they took away a piece of wall and turned everything around. You just guessed when they said 'mark' and not to *overlap*. You don't want to ask because they'll think you're dumb."

"When I'm behind the wheel, I'm the boss. You're goin' fast, see, somebody crowds you, you push 'em back. Like a guy swattin' flies."

STAKEOUT ON DOPE STREET (May, 1958) Warner Bros.

M Richard Markowitz, W Irvin Kershner, Irving Schwartz, Andrew J. Fenady, P Andrew J. Fenady, D Irvin Kershner

After arresting a drug dealer, with two pounds of un-cut heroin in his briefcase, one of the policeman is killed and the other one wounded by a couple of gangsters. Before they can shoot the dealer, he disappears into the night, tossing the briefcase along the way. The sound of approaching sirens scares the gangsters off before they can find the briefcase. The next morning, Julian "Ves" Vespucci (Jonathan Haze) spots the briefcase in the bushes. He brings it back to the gang's hangout and shows it to his pals, Jim (Yale Wexler) and Nick (Morris Miller). They pry the lock open and find samples of women's cosmetics. There's a large canister, marked "Face Powder" that they toss around like a football and then Ves pitches it into the trash as they march off to the pawnshop to hock the briefcase for a whopping five bucks. Jim gives a couple of the samples to his girl Kathy (Abby Dalton), then reads about the

Abby Dalton and Yale Wexler.

robbery and the heroin in the newspaper. The trash has been emptied by the time the boys return. They search through the garbage until they find it. They decide to sell "the face powder" in small quantities to a dealer Nick knows named Danny (Allen Kramer). Ves and Nick use the money to buy clothes. Jim buys a bracelet for Kathy. She's appalled when he tells her where the money came from and won't take it. And after listening to Danny explain how he became an addict, Jim wants to call it quits and turn the drugs over to the police. But Ves and Nick want to buy fancy clothes and fancy cars. Meanwhile, the police and the gangsters are closing in.

Tight little thriller, independently made for $30,000 by a couple of first-time filmmakers, and photographed by Haskell Wexler, the man responsible for the breathtaking **Days of Heaven**, for which he won an Oscar in 1978. He used a pseudonym for this film—Mark Jeffrey. He and Kershner were both working on TV's *Confidential File* when Wexler mentioned that he wanted to get into features. Kershner showed him his **Dope Street** script and Wexler liked it. He agreed to put up half of the money to make it. Roger Corman kicked in the other half. "I liked him immediately," Wexler said, "but mostly because he was putting up half the money. We shot in this place where they shot some porno films. And when the union rep came by I would have to hide behind the scenery because I wasn't in the union and I wasn't supposed to be making the film."

Said Corman, "I was doing fairly well as a young producer-director and I knew people around town who moved in a certain milieu. And I'd made a little bit of money and was looking for some way to invest it. A friend of mine—I think it was Al Kallis—came to me and said he knew Irv Kershner and Andy Fenady who wanted to make a very low budget film. Al wanted to know if I'd back them. They were just out of school, doing TV documentaries for one of the local television stations. I put up the money and they made a little picture called **Stakeout on Dope Street** which we sold to Warner Brothers [for $75,000 or $80,000], and did extremely well. Irv Kershner was laughing as we handed out the checks. He'd heard all of these terrible stories about people suing each other for profits and here we were, laughing and drinking champagne. It was a great evening."

Dick Miller was offered the lead in the picture, but he didn't want to work on weekends. "Jonathan told me that when I quit, the three leads were moved up," Miller told me. "He had a small part and they moved him into one of the leads. That cost me a lot of work. The people who made that wound up doing a bunch of TV series later on in life and would never use me because they thought I had walked off the picture. What they didn't know was when I walked off, Roger asked if I was walking off because it was a bad picture. I said, 'No. I think it's a good picture. I think you should go ahead and make it.' It was pretty much my final say that got them the financing to do that picture."

What happens when kids get their hands on dope?

SUMMER LOVE (June, 1958) Universal-International
M Henry Mancini, W William Raynor, Herbert Margolis, P William Grady, Jr., D Charles Haas

Look out Lake Tahoe! Those **Rock Pretty Baby** kids are back and they're headed your way—Jimmy (John Saxon), Ox (Rod McKuen), Mike (John Wilder) and, of course, little Twinkie (Shelley Fabares), 14 and feisty and still hot to trot. They're all rockin' and rollin', laughin' and scratchin,' eatin' and sleepin' in the screen's happiest summer hit, **Summer Love**, where the big beat meets the summer heat. And boy, oh boy, the temperature really rises when Jimmy gets an eyeful of newcomer Jill St. John. Ooh, la, la! This is one curvaceous cutie who really knows how to beat that meat. Watch the fireworks fly when Jimmy's girl (Judi Meredith) sees the two of them making goo-goo eyes. But when Jimmy's parents (Ed Platt and Fay Wray) show up unexpectedly, all bets are off and it's every man for himself! **Summer Love**, staring John Saxon, in his most challenging role since **Rock Pretty Baby**. With Shelley Fabares, the singing sensation from **The Donna Reed Show**. And Elinor Donahue. You know her as Princess on **Father Knows Best**. And won't the bobbysoxers melt like cheese on a hamburger when they hear Rod McKuen's new hit, "Calypso Rock." Yes, the joint's really jumpin' when Jimmy and His Ding-a-Lings pull out all the stops. And who better than Henry Mancini, that wild man of rock and roll, to keep the soundtrack hopping with 14 hard-rockin' instrumentals, guaranteed to keep your pulse pounding. **Summer Love**! It's hotter than hot!

Molly Bee got me through this film. Without her, I wouldn't have made it. She is just as cute as she can be and sounds a lot like Julie London, only better. Why we didn't see more of her is a mystery. She sings three songs, "Beatin' on the Bongos," "Love is Something," and with Rod McKuen "To Know You is to Love You." McKuen also sings "Calypso Rock." Jimmy Daley and The Ding-A-Lings (whoever they actually are) perform "Summer Love," "Sock Hop," "Walkin' the Rock," "Ding-A-Ling," "Night Walk," "Boppin' at the Bash," "Theme for a Crazy Chick," "Soft Touch," "Sad Sax and "So, Good Night."

Variety didn't think **Summer Love** was as good as **Rock Pretty Baby**. *Film Daily* called it "pleasing." The *New York Times* found it full of sound and fury "and very little originality." "This is a fine family and teenage picture with none of the rough stuff that one finds as a rule in pictures aimed at teenagers," said exhibitor Victor Weber. He added, "Maybe it would have been better if it had some rough spots in it for it did not do too well!" It did all right for Ken Christianson. "I believe it was the magic of Molly Bee," he concluded. Said Frank Sabin, "The high school set was pleased. Very few adults. I wouldn't give it much."

"Are you crazy, man? We never work for free. We gotta pay them."

A SUMMER PLACE (November, 1959) Warner Bros.
M Max Steiner, W-P-D Delmer Daves

Melodrama at its overblown, trashy best, as writer-director Delmer Daves brings his usual ham-fisted approach to his screen version of Sloan Wilson's best-selling and somewhat scandalous novel of sex and love and hate. It was generally lambasted by the critics. *Variety* said in his capacity as writer and director, Daves "missed the mark by a mile," and the *New York Times* called it a "civilized shocker" with a "tedious bluntness of speech and imagery that few people should accept as adult realism." It was, nevertheless, a big hit for Warner Bros. and made a teen idol and star out of Troy Donahue, whose sole asset was a good looking pan.

"I saw it in a regular theater for the first time in Pasadena," said Donahue. "[Looked] around, heard the music, and thought, 'We might be something here.' It was pretty heady stuff for a kid 22-years old."

The *New York Times* hated Max Steiner's score, too, "hammering away at each sexual nuance like a pile driver." The main title was a lift from **A Stolen Life** (1946), but it was Steiner's theme for the young lovers in the film, Molly and Johnny (Sandra Dee and Donahue) that became a major hit for Percy Faith. The record quickly climbed to number one and remained there for over a month, the record that everyone wanted to dance to, and was made to order for Muzak.

Now, sixty years later, I see on the net that the film is still being critically lambasted, largely for its excess. It is a melodrama, and in melodramas the characters are either good or bad, they often climb on soapboxes to say what they have to say, everything is milked for all its worth, and these sudsy tales generally run fifteen or twenty minutes too long. To criticize a melodrama for being melodramatic is simply ridiculous. A film should be partially judged by the other films that were being made at the time, and the climate that hammered them into shape. To ignore these factors is doing any film a disservice, and the critic as well, who is announcing to the world that his or her opinion is an uninformed one. Believe me, in the sexually repressed fifties, this film was a breath of fresh air, and should be applauded for not only talking about sex and desire, but for saying there was nothing wrong with it.

Helen Jorgenson (Constance Ford) thinks sex is dirty, thanks to her soulless mother. The only reason she and her husband Ken (Richard Egan) have a child is because it was her wifely duty, and a way of keeping Ken tied to her. There's not a drop of love or compassion in her. She reports, with disgust, that she's seen their daughter, Molly kissing Johnny Hunter, a boy she has just met, in the garden, right below her window! "If they had anything to hide, you think they'd do it right under your window?" Ken asks. She insists, "No decent girl lets a boy kiss and maul her the very first night they meet! I suppose it's your Swedish blood in her. I've read about how the Swedes bathe together and…and have trial marriages and free love. I've read all about that. Anything goes." Ken is taken aback. "So, now you hate the Swedes. How many outlets for your hate do you have, Helen? We haven't been able to find a new house because of your multiplicity of them. We can't buy near a school because you hate kids. They make noise. And there can't be any Jews or

Sandra Dee and Troy Donahue.

Sandra Dee, Troy Donahue, Constance Ford, Dorothy McGuire, Richard Egan and Arthur Kennedy.

Catholics on the block, either. And, oh, yes, it can't be anywhere near the Polish or Italian sections. And, of course, Negros have to be avoided at all costs…And, oh, yes, you won't use a Chinese laundry because you distrust Orientals. And you think the British are snobbish, the Russians fearful, the French immoral, the Germans brutal, and all Latin Americans lazy. What's your plan? To cut humanity out? Are you anti-people and anti-life? Must you suffocate every natural instinct in our daughter, too? Must you label young love-making as cheap and wanton and indecent? Must you persist in making sex, itself, a filthy word?" During its opening week at Radio City Music Hall, the audience gave this little speech a standing ovation.

Ken and Helen, and their daughter Molly (Sandra Dee), have come to Fire Island, off of the coast of Maine, to stay at the inn where Ken worked as a lifeguard twenty years ago. He's become a millionaire since and he's trying to get back to his roots. He's also hoping to rekindle his romance with Sylvia (Dorothy McGuire), who is married to Bart Hunter (Arthur Kennedy), the owner of the inn. Things have not gone well for Bart. An undeserving son of the privileged class, he's mismanaged his fortune and has become a bitter drunk. The inn fell into disrepair, and in order to stay afloat, he and Sylvia have had to turn their home into a bed and breakfast. Bart assumes Ken has come back to flaunt his wealth, and now he has to move out of his own bedroom so that the Jorgensons will have the best room in the place. Their son, Johnny (Donahue) falls for Molly and her for him. Ken and Sylvia admit that the only reason they've stayed in their loveless marriages was for the sake of the children. "Why did you come back?" she asks. "I came back because I had to," he replies. They agree to meet later that night and are seen by a night watchman who tells Helen. Let the fireworks begin.

A lot of my friends weren't allowed to see this movie which, of course, only made them want to see it all the more. For all of its faults, I still like **A Summer Place**. It isn't boring. Except for Donahue, the cast is solid. And though I may laugh sometimes at the excess, I think it has a lot to say and for once, even after Johnny gets Molly into "trouble," they're never shown to be anything more than a couple of decent kids.

Daves had a couple of kids of his own, about the age of the kids in his film. He understood the communication problem between parents and their children. "And while this may sound corny, it can be assisted by love and understanding," he said. "Frankness and impatience will help pull the cork on a situation blocked by intolerance. What we are trying to do is dramatize that pulling of the cork."

Said exhibitor Mel Danner, "Sandra Dee is about the best thing that has happened to the movies in a long time," and Paul Gomoche was surprised the movie did so well. "Appealed to teens and adults."

"I haven't done anything wrong! I've been a good girl!"

TAMMY aka TAMMY AND THE BACHELOR (June, 1957) Universal-International
M Frank Skinner, W Oscar Brodney, P Ross Hunter, D Joseph Pevney

Shamelessly corny film, even for Universal, finds Pollyanna, the 11-year old orphan of Eleanor H. Porter's children's classic, alive and well in the form of 17-year Tammy Tyree, living in Mississippi, on a houseboat with her Grandpa and her pet goat. This barefoot lass may lack polish, but she's got all of the wisdom in the world. Before the film is over, she has changed the lives of everyone she meets, for the better.

Debbie Reynolds.

Debbie Reynolds and Walter Brennan.

Tammy (Debbie Reynolds) and her Grandpa (Walter Brennan) hear about a plane crash and rush to the rescue. They fish Peter Brent (Leslie Nielson) out of the water, and he doesn't look good. He lays unconscious for five days and nights with Tammy watching over him. "He come this far, Lord," she says. "It wouldn't make sense to take him now, would it?" Once he recovers, to show his gratitude, Peter promises Grandpa he'll take care of Tammy if anything should happen to him. "I'll never forget you, Tammy," Pete tells her, and as she sadly watches him walk away, we know that Tammy's in love because Frank Skinner is doing wonderful things to the "Tammy" melody on the soundtrack. *Does my lover feel what I feel when he comes near? My heart beats so joyfully, you'd think that he could hear.*

Grandpa's tossed in jail for making and selling corn liquor. "No need to be ashamed, girl, because of some fool law some fellas made up in Washington," he tells her and sends her off to Pete. Tammy walks all of the way to Brentwood Hall with her goat, but there's a party going on, or at least, that's what it looks like, so she parks herself outside, not wanting to disturb anyone. They're rehearsing for The Rebel Ball, a grand show for Pilgrimage Week. That's when Brentwood Hall opens its doors to tourists who want to experience a slice of the grand old South, like it was in Brentwood Hall's glory days, with everyone in costume. Now, the house has become an albatross, but Peter believes with the new strain of tomato he's been developing, he can make the place pay for itself. His fiancé, Barbara (Mala Powers) thinks he's being silly, but Tammy thinks it's a wonderful idea. "I wish mother and Barbara had your confidence," Pete sighs. Barbara's uncle Alfred (Philip Ober), stopping for a visit between business meetings, wants Pete to come to work for him.

Tammy is an enigma to everyone, especially Alfred. She brings him breakfast in bed without expecting a tip. He can't eat her pancakes. "Never anything more than dry toast and coffee. Indigestion," he explains. He brags about putting all of his efforts into his business with no time for love or family. Love, as far as he's concerned, is a disease. "How sad," Tammy ponders. "A man alone with nothing to show for his life but indigestion."

Peter's mother (Fay Wray) is not at all happy with this backwoods little ragamuffin, who talks about things like the hair in men's noses. "You have a tendency to say things that upset people," Mama Brent tells her. Worried that she'll say something embarrassing at The Rebel Ball, she adds, "Please learn not to talk too much." Tammy's got her number, too. Pete laughs when she tells him that his mom is scared. "Most people are scared of her," he remarks. Tammy thinks she's afraid of losing her way of life, and it makes sense to Pete. He wants to know what she thinks of him. "You're like driftwood, Pete, with Barbara pulling you one way and your mother another." And that makes sense to him, too.

Aunt Renie (Mildred Natwick), a bit of a bohemian, thinks Tammy is charming. When Ma Brent makes Tammy feel unwelcome, Renie tells Tammy, "This house is mine as long as I'm alive. And I've felt better ever since you arrived." Peter's fiancé, Barbara (Mala Powers), looks right through Tammy when she's introduced, calling her "Peter's little goat girl." She changes her tune pretty quick when she sees Pete racing off to rescue Tammy from the clutches of his best friend Ernie (Craig Hill). Ernie's more than a little miffed. Barbara was his girl before Pete came along. He doesn't feel like stepping down twice but drives off anyway. Tammy doesn't understand what all of the fuss was about. "You don't know about wolves like Ernie," Pete explains. "He might have some ideas that you might not find very pleasant." Tammy mulls it over. "You mean it might be of a carnal nature."

It isn't until the Rebel Ball, when Aunt Renie dresses Tammy in the gown worn by Pete's grandmother, that Pete sees her as a woman for the first time. It's exactly

Leslie Nielson, Debbie Reynolds and Mildred Natwick.

what Renie wanted. "I never did think Barbara was right for him in the first place," she tells Tammy. Of course, Tammy is a big hit with everyone, enchanting the room, playing the part of Pete's grandmother with her story of how she came to live in this great house, a story told to her by Renie. Ernie waits until she's broken away from the crowd. "I'd like to ask you out again," he tells her. "Last time was for laughs. This time I'll take you anywhere you want to go." But Tammy knows he's still carrying the torch for Barbara. "Don't you see? You'd be thinking about Barbara, and I'd be thinking about Pete. It wouldn't be no fun at all."

Based on Cyd Ricketts Sumner's novel *Tammy Out of Time*, this was one of the studio's "A" pictures, so it's a mystery why they would give it to a run-of-the-mill writer like Oscar Brodney. There must have been somebody on the payroll who was better qualified. If you want to see how it's supposed to be done, watch Disney's **Pollyanna** (1960), written and directed by David Swift, also responsible for **The Parent Trap** (1961), two of the best live action movies in Walt's library.

However, if you're a sucker like me, and you like the song by Ray Evans and Jay Livingston, which is every bit as sentimental and sugary sweet as the film, then let yourself enjoy a guilty pleasure. Play the song ahead of time to get yourself in the mood, and pretend that Debbie's not too old for the part.

Originally titled **Tammy**, the critics were hardly won over by it and nobody was lining up to see it. "My recording wasn't released until after the movie had come out, but unlike the picture, it took off right away," said Reynolds. "Seeing a big promotional possibility, Universal immediately pulled the picture for a few weeks until the record built momentum." The record went all the way to number one, and before long, Universal had a hit movie on its hands, and another franchise.

"Our normal playdates are Wednesday, Thursday with change on Friday. However, we played this four days and business was great," said exhibitor Val Dage. Jess Jones and Victor Weber were both amazed. Said Weber, "People who have not been to the show for the last three or four years showed up for **Tammy**," and Jones said weeks later "people were still raving about Debbie." Velva Otts recommended that her fellow exhibitors stroll up and down their aisles every now and then, "and enjoy those smiles on the faces of your patrons."

"If you don't know by now Tammy's in love with you, Peter, you're just plain stupid, even for a man."

THE T-BIRD GANG (October, 1959) The Filmgroup
M Shelley Manne, W John Brinkley, Tony Miller, P San Bickman, D Richard Horberger

John Brinkley and the gang.

Sadistic Ed Nelson runs a gang of thieves known as The T-Bird Gang. During a robbery, a troublesome night watchman is struck on the head and dies from the concussion. His son, John Brinkley, wants to know why the cops don't arrest Nelson. Everyone knows he's behind the robberies. "You don't just go get 'em," Cpt. Coleman Francis reminds him. "You've got to have evidence. The only way we can prove anything on this bunch is from the inside."

Brinkley incites an encounter with one of Nelson's gang and the two trade blows. Nelson places bets on who'll win. He picks Brinkley, and is impressed when Brinkley cleans the guy's clock. Nelson buys him a drink. Before the ice has had a chance to melt, he gives Brinkley fifty bucks (his share of the winnings) and offers him a job. Brinkley tells Cpt. Francis that when he finds the killer, he's going to give him what he gave his old man. "That's not something you're supposed to say to a cop," the Captain reminds him.

Nelson sends Brinkley with a couple of punks to rob a gas station. The police show up and the punks take off, leaving Brinkley behind to take the rap. It was all part of the plan. Nelson wanted Brinkley to have a record, something to blackmail him with later on, if necessary. Nelson thinks of everything. Or so he thinks. As he's conducting his business, he's playing chess with his seemingly bubble-headed girlfriend, Pat George. But a closer look shows that there's a light on in the young lady's eyes. The second Nelson takes his attention off of the board, she swipes one of his men and puts one of her own pieces in its place, putting him in check.

Roger Corman had a stable of actors that came to be known as the Corman Stock Company Players, and this film is loaded with them. Charles "Beech" Dickerson. Tony Miller. John Brinkley. Ed Nelson. Nelson, normally a very good actor, seems uncomfortable here. The performances are uneven throughout, and though the film isn't a washout, it's never as good as it needs to be. There are a couple of dead spark plugs in this T-Bird.

"*A very aggressive young man. I like that.*"

TEENAGE BAD GIRL aka BAD GIRL aka MY TEENAGE DAUGHTER
(June, 1956) DCA
M Stanley Black, W Felicity Douglas, P-D Herbert Wilcox

Well-made British film, more appropriately titled **My Teenage Daughter**. Sylvia Simms is Janet, the daughter in question, and she's really not all that bad. She stays out late with ne'er-do-well playboy Tony Black (Kenneth Haigh in his first screen role) and his bunch, but besides driving without a license, all they do is hang around a sleazy nightclub, smoking and drinking and dancing to "Get With It," a song written by Stanley Black and Dick James, which apparently is the only record the club could get their hands on. Nevertheless, her war widow mother, Valerie Carr (Anne Neagle), whose job as the fiction editor for a teenage magazine often takes her away to New York, returns from one of her meetings to find her daughter hopelessly involved with Tony and his bunch. Tony is caught stealing money from an elderly aunt and the woman dies of a heart attack. He's arrested for murder and Janet along with him as his accomplice.

Being the star of the show, we get to spend a lot of time with Miss Neagle, watching her wringing her hands as she strolls about her huge, elegant home, wondering what went wrong, allowing the melodrama to tread on campy grounds. Simms transformation from a timid little thing to an emotional ball of fire is the film's saving grace. She's the best thing about the picture.

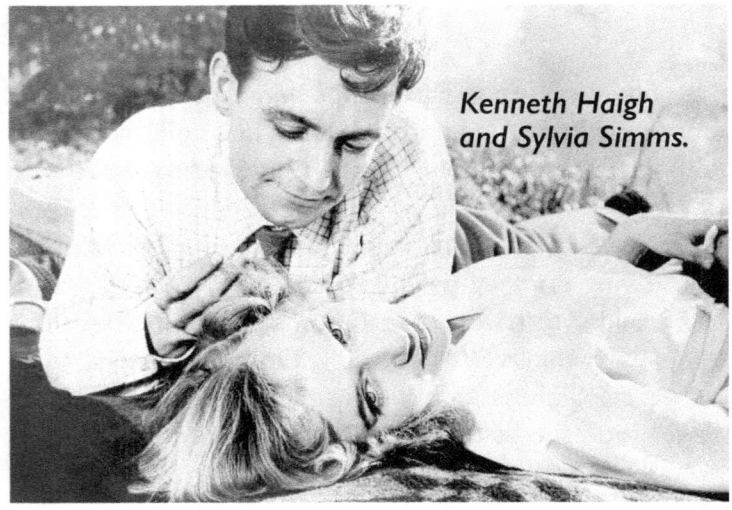

Kenneth Haigh and Sylvia Simms.

Motion Picture Herald called it "mildly engrossing" and *Boxoffice* blew the whistle by revealing the film was "on the wholesome side, with ethics and moral values being neatly upheld without preachment."

Don't look at me like that. I didn't ask to be born!

TEENAGE CAVEMAN aka TEENAGE CAVE MAN aka PREHISTORIC WORLD aka OUT OF THE DARKNESS aka PREHISTORIC PRATTLE
(1958) American International
M Albert Glasser, *W* R. Wright Campbell, *P-D* Roger Corman

Roger Corman and his crew were in Bronson Canyon (where most of this picture takes place), and Beach Dickerson was sitting in the wardrobe truck, watching everyone getting ready to shoot his funeral sequence. The day before, they were shooting scenes at the Arboretum in Arcadia, where a lot of the old Tarzan movies were filmed. Dickerson was supposed to fall off of a log and drown. He had hoped that if he flailed around enough, Corman wouldn't make him go all of the way under, because the water was so filthy it almost made him throw up. Roger knelt beside him. "I don't believe your drowning," he said. "You're not convincing me." Holding his breath, Dickerson went all of the way under and floated to the surface. Well, he thought, sitting in that wardrobe truck, at least the worst of it was over with.

"What are you doing here?" Corman asked testily. "Well," Dickerson replied, "I can't be out *there*. It's *my* funeral." Corman scoffed. "Who would recognize you anyway?" Dickerson can be seen in the front row, in a bearskin and a fright wig, beating a tom-tom.

In this barren, rocky terrain dwells a primitive, superstitious tribe, bound by a law that forbids them from going across the river, to the land of "sinking earth," and its "great animals" and "the God who kills with his touch." Robert Vaughn, the son of symbol-maker Leslie Bradley, thinks the law is crazy. The land is rich and green across the river. And there's food. The deer can be seen prancing about the trees. Nope. Makes no sense at all. Vaughn takes a small group beyond the river and one of them is swallowed by quicksand. The tribe wants Vaughn put to death, but Bradley talks them out of it, only to have Vaughn run off again, in search of the truth.

The title, imposed on the film by AIP's Jim Nicholson, is silly and stupid but the film isn't. "I couldn't wait to do it," said Vaughn. "It was a magnificent script written in blank verse about the end of mankind." According to the writer, R. Wright Campbell, it was an allegory. The "surprise" is the audience believes they're watching a story about our prehistoric past, but it's really a story about our prehistoric future, after the bomb, and how people make up rules to restore order and survive, and how eventually those rules will be challenged. (Which doesn't explain the presence of dinosaurs, but we'll let that slide.)

Ed Nelson kept feeling Frank de Kova's spear poking at his back. He was running with a pack of guys and everyone was supposed have their spears pointed up. The actor had been told several times to keep his spear up. "Ed, keep in close!" Roger yelled. "I can't," Nelson screamed back, "the guy's gonna get me!" When Corman called cut, Nelson turned on de Kova. "What the hell is the matter with you?" he said angrily. "Well," de Kova grumbled, "no Number One Bad Caveman carries his spear up in the air like that!" Confronted with someone who had temporarily lost his mind, Nelson replied, "He'd carry it up in the air if the director *told* him to carry it up in the air!"

Nelson was minding his own business when he heard the dog wrangler yell, "Tiger, get over here! Fang, come here! Killer, let's go!" Nelson saw the wrangler and his dogs coming his way. "You're the guy my dogs are supposed to attack," he confirmed. "Watch out for Missy here, cuz she's the one, she'll go right for the throat." Nelson started to say something about having no padding when the guy cut him off. "You're not carrying that spear, are you? The dogs see ya with the spear, they're gonna become very aggressive." Nelson pointed out that it wouldn't make sense to throw the spear away with a pack of dogs about to attack him. "Yeah, well, I'm just tellin' ya fer yer own protection. You figger out the rest." Fearing the worst, Nelson concocted a reason for not having the spear. He could get tired just before the attack, and set his spear down. He asked Corman if it would be okay and Corman agreed. "And you know Roger," said Nelson. "We gotta get it on the first take, we were losing light, or he only had the dogs for ten minutes or some damn thing. So I put the spear down, I hear the dogs coming, I brace myself and I go, AAAAARRRRGGGGHHHH! The dogs stop, stare at me, and they take off!" It took a while to round them up again. Wanting nothing more to do with Nelson, the dogs had to be thrown at him for this so-called attack. "The dogs now are so frightened they're pushing against my body to get away from me, and I'm havin' to hold onto them and force one of 'em's mouth open and stick my arm in it! Now, if you watch that movie, you'll see that those dogs are afraid I'm gonna choke 'em to death with my arm. It's one of the funniest things that ever happened to me, and that was **Teenage Caveman**."

They were getting ready to shoot the scene where a character called The Man from the Burning Plains rides into camp and gets stoned to death by these superstitious fools. Beach Dickerson saw someone ushering the horse into position. Pitiful looking thing. Dickerson didn't envy the stunt man. The guy was going to have to take a fall off that horse and the ground was as hard as cement. Then he saw someone coming his way with a bearskin and a beard.

Robert Shayne, best known for his role as Inspector Henderson on the **Adventures of Superman**, television series, had a son and a daughter who'd heard about **Prehistoric World** and wanted to be in it. "I made a deal with Corman to put them in, and I would do a small part *if* I were disguised," said Shayne. "Therefore, the heavy wig, beard, etc. No one knew it was me. [He wishes!] It was a crappy little part."

"Then we went to Iverson's Ranch," said Dickerson, "and they were going to do this scene where they hunt and kill this bear. I was waiting for the trainer to show up with the bear when I see this guy coming toward me with a bear suit."

Robert Vaughn was supposed to hunt and kill a deer with this puny little bow and arrow of his, and Corman was unhappy with the stuffed deer the prop man brought him. "It's this stuffed deer or no deer," the guy told him. "At the sneak preview the picture was really playing well," Corman said, "I mean the people liked the film. Then that shot came on, and the people laughed as they saw the ridiculous deer. It was the only thing I later cut out of the picture."

Frankly, I can't imagine the picture "really playing well" with any audience at any age, but one thing I know for sure. That scene was never cut.

"The producer hired the worst actors in the world and changed the title to **Teenage Caveman**," said Vaughn. "That was me. It was one of the great bad pictures of all time." It's certainly his worst performance.

Corman called this film a missed opportunity. If he'd just had a little more money. But how much money did he need? It's a bunch of guys sitting around Bronson Canyon in bearskins. If he was shooting the same script, all of the money in the world wouldn't help it. It would still be a pompous bore.

Said *The Los Angeles Times*, "the ten cent title notwithstanding, this is an interesting motion picture and judged with the context of its intent remarkably good." *Variety* gave it a nod for "restraint and good taste," while *Motion Picture Herald* called it "a modest budget film with some stature."

"I wondered as you do, and because I did I tell you to listen to the law, and hold to it."

TEEN-AGE CRIME WAVE (1955) Columbia
W Harry Essex, Ray Buffum, P Sam Katzman, D Fred F. Sears

Tommy Cook and Molly McCart attempt to separate a man from his wallet, but the robbery is foiled by the arrival of the police. Tommy gets away but Molly and an innocent bystander, Sue Englund, are thrown in the slammer, effectively putting an end to this so-called crime wave pretty early in the game. We get a look at how Molly handles herself behind bars. She's no one to mess with.

Tommy springs Molly, and they take Sue with them, and the three take refuge in the rural home of James Bell and Kay Riehl, a religious, elderly couple. "You don't need a gun with an old man like me, son," the old man tells Tommy. Kay asks Molly if she's ever read The Bible. "Only thing I read is the comics," she replies. "I need laughs."

The film places some of the blame for the antics of the Bonnie and Clyde couple on their upbringing, or rather the lack of it. The more we learn about these two kids it becomes very clear that they never had the kind of home they've taken refuge in, or parents as kind and as understanding as Jim and Kay.

Poor Sue is horrified to see her picture on the news, branded as a thief and a fugitive, but our two partners in crime are delighted. "Look," Tommy says with a grin, "they're really playing it up." How else could they ever hope to see themselves on television? They're the kids nobody had time for. As one of the cops in the movie puts it, "I think we lock up the wrong people."

As the police close in, Tommy and Molly race up a mountain road, hoping to become lost in the crowd at the Griffith Park Observatory. But the park is closed. And there's no turning back. Molly, defiant to the end, is shot. Before she dies, she tells the cops that Sue had nothing to do with the robbery. Tommy is taken away in tears and in handcuffs.

A modest supporting feature from producer Sam Katzman, **Teenage Crime Wave** surprised both the critics and the exhibitors. Said the Citizen News, "Under the direction of Fred F. Sears, these youngsters have delivered what the trade likes to call a 'sleeper.' The film pulls no punches." Unlike Senator Kefauver and his ilk, Kansas exhibitor Ben Spainhour not only thought the film was "good entertainment" but "one that you wish every teenager would see."

"I'll take it out on your old man right now, right before your eyes!"

Molly McCart.

TEENAGE DOLL aka THE YOUNG REBELS (1957) Allied Artists
M Walter Greene, *W* Charles B. Griffith, *P-D* Roger Corman

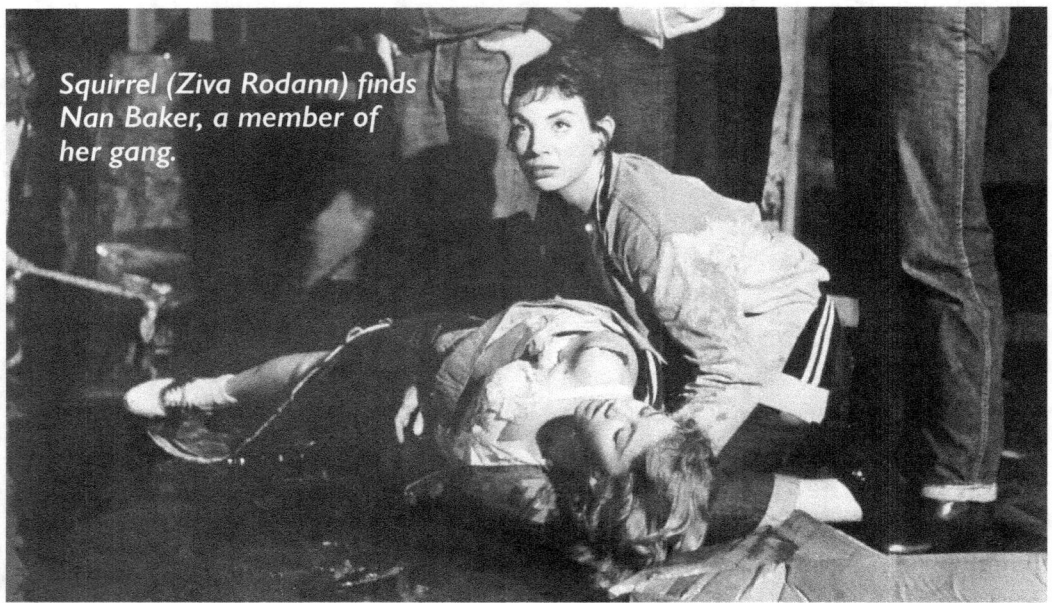

Squirrel (Ziva Rodann) finds Nan Baker, a member of her gang.

> This is not a pretty picture. It could not be pretty and still be true. What happens to the girl is unimportant. What happens to the others is more than important; it is the most vital issue of our time. This story is about a sickness, a spreading epidemic that threatens to destroy our very way of life. We are not doctors. We can offer no cure. But we know that a cure must be found.

Grim and gritty look at the underbelly of street life from producer-director Roger Corman, is rarely mentioned in any discussion of his work. The story takes place in real time, during a single night, in a lower class, urban neighborhood.

June Kenney is Barbara Bonney, on the run from the police and an all-girl street gang known as The Black Widows. She's killed one of the Widows, in a fight over Eddie Rand (John Brinkley), the leader of The Vandals, who Barbara has fallen in love with. All of this takes place before the film opens. After the wonderful Bill Martin credits, we see Barbara running away from the scene of the crime. She goes home to change her torn and bloodied dress. Her mother (Dorothy Neumann) knows she's in trouble. She was involved with a no-good bootlegger once. "Maybe someday you'll meet a man like that," she tells her daughter. "You'll know he's cheap and worthless and treacherous but you won't care. You'll do anything he wants, any time, and be glad for the chance to do it. And you must never, ever fall in love with one of them."

The Widows find Baker's body and their leader, Hel (Fay Spain), knows that Bonnie did it and assumes she'll turn to Eddie. "Eddie'll sell his grandmother's teeth for

Ziva Rodann and Fay Spain.

a ticket to the burlesque and he'll sell Barbara Bonney for not much more," she tells the gang.

Barbara is very disappointed to discover that Eddie is exactly the sort of scum her mother was talking about. He couldn't care less about the trouble she's made for herself. "You don't go looking for a con man and expect to find a boy scout," he glibly tells her.

In the first draft of the script by Charles Griffith, the Black Widows were going to kill Bonney with home-made weapons. "I invented something I called a potato grenade," said Griffith, "which was a potato impaled on a peeler with razor blades stuck in it. The script I wrote was rejected by The Hays Office (or whatever it was called at the time) so I had to rewrite it over the weekend, or should I say I had to ruin it over the weekend. We had to change the story so that gang hires someone else to do their dirty work for them. That really ruined it. We also had a very unsatisfactory ending because we couldn't figure out what the hell we could get away with."

"Roger Corman got me started," said June Kenney. **Teenage Doll** introduced her, though she'd been in TV shows and commercials. She made three more films with Roger and two for director Bert I. Gordon, and quickly found herself typed as a B-movie actress. "When you go on an interview and your past credits are reviewed and all they see is 'teenage' this and 'monster' that, it's a turn-off."

Kenney had some reservations about a scene with Jay Sayer. He was supposed to attack her and she was supposed to smack him in the head with a bottle. She didn't want to hit him any harder than she had to, but she had to hit him hard enough to break the bottle, and she knew she had to get it right on the first take. "June was

June Kenney and John Brinkley.

very apprehensive about it," Sayer recalled, "but she did it and knocked me cold!" Someone had filled the candy-glass bottle with water.

"Unremitting unconvincingly downbeat tenor, clumsily executed, deaden [boxoffice] chances for any audience outside of sex-and-sadism fanciers," said the disappointed critic from *Variety*. *The Hollywood Reporter* thought audiences would be amused by all of the luscious, tough-acting babes "with their perfectly made-up faces, they should have been attired in décolleté evening gowns rather than blue jeans and windbreaker jackets." *Boxoffice* called it "a veritable marathon of unmitigated mugging."

I say those people don't know what they're talking about. This is one of Corman's best pictures, and it certainly delivered the kind of nasty action the kids always hoped for but rarely got.

"You did one thing wrong. The worst thing anybody can do. You stepped out of your class."

*TEENAGE MENACE (1953) Broadway Angels

Chuck and Jimmy and their girlfriends hang out in Chuck's place after school, and during their conversation, Chuck happens to mention that his father deals in "junk." Jimmy's heard some bad things about heroin. "It's only dangerous if you don't know how to use it," Chuck assures him. Ultimately, after smoking some grass, Jimmy is won over when Chuck tells him that heroin "will take you up there and *keep* you there." Once Jimmy gets hooked, he's in constant need of money. He pawns everything he has of value, then steals from his parents. With his back against the wall, he goes with his hand out to his girlfriend Jeannie. She feels sorry for him and gives him her savings. Chuck tells Jimmy he'll get more bang for his buck if he stops "skin-popping" (injecting into his muscles) and starts "mainlining" (injection into the artery). Once Jimmy hits bottom, Chuck's conscience kicks in. He finds Jimmy's peddler and threatens to expose him if he doesn't keep Jimmy supplied. The peddler simply gives Jimmy a little poison in his fix. Goodbye, Jimmy.

In 1952, William Free, the owner of Broadway Angels and the man behind **Teenage Menace**, petitioned New York State for permission to show his film. Since the board had never given its approval to any film dealing with drug use—20 requests, 20 denials—Mr. Free had every reason to believe, and counted on receiving the same treatment. His lawyer told him the publicity would mean an extra $150,000 at the boxoffice. As expected, Free was denied permission, in spite of his insistence that the film was "conceived, produced and completed as a tool in fighting dope addiction in the interest of welfare and American youth." Scenes like the one of the pusher flashing a roll of cash at a shoeshine stand, suggested that some people prospered from the drug traffic. Therefore, "the use of narcotics is presented in an attractive light." Free was ready for them. "Obviously," he said, "these are the stock terms used as grounds for rejection of all narcotics pictures. There is no written word forbidding exhibiting a picture on the subject of narcotics as such, which would be the only conceivable reason for such a denial." Much to the horror of Charles Brind, the head of the New York Board of Regents, Free was right. The Board was overruled.

TEENAGE MONSTER aka METEOR MONSTER aka THE BIG GYP
(Jan, 1958) Howco- International
M Walter Greene, *W* Ray Buffum, *P-D* Jacques Marquette

The blast from a falling meteorite horribly disfigures little Charlie Cannon (Gilbert Perkins) and kills his father. Everyone believes that they're both dead because that's what his mother (Anne Gwynn) wants everyone to think. Charlie's brain was damaged and every now and then he just has to kill somebody.

55-year old Gil Perkins played the *teenage* monster. A stunt man, he stood well-over six foot, and with some lifts he was head and shoulders above the rest of the cast. You can't understand anything he says, yet somehow everybody in the movie knows what he's saying. Perkins said he originally had dialog but the writer thought he sounded too intelligent, so Perkins spent an afternoon dubbing the gibberish. According to producer-director Jacques Marquette, everyone was supposed to intuitively understand him. The only thing more astounding than that remark is the idea that anyone listened to the writer.

The real teenage monster here is Kathy North (Gloria Castillo), a nasty little piece of business if ever there was one, and the only interesting character in the film. She makes friends with Charlie, then sends him out to kill a few of the troublesome people in her life.

Amazingly awful western and most certainly a contender for one of the worst movies ever made. Shot in seven days as **The Monster on the Hill**, the title was changed to **Teenage Monster**, hoping to ride the current cycle of teenage horror films. On television it became **Meteor Monster**. Touted as "the year's shock suspense sensation," this "whispy bit of utterly unbelievable nonsense" (as *Boxoffice* put it) will leave you with the feeling that you've just been mugged.

Gilbert Perkins and Gloria Castello.

"*You've been a bad boy again, haven't you, Charlie?*"

TEENAGE REBEL (1956) 20th Century-Fox
M Leigh Harline, W Walter Reisch, Charles Bracket, P Charles Brackett, D Edmund Goulding

With Ginger Rogers, Michael Rennie and Mildred Natwick headlining the cast, this movie promises far more in the way of adult conversation than it does teenage rebellion, and in that regard it doesn't disappoint. Adapted from Edith Sommers' play, *A Room Full of Roses*, it is a sincere (and exhausting) look at some of the problems faced by the children of broken homes. As one critic noted, the teenagers in this film "behave perfectly, maybe even more perfectly than the teenagers in the Hardy family."

Reprising her role from the stage, Betty Lou Keim plays Dodie McGowan who, since her parents divorced, has adopted an air of snooty indifference to hide her fear that nobody loves her. After eight years of living with her father (John Stephenson), she's given back to her mother (Ginger Rogers), so he can devote all of his time to his new girlfriend. When her mother tells Dodie that she loves her, Dodie fires back, "Sure. You loved me so much you left me!" Toward the end of the movie, and at the end of her rope, Nancy finally tells her, "Don't blame everyone you meet for something that happened a long time ago."

"When I walked on the set of *Teenage Rebel*, the crew would hiss and boo, so mean was my character," Keim recalled.

Michael Rennie, Betty Lou Keim and Ginger Rodgers.

"And what a wonderful rebel she was," declared exhibitor Harold Bell. "Our customers want more like this." F.A. Fillips was delighted the picture didn't draw "the vandal type crowd" (who would have known better) that he'd expected, and Jim Goggin reported "a good turnout" on an "excellent picture," though he admitted that a big crowd made the picture better to him. Any kid worth their salt would have run screaming from the theatre as soon as they heard the bouncy main title, "Dodie," sung by the Hi-lo's, dashing all hope for any true rebellion. It was, as *Boxoffice* noted, a woman's picture.

A grown-up motion picture for grown-up emotions.

TEEN-AGE THUNDER (1957) Howco-International
M Walter Greene, W Ray Buffum, P Jacques Marquette, D Paul Hemlick

Jacques Marquette was a very good cinematographer, one of those guys who could light a picture quickly, and still make it look like something, which made him a much sought after commodity in television. When he was just starting out, however, he couldn't get a job to save his life. So he formed a production company and hired himself. **Teenage Thunder** was his first feature, made with people that Marquette knew would be willing to work for scale. Ray (**Girls in the Night**) Buffum wrote it. He was a friend of Marquette's. His script pretty much covers all of the bases—drag races, chicken runs, juke boxes, dancing, misunderstood kids and their bone-headed parents.

Marquette was two days into production when he got a curious call from someone at Howco-International (probably Joy Houck or J. Francis White). Somehow, they'd gotten their hands on the script and wanted to invest in the picture, and then distribute it. "We'd been running a pretty lean operation, you know," Marquette recalled, "and this was like money from heaven. Their contract seemed to be all right so we signed it and finished the picture with their money."

Johnnie Simpson (Chuck Courtney) is the focus of Buffum's scenario, the sullen son of widower Frank Simpson (Tyler McVey), a real estate salesman who lives with his sister Martha (Helene Heigh). He's pretty hard on Johnnie, and in her own quiet way, she often comes to the boy's defense. "Look, Martha, you're forgetting one thing. I was a child myself."

Charles Courtney and Robert Fuller.

The big bone of contention is over the hot-rod that Johnnie wants. He's a big nothing without a set of wheels, so to earn a little bread, he takes a job at a service station owned by Bert Morrison (Paul Bryar), a surrogate father to Johnnie. "In a service station!?" Frank says disdainfully. "As a grease monkey?!" Frank orders him to quit and come to work in his real estate office. Johnnie tells his girl, Betty Palmer (Melinda Byron), he'd rather work for Bert. But his father doesn't want him working in some cheap place, getting grease under his nails. Betty, who works as a waitress, replies, "My father says places are never cheap. Only people are cheap." Betty is one bright lady, and way too good for Johnnie.

Johnnie's got another problem. Even if he could afford to buy a car, his dad doesn't think he's responsible enough to drive one, and as much as one may hate to side with his dogmatic, hard-ass father, after seeing Johnny in action, one has to admit that he's right. The first time we Johnnie behind the wheel, he gets a speeding ticket for trying to pass the car that cut him off.

Maurie Weston (Robert Fuller) has made it his job to rattle Johnnie's cage every chance he gets, and he gets quite a few because he seems to be wherever Johnnie is. He cons Johnnie into a chicken run by simply calling him "chicken." Betty tries to reason with Johnnie but he's gotta do what a man's gotta do. "Chicken may be just a word to you," he snaps, "but it means a lot more than that to me." Betty has the good sense not to let him use her car, so he steals one. As the two cars race toward each other, Betty steps into the middle of the road, and closes her eyes. The boys are forced to swerve to avoid hitting her, after which she collapses. As far as Maurie is concerned, nothing has been settled. "Let's go mess him up a little," he tells his stooges, but before they can take action, the cops show up and take Johnnie to the station.

Johnnie's dad is fit to be tied. Before the film is over, he manages to cover all of the bases when it comes to those generic remarks that parents often feel obligated to say to their offspring, often ending with "and this is the thanks I get."

In real life, Charles Courtney and Robert Fuller were the best of friends. "Chuck had the pull at the time to get the director, Paul Helmick, to use me for the bad guy and not another actor that he really wanted," said Fuller. "It was the gateway to many other roles which led to the **Laramie** series [1959-1963] and so on and so forth."

Teenage Thunder isn't likely to end up on anyone's list of favorites, but it's entertaining enough, and if you're in the right frame of mind, it's funny without being campy. "It did very well for Howco," said producer Marquette, "but we never saw a dime. We made two more pictures for them before we found out they were crooks."

Said *Boxoffice*: "…a more realistic, less hysterical and sanguinary view of what—if anything—is wrong with the young generation."

Chicken is not just a word…its murder!

TEENAGE WOLF PACK aka DIE HALBSTARKEN aka WOLFPACK
(September, 1956) DCA
M Martin Boettcher, W Will Tremper, P Wenzel Ludecke, D Georg Tressler

Think of a law…they've broken it! Think of a crime…they've committed it!

They must have done all of that stuff before the film opens because this has to be one of the most uneventful tales in the juvenile delinquency arsenal. It's the story of two brothers, Freddie and Jan Borchert (Horst Buchholz and Christian Doermer), and Freddie's sleazy, emotionally unstable girlfriend, Cissy (Karin Baal), the most interesting character in the film. Freddie has been kicked out of his home by his cranky, abusive father (Paul Wagner), who has been worse than usual since he's taken on a debt incurred by his wife's brother. Any complaint she has about the way things are run is trumped by, "You insisted that I help your rottin' family!"

Horst Buchholz would land a great role in Tiger Bay *(1959) opposite Haley Mills in one of her best films.*

Upon hearing Jan tell his mother that he's seen Freddie, his father forbids him to see him again. "Freddie doesn't know he's a fool that's going to end up with a 45 caliber bullet in his back," he says reproachfully. Jan, not knowing that Freddie is the leader of a gang of crooks, tries to defend Freddie. His father kicks him out, too. Now that Jan has nowhere else to go, he joins Freddie's gang. Freddie has a big job in the works, one that we know will go badly, if only because the production code insisted on it.

Variety called it a "mediocre" film with a "corny" story, while *Boxoffice* accurately described it as having "the curious unnaturally slow pacing of something glimpsed under water."

"*Shoot! Don't just talk! Shoot!*"

TEENAGERS FROM OUTER SPACE (May, 1959) Warner Bros.
W-P-D Tom Graeff

There are those, like the critic for *Variety*, who saw glimpses of "brilliance" and "artistry" in this amateurish effort from writer-producer-director-editor-photographer-actor Tom Graeff, but rest assured you will more likely agree with the critic from *Boxoffice* who wrote, "[The] plot is so incredible, even for a film of its type, that its appeal would be one only of amusement."

We are told that these gestapo-like, alien delinquents were raised in cubicles, never knowing their mothers or fathers. The first one out of the spaceship sees a little dog and, for no reason, shoots it with his ray gun, turning the helpless little critter into an assembled skeleton. The only one of the bunch who seems to have a heart is Derek (David Love). He tries to talk his comrades out of using the Earth as a breeding for Gargons, a lobster-like giant of a creature. When his efforts fail, he defects.

Graef borrowed money from just about everyone he knew to make this show. Some of it came from Bryan and Ursula Pearson who wanted to be in the picture. Bryan is Thor, the villain of the piece. "[Tom's] direction was very stilted and [it] comes across that way in the film," he remarked. "Everybody talked like robots, because that was his idea as to how aliens would talk." Said his wife Ursula, "He conned everybody into doing the movie for nothing." And nothing was what they got. When Graeff finally sold the picture to attorney Paul Schriebman for $28,000, he kept every penny. The investors had to sue him.

Many viewers would discover that by the time the Gargon made its appearance in this sci-fi shocker, the movie had had the effect of The Gorgon.

Said *The Hollywood Reporter*, "Tom Graeff's production constantly struggles to overcome the disadvantage of his own bad direction which, in turn, is gravely handicapped by a script written by himself." *Motion Picture Herald* referred to the picture as a "triple-threat effort" from Graeff. Exhibitor Paul Fournier was aghast. "This is the poorest picture we have played in this theatre since it opened 15 years ago. I can only say to leave it in the cans." William Duncan concurred. "[Would] have been better off to leave the house dark for three nights."

"I have found no evidence of intelligent beings on this planet."

THE UNGUARDED MOMENT (November, 1956) Universal-International
M Herman Stein, W Herb Meadows, Larry Marcus from a screenplay by Marcus and Rosalind Russell, P Gordon Kay, D Harry Keller

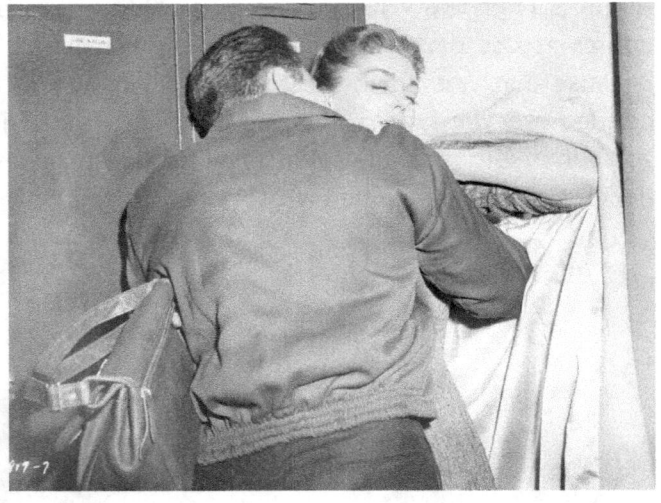

Where I come from, this is not what we called a student-teacher conference.

For eight years, Esther Williams was one of the most popular stars on M-G-M's payroll, swimming her way through a series of colorful, romantic cream puffs. When they let her go, Universal had the good sense to snap her up and put her in this picture. Said the actress, "I thought it was a curious choice for Universal to offer me a lead in a 'dry' psychological thriller, and I wasn't sure the public would accept me without my glittering gowns and sparkly swimsuits. Nevertheless, Universal offered me $200,000, which was more than I ever made for a single film at M-G-M, in or out of water."

Williams is Lois Conway, a high school music teacher in small town America. A woman was found murdered recently near the school, and it has everyone on edge. Lois begins receiving notes from an anonymous admirer that take on an unsavory tone as time goes on, and Lois foolishly agrees to a late night rendezvous in the locker room, hoping to put a stop to it. She is attacked by someone, and though it's too dark to be positive, she's pretty sure it's the school's star football player, Leonard Bennett (John Saxon in his first starring role). She drops her purse in her struggle to get away, and when she sees it on the table in her home, having just come from the police station, she realizes the thief might still be there. She opens the front door and begs him to leave. A shadowy figure races past her, his face revealed in the glare of headlights as he runs across the street. It's Leonard all right but Principal Pendleton (Les Tremayne) just can't believe it. Why would a minor god like Leonard need to throw himself at an older woman? It didn't make sense. Pendleton needed

John Saxon with Dani Crayne, married to long-time friend and sparring partner David Janssen for five years until his death. "I didn't drink. I didn't dope. I didn't smoke," said the actress "But when I lost David, I said, 'Oh, well, what the hell,' and I lit a cigarette."

only to follow Leonard home that night and it would have all made perfect sense. Leonard's father (Edward Andrews) is as crazy as he can be and he's taught the boy well. All women are just like his mother—dirty liars and cheats—and "ought to be wiped off the face of the earth!" Understandably, his wife fled for her life, and now Bennett plays the suffering single parent. Fearing that Leonard may have done something that might get him into some real trouble, Bennett warns him, in a voice as gentle and sweet as if he were telling the boy to sleep tight, "If you knock down what I've spent years building up, I'll break every bone in your body."

Lois becomes the target of malicious gossip and Pendleton fears a scandal. Lois's only ally is soft-boiled police Lt. Harry Graham (George Nader). He believes her and wants her to press charges, but she insists on protecting Leonard because he's "just a boy." Graham dully remarks, "I ought to drag you up to the reform school and show you some of the angel faces roosting there." Later, when Leonard grows tired of Graham hounding him, he reminds the Lieutenant that he's only eighteen. "So was Billy the Kid," Graham quips. Lois's kindness eventually works its magic on Leonard who confesses everything. "There's something about her that gets under your skin." Graham hurries to Lois's place to tell her the good news in person. Good thing, too, because Leonard's father, fearing the police might be on to something, has broken

Esther Williams, George Nader and John Saxon.

into Lois's house, hoping to find some skeleton in her closet with which to blackmail her, and ends up hiding in one instead, when she unexpectedly returns. Bennett cracks the door and becomes aroused as he watches her undress. By the time Harry arrives, Bennett is wheezing and slobbering as he chases Lois all over the living room. It is the film's finest moment.

Actress Rosalind Russell walked up to Williams at a party and said, "I hear you're doing my script." Williams looked at her blankly. Russell explained she'd written the original screenplay for **The Unguarded Moment** with Larry Marcus in 1951, under the pseudonym C.A. McKnight. "I wrote the part for me, but I got too old."

The Unguarded Moment is surprisingly grim for a Universal picture, and all the better for it. Edward Andrew's super creepy performance may well qualify it as

George Nader and Esther Williams.

a film noir. Let's hope that Universal can come up with something better than that 16mm print they released to DVD and television.

"Goodness, what a suspenseful motion picture," declared exhibitor Jerry Walden. James C. Balkolm said it "held the audience spellbound." Moz Burles wrote, "Certainly happy to have had this fine show to start the New Year—Universal scores again with an exciting, well-produced, superbly cast picture, as far as our patrons were concerned."

"I guess if you love them, they grow up."

UNTAMED YOUTH (March, 1957) Warner Bros.
M Les Baxter, W John C. Higgins, P Aubrey Schenck, D Howard W. Koch

Deceptively titled melodrama, is almost a satire. John Russell marries Lurene Tuttle, gets her elected judge, and convinces her to send short-term prisoners to his farm for "rehabilitation." He gloats. With all of this free labor, no other farmer could hope to compete with his prices. But he pays a price. Every now and then he has to make love to Tuttle to keep her in line. We watch him grit his teeth as he holds her in his arms. It's hysterical. His love life at the ranch isn't so hot either. His slutty mistress, Jeanne Carmen, has just performed the horizontal tango with one of the ranch hands, and is fixing her make up when she hears Russell's car. She races to the vacuum and has it running before he clears the porch.

Mamie Van Doren, Jeanne Carmen, Lori Nelson and John Russell. Carmen said that she and Mamie didn't really get along. "All the guys were kind of ogling me, and that didn't please her." Yeah. Yeah. Sure. Sure.

Sisters Mamie Van Doren and Lori Nelson, on their way to a gig, are arrested on trumped up charges by the corrupt Sheriff (Robert Foulk) in Russell's pay, and sentenced to thirty days of cotton-picking by Judge Tuttle, "where hopefully you will regain your self-respect," she tells them. "We never lost it, your Honor," Nelson tells her.

Tuttle's son, Don Burnett, falls in love with Lori and is appalled at the conditions of Russell's farm. He tells his mother the kids are living in shacks with inadequate toilet facilities. They sleep on canvas cots and eat dog food disguised as beef stew. The little money they earn is used for their clothing, food and medical expenses. Worse, a pregnant girl (Yvonne Lime) died because she was never medically examined. "I can't help myself," Tuttle sobs. Only when she learns that Russell regularly samples the lovely young prisoners does her moral outrage surface.

This was Mamie Van Doren's favorite of the pictures she made. "I got to sing and dance and do my own gyrations." She sings four songs, "Go Go Calypso," "Oobala Baby," "Rollin' Stone," and "Salamander." Eddie Cochran has one number, "Cotton Picker." He would come into his own the following year with his hit record "Summertime Blues."

"Eddie was blue-eyed and skinny, with curly blond hair and an all-American smile that won me over right away," Van Doren reported in her autobiography, *Playing the Field*. She fondly recalled the afternoon when husband Ray Anthony was away at rehearsal and she and Cochran engaged in a little rehearsing of their own. "All at once Eddie leaned over and kissed me. In a few moments we were in each other's arms. Suddenly, the front door slammed—Ray was back from rehearsal! Eddie and I straightened ourselves out, and I flipped on the record player with one of [Eddie's] demos on it." Anthony, who hated rock music, poked his head in just long enough to express his displeasure before storming off to his room. Had he not been in such a hurry, he might have noticed their flushed faces.

Lori Nelson, the actress playing Van Doren's sister, had been working with comedian-

Lori Nelson and Mamie Van Doren.

dancer Leon Tyler on a nightclub act. "The jitterbug number I did with him was not in the original script," said Nelson. "We did a little demonstration for Howard Koch, the director, and he put it in the movie."

Tyler was thin little guy with thick-rimmed glasses who can also be seen in **The Girl Can't Help It**, **Carnival Rock** and **Don't Knock the Rock!** He really knows how to cut a rug!

"Best part of the picture is the driving beat of the music, four [rock] pieces and one calypso, and it does more to hold the footage together than the actual story development," said *Variety*. "The picture isn't much but who cares if the crowd comes," said exhibitor Victor R. Weber. "Man, oh man!" exclaimed I. Roche. "This is a show right down the alley for the young folks. A real gone thing, they told me. It held its own in competition with a homecoming football game."

"Here's to cotton pickin', and the little gal cotton-pickers."

VIOLENT PLAYGROUND (March, 1958) The Rank Organization
M Philip Green, W James Kennaway, P Michael Relph, D Basil Dearden

Taking a cue from **Blackboard Jungle**, a rock 'n roll song, "Play Rough," written by Phillip Green and Paddy Robertson, blasts behind the main titles, and is heard again when it causes a group of thugs to have evil thoughts. Referring to the character played by David McCallum, producer Michael Relph said, "I believe rock 'n roll could affect this kind of boy."

In the middle of looking for the pyromaniac responsible for a series of fires, Detective Sergeant Jack Truman (Stanley Baker) is asked to fill in as the division's Juvenile Liaison Officer, and he isn't happy about it. "I don't even like kids," he tells his boss. His new job is to prevent crime before it happens by (as the people in the neighborhood see it) sticking their nose into other people's business. "You blue bottles make my flesh creep," Cathie Murphy (Anne Heywood) tells him. She has three kids. The two youngest (Brona and Fergal Borland) have been caught shoplifting. The oldest is Johnnie (David McCallum). As the leader of a gang of troublemakers, he's of special interest to Jack. He watches as Johnnie, sitting like a guru, oversees his gang as they pick on a Chinese laundry guy. Johnnie stops them from pelting his van with stones when the guy tells Johnnie he could lose his job, then lets them toss bundles of laundry around. It's a show of power. Nothing more.

In another show of power, Johnnie takes Jack to a party. As they watch everyone dancing to rock 'n roll music, Johnnie suddenly jumps into the middle of the crowd and works himself into a tortured frenzy. Then, as if rehearsed, the group stops dancing and like something out of **Night of the Living Dead** (1968), they ominously move toward Jack as if they're going to kill him. It's very creepy. There's just no other word for it.

The Monthly Film Bulletin called the film "stiff" and "lifeless" and "false," which shows you what I know. I enjoyed it. It's no great shakes, and the old soap box is hauled out every so often, but it's entertaining enough. The cast is solid. David McCallum is positively striking as the leader of the thugs. Stanley Baker plays his fish-out-of-water part very well. It's fun to watch him doing the best he can, feeling put upon and helpless the whole time, and eventually having a change of heart about the way he looks at his job in general. Once he suspects that Johnnie is the arsonist he's been after, he asks a priest who knows Johnnie well, if he's capable of such a thing. He's hoping he's wrong, for he has fallen in love with Johnnie's mother, Cathie. Unfortunately, the priest has a story from Johnnie's childhood that only supports Jack's suspicions. Peter Cushing is the priest. He guesses that Jack is in love with Cathie. "I'll tell her it wasn't easy for you," he assures him. "That's what you came for, isn't it?"

The film didn't get a U.S. release until sometime in the sixties, when The Beatles put Liverpool on the map, and McCallum had gained worldwide popularity from his role on *The Man From U.N.C.L.E.* TV series.

"It's as if I'm nothing to do with anything anymore."

THE VIOLENT YEARS (1956) Headliner Productions
M Louis Palange, W Edward D. Wood, P Roy Reid, D William Morgan

Newspaper headline: *Young man robbed! Criminally attacked by four girls*! Not surprising. We've seen the girls. Paula (Jean Moorhead). Phyllis (Gloria Farr). Geraldine (Joanne Cangi). Georgia (Theresa Hancock). We watched them walk past the classroom blackboard, each stopping just long enough to scoff at the words written there—*good citizenship, self-restraint, politeness, loyalty*. Yep. These girls are a bad lot.

Playboy's October 1955 Playmate Jean Moorhead is the leader of the gang. She also has a small role *Motorcycle Gang* (1958). Fans of fifties sci-fi remember her as the girl in the bathtub that giant Glenn Langan is ogling in *The Amazing Colossal Man* (1957). She's also the secretary at the opening of *Attack of the Puppet People* (1958) who ends up six inches tall in a glass jar. She seems to be an okay actress. One has to make allowances for the fact that she's trying to sell dialog written by Eddie Wood. A glimpse of her home life is supposed to tell us everything we need to know about her character. Her father (Arthur Millan) is too busy with his police work to help her celebrate her birthday, and mom (Barbara Weeks) has to run off to one of her many charities, and won't even stop to talk to her. "What could be so important in your young life that you warrant my attention so drastically?" she says on her way out the door. Nuff said?

Long before she ends up with a tommy gun in her hand, we see Paula and the girls rob a gas station. As a cost saving measure, this sequence is accomplished without dialog, saving the need for sound equipment or dubbing, which would have taken all of five minutes since the girls are wearing masks. You can't see their mouths. The only character they would have had to worry about is the service station attendant and they could have kept the back of his head to the camera whenever he opened his mouth.

It's their next outing that provoked that shocking newspaper headline, an event more shocking than the headline revealed. The ladies ambush a young couple in a car. The girl is bound and gagged and the young man is dragged off into the woods. As he struggles with the two women who hold his arms, Paula eyes him lustily. As she slowly unbuttons her blouse (or sweater; please don't make me watch it again), there is no question what she has on her mind. She's going to rape the guy. And it stands to reason that once she's had her way with him, he's fair game for the others. The scene fades to black, leaving the viewer to fill in the details. Pretty heady stuff for 1957.

Otherwise tedious tale of girls gone bad, written by the infamous Ed Wood, is as inept as any of the films he directed but not nearly as much fun. Wood loves to get on a soapbox and what better way to do it than to set the climax in a courtroom, and let the judge (I. Stanford Jolly) serve as his mouthpiece. With the parents of the four girls in front of him, the judge pulls a Paddy Chayefsky. "Having proven yourselves incompetent," he begins, and then beats them and the audience over the head with the dos and don'ts of raising children. It's curious that people like Wood, who have never had any children of their own, believe their lack of experience somehow qualifies them to give advice on the matter.

Teenage killers taking their thrills unashamed.

THE WILD ONE aka HOT BLOOD (December, 1954) Columbia
M Leith Stevens, *W* John Paxton, *P* Stanley Kramer, *D* Laslo Benedek.

There was no better visual metaphor to illustrate the eruption of a counter-culture than the pre-credit opening of this picture. Looking down an endless stretch of highway, in what looks like the desert, a black shape appears too far in the distance to make it out at first, when suddenly the tranquility of a quiet afternoon is shattered by the roar of motorcycle engines, as a group of biker boys in their black leather jackets race toward the camera.

The film is based on Frank Rooney's Harper's magazine story, "The Cyclists Raid," in which four thousand members of a motorcycle club descended upon the sleepy little town of Hollister, California on Fourth of July weekend and tore the place apart. He based his story on an explosion of violence that occurred in a small town in the late forties that some say was blown all out of proportion. Rooney's story is told through the eyes of an intelligent, introspective hotel proprietor named Joel Bleeker who has a daughter named Cathie. He's disturbed by the gang's disciplined, military precision. The cyclists think and act as one, further accentuated by the

Johnny and The Black Rebels.

similarity of their clothing. As a former lieutenant-colonel during the war, Bleeker "had always hated the men surrendered their individuality to attain perfection as a unit." He takes the precaution of hiding Cathie in her upstairs bedroom before having a drink with Simpson, the group's leader. They talk about the gang which Simpson describes as constantly expanding. "Our hope for the future." After a few beers, the bikers become drunk and violent and go on a destructive rampage. Two of them come crashing into Bleeker's hotel, killing Cathie. The gang scurries off but one lone member returns to beg for forgiveness. Bleeker goes crazy and beats the boy senseless. By the time Bleeker comes to his senses, he realizes his grief is as great as ever, only now he's haunted by an inner loathing for his own capacity for violence. Bleeker is the town sheriff in John Paxton's scenario. His introspection is replaced with action. Collectively, the townspeople erupt into violence, but in Pax-

Mary Murphy and Marlon Brando.

ton's account there is no evidence that any of them suffer any inner turmoil over it. The bikers in **The Wild One** are far more sporadic than the neo-fascist gang in Rooney's story, their leader an inarticulate rebel named Johnny Strabler, played by Marlon Brando. Cathie is a wholesome waitress, hypnotically drawn to Johnny and his unconventional lifestyle, refreshingly intoxicating when compared to her own mundane life. Mary Murphy was cast in the part, and she was feeling very sure of herself as she approached the set that had been built on Columbia's ranch in the San Fernando Valley. But when she saw all of the lights and the cast and the crew, she couldn't speak. "My mouth seemed as though it was sealed shut, and Marlon was like a cat because he picked it up instantly," Murphy remembered. "He saw that

I was tense and a bit scared. He sat with me for a while and clasped my hands in his and was wonderful. He was a gentleman and there was no flirting. He knew I was scared and he wanted to build my confidence up again so we could move on."

In their first encounter, Cathie and Johnny aren't even speaking the same language. His attempt to explain his philosophy of life is an early example of "jive" talk. "Now, if you're gonna stay cool, you've got to wail," he tells her. "You gotta put something down. You gotta make some jive. Don't you know what I'm talking about?" "Yeah. Yeah. I know what you mean," she replies. "Well, that's all I'm saying," he assures her. "My father was going to take me on a fishing trip to Canada once," she adds. "Yeah?" Johnny replies, waiting for the rest of it. "We didn't go," she says dully. "Crazy," he replies.

After the opening credits, Johnny and his Black Rebels disrupt a "legitimate" motorcycle race and steal the second place trophy as they ride off. Choosing to believe that Johnny would have won it fair and square if he'd been allowed to participate, they give it to Johnny, who mounts the trophy on his bike, an act of defiance against society that reveals his desire to be a part of it. Their next stop is the peaceful, rural town of Wrightwood, where Johnny meets Cathie.

Her father, the sheriff, is an ineffectual man, hoping the gang will move on before he has to deal with them. With all of the booze and food they're selling, the business community is happy to have them. Until the bikers realize they can do anything that they want.

Chino (Lee Marvin) and his biker boys, who call themselves The Beetles, blow into town. Johnny used to ride with them and there's bad blood between him and Chino. "I love you, Johnny," Chino says with a great big grin. "I've been looking in every ditch from Fresno to here, hoping you was dead." Chino has Johnny's trophy tied to his bike. The two of them get in a fight over it, and Johnny takes it back. It isn't until Chino is arrested that things get out of hand. The sheriff has to call for help.

For the sequence where Chino's gang circle Cathie and terrorize her, director Laslo Benedict had five or six cameras running. As they zigged and zagged, and tugged at her sweater, Murphy felt her skirt lift as one of the cycles nearly scraped her leg. As things got more intense, so did her performance. She was really scared and knew enough to "go with it." When they were done, she broke down in tears. "John Paxton, the writer, came over and we went off into his car, and I cried my eyes out," she said. "It's amazing to me when I think of it, because off camera we would all clown around and were friends, but it actually became reality for me doing that shot. I was really terrified."

Earlier, Johnny had offered his pilfered trophy to Cathie. "Why don't you take that back so they can give it to someone who really won it?" she tells him. After Johnny rescues her from the bikers, she expresses some interest in it. In the end, just before Johnny leaves town, she finally accepts the trophy as an act of mutual respect.

J. C. Flippin, Robert Keith, Mary Murphy and Marlon Brando.

The censors didn't take kindly to Kramer's story of middle-America's intolerance and greed, and ordered revisions that downplayed and diluted the hypocrisies of the businessmen, while stripping away any attempt to justify the behavior of the bikers. Studio head Harry Cohn hated the picture, and only released it on the basis of Kramer's and Brando's track records.

"We started out to do something worthwhile, to explain the psychology of the hipster," said Brando. "But somewhere along the way we went off track. The result was that instead of explaining why young people tend to bunch into groups that seek expression, all that we did was show the violence."

There were many critics who accused this film of condoning anarchy because it doesn't take a moral stand. "On the contrary," claimed director Benedek, "incidents that happened were based on actual fact. Before writing the screenplay, John Paxton and I spent weeks in research." So did the producer, Stanley Kramer, who interviewed a number of gang members. Their conversations were used verbatim in the film.

Boxoffice called it a "rugged, frequently raw, drama-packed, off beat film," and *The New York Times*, unsatisfied with the climax, still found it to be "tough and engrossing, weird and cruel, while it stays on the beam." *Variety* criticized it for being "long on suspense, brutality and sadism," and the *Hollywood Reporter* called it "an unpleasant absorption that certainly cannot be classified as entertaining." Exhibitor J. C. Balkcom thought it "should be banned from all theaters" and called it "one of the year's worst."

"*A picnic? Man, you are too square. I have to straighten you out.*"

Lili Gentle, Mark Damon, Ann Doran and Dabbs Greer.

*YOUNG AND DANGEROUS (October 1957) 20th Century-Fox
M Richard LaSalle, W James Landis, P-D William F. Claxton

The "dangerous" part of this movie pretty well plays itself out before the opening credits. Mark Damon gets into a fight with a guy who catches him making time with his girl. Damon leaves the guy lying in the street then races off with his buddies. Later, feeling his oats, he makes a bet that he can deflower the very sweet and very proper Lili Gentle. When Lili agrees to go out with him, her parents are horrified. Damon may be a doctor's son but he has a well-deserved reputation as a troublemaker. As it turns out, Damon is as surprised as the audience that he's the one who gets seduced. What began as a promising J.D. drama turns into a gentle romance.

This was one of Robert Lippert's RegalScope pictures, released by Fox, and coupled with another Lippert film, **Rockabilly Baby**. Fox gave the package a first class campaign, prompted by a couple of test screenings where audience reaction was enthusiastic. Look for Connie Stevens as Candy.

Variety called it "well-made," the Los Angeles Examiner said it was "intelligent," and it was "realistic" according to *Motion Picture Herald*. *Boxoffice* thought it was the "most impressive and promising" Regal film to date, and the *Hollywood Reporter* said it was "one of the best small budget pictures of the year."

"These teenage [double bills] have become my bread and butter here of late," said Victor Webber. Most of the exhibitors reported a better-than-average take.

"You've mistaken me for a fast girl."

*THE YOUNG AND THE DAMNED aka LOS OLVIDADOS (March 24, 1952) Ultramar Films

M Rodolfo Halfter, *W* Luis Alcoriza, Louis Buñuel, *P* Oscar Dancigers, *D* Luis Buñuel

The original release date of this uncompromising look at the poverty, despair and violence in a Mexico City slum was December of 1950. The focus is on two characters—Pedro (Alfonso Mojia), trying to go straight, and Jaibo (Roberto Cobo), determined to see that he doesn't. Jaibo has recently escaped from juvenile jail and is out to get the boy he thinks turned him in, Julian (Javier Amézcua). But the first order of business is to beat and rob the guitar-playing blind man (Miguel Inclán) who sells fake elixirs and preys on small children. For good measure, with the fellow lying in a heap, Jaibo smashes his guitar. Later, with his arm in a sling, Jaibo and Pedro find Julian and Jaibo challenges him to a fight. Julian won't because it wouldn't be a fair fight. As he turns to leave, Jaibo clobbers him in the back of his skull, with the rock he had hidden in the sling. Pedro tries to stop Jaibo from beating the boy to death but it's no use. Jaibo steals his money and gives some of it to Pedro, warning him to keep his mouth shut, making him an accomplice to murder.

In the most talked about sequence in the film, Pedro has a dream in which he finds Julian's blood-stained body beneath his bed. His mother (Stella Inda) rises from her bed and is the loving mother Pedro has always needed, and when she gives him the meat he wants, Jaibo comes out from under the bed and grabs it.

The police start asking questions about Julian's death. Jaibo steals a knife from the blacksmith shop where Pedro has taken a job as an apprentice, still hoping to win the love of his mother. Pedro is blamed for the theft and in an ultimate act of betrayal, his mother turns him into the police and has sex with Jaibo.

The film is so relentlessly brutal, with an ending that offers no hope, that it was necessary to film an alternate, happier ending, undiscovered until 2002. "The film was so harsh and innovative, so critical and daring in its statements that during its first screenings, spectators opening aired their indignation towards the features of Mexican identity presented by Buñuel," wrote Juan Carlos Ibáñez and Manuel Palacio.

"I wish Buñuel had made **Los Olvidados** before I made **Knock on Any Door**, because I would have made a hell of a lot better film," said director Nicholas Ray. He rented the film when he was making **Rebel Without a Cause**.

"A triumph of craft," said the *New York Herald Tribune*, a film of "terrifying power" praised the *New York World Telegram*. The *New York Times* called it "a vicious and shocking mélange of violence, melodrama, coincidence and irony," its qualifications as "dramatic entertainment" or "social reportage" dim. It has since been hailed as a masterpiece of Latin American cinema.

"I'm falling into a black hole. I'm alone. Alone. As always, boy, as always."

YOUNG AND WILD (March 9, 1958) Republic Pictures
W Arthur T. Horman, P Sidney Picker, D William Witney

Scott (**The Cool and the Crazy**) Marlowe is back as another loser, a psychopathic bully named Rick Braden. He has the hots for Valerie Whitman (Carolyn Kearney). At the local burger joint, Valerie is waiting in the car for her boyfriend, when Rick and his buddies pull up beside her. He thinks he's being cool but she finds him repulsive. "You think you're better than me?" he snarls. Well, of course she does. *Everybody* does. Rick has the morals and manners of goat. Not one to be spurned, however, which one would think he would be used to by now, Rick and his two pals, Allie and Beejay (James Kevin and Tom Gilson), run Valerie and her boyfriend, Jerry Coltrin (Robert Arthur) off of the road. While Allie and Beejay beat Jerry senseless, Rick tries to rape Valerie. She is saved by an approaching truck.

The three delinquents hop back into their stolen car and speed away. Being the boneheads that they are, they lose control and smack into an old woman. The police find the abandoned car but have no way of knowing who drove it because (unless I dozed off) they never check for fingerprints. And don't tell me the three nitwits thought to wipe the car clean. I won't buy it.

Valerie and Jerry can't find their attackers in the mug books, so with nothing else to go on, the Detective assigned to the case, Sgt. Fred Janusz (Gene Evans) throws his hands in the air. Valerie remembers the name of a school

Scott Marlowe and Carolyn Kearney.

that Rick mentioned when he was trying to pick her up. She thinks she and Jerry should look through the old year books. Janusz, with no ideas of his own, thinks it's a waste of time. They find Rick's picture and he's asked to come to the station for a line-up. Valerie's parents (Ken Lynch and Emlin Davies) give a very poor account of themselves as they allow Rick and his stooges to push their way into their home. They lift nary a finger to help poor Jerry who shows up in time to take another beating. At the station, the youngsters refuse to identify Rick at their parents' insistence. Emboldened, Rick accosts Valerie again as she walks home from school, telling her that from now on, she'll do whatever he wants. Once again, it's Valerie who comes up with a way to catch Rick in the act, using herself as bait. She tells Janusz to spread the word that she'll testify. Her plan works, but with Janusz on the job, it almost backfires.

Instead of planting himself inside of the house, Janusz and his partner aren't even nearby when Rick shows up to kill her. Approaching the house, Janusz sees Rick's car out front, but instead of racing to her rescue, he stops his car a goodly distance from the house, then he and his partner take a leisurely stroll to the door, successfully turning what could have been a high tension sequence into Monty Python-style buffoonery.

Young and Wild with Gene Evans is like **Rockin' Your Socks Off** with Perry Como. I have nothing against Evans. I think he's a terrific actor. His name just shouldn't be the first one you see. Filmed in Naturama, it's stupid but fun.

"That its theme is nothing to shout with joy about will have no bearing on its boxoffice returns," said *Boxoffice*. Exhibitor Victor Webber reported that he ran it with **Juvenile Jungle** to average business and a happy audience. "Not all dull moment in either, and at times the action get a little rough, but that's what they want here, and in this double bill they got it."

The scorching, reckless joy rides of wild girls of the road!

*THE YOUNG CAPTIVES (February, 1959) Paramount
M Richard Markowitz, W Al Burton and Andrew J. Fenady, P Andrew J. Fenady, D Irvin Kershner

Ann Howell and Benjie Whitney (Luana Patten and Tom Selden) are young and in love and getting that old itch. But Ann is saving herself for marriage and their parents want them to wait a couple of years. But then, they're not the ones itching. The two take off for Tijuana to get married and make the mistake of picking up a hitch-hiker, Jamie Forbes (Steven Marlo), and the audience *knows* it's a mistake.

Luana Patten and Tom Selden.

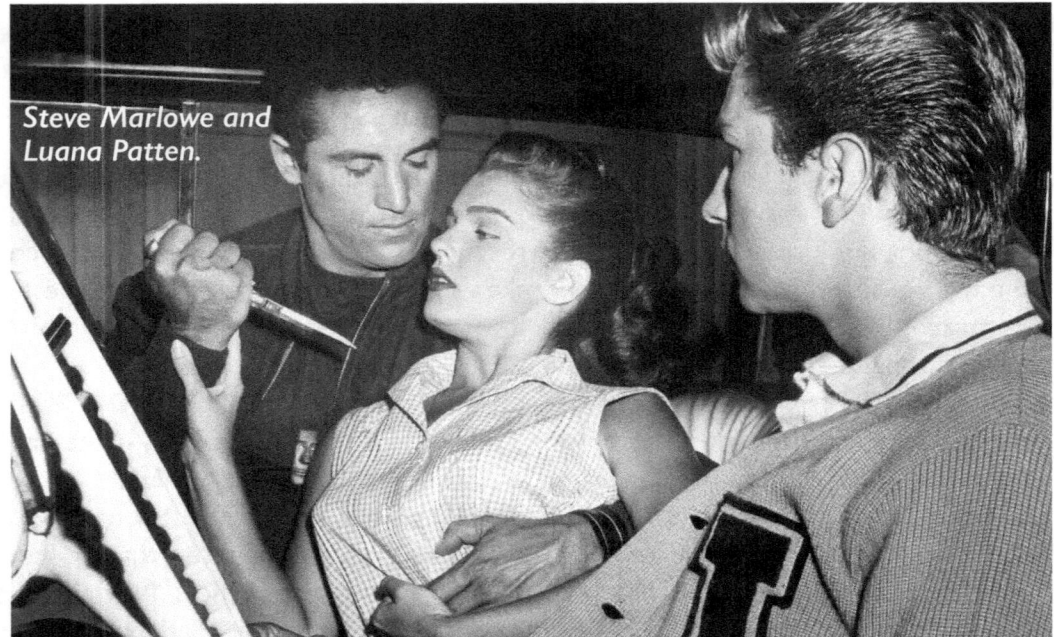
Steve Marlowe and Luana Patten.

They've just seen him beat his boss to death with a wrench, after being fired for sleeping on the job. Jamie took the man's wallet and tossed the body into the oil well.

The three stop for breakfast at a diner. Jamie excuses himself to make a call, disables their car radio, and then tries to put the make on a blonde (Marjorie Stapp) who wants nothing to do with him. He stabs her and dumps the body in the trunk of a Cadillac convertible.

Back on the road, Jamie puts a knife to Ann's throat and tells Benjie there's a new plan in the works. Jamie is not going to marry Benjie. She's going to marry him. "Now, I could tell from quite a ways back she's been giving me the big eye—bet you didn't see that, huh, Benjie boy?" Sounds like Jamie's got that old itch too.

Boxoffice called it "sure-fire entertainment for the teenagers and male adults, but will run the risk in some areas of being labeled too sensational." "Leave it alone," warned exhibitor Paul Gomoche.

"I'm Mister In. You're Mister Out."

THE YOUNG DON'T CRY (July, 1957) Columbia
M George Antheil, W Richard Jessup, P Phillip Waxman, D Alfred L. Werker

Sal Mineo and James Whitmore head an exceptionally fine cast in this screen version of Richard Jessup's semi-autobiographical novel, *The Cunning and the Hunted*. The result is a pretty good little picture.

Mineo plays Les Henderson, a resident of the Brockton Orphanage for Boys, an institution somewhere in one of the southern states. He's a good kid at a turning point in his life, trying to decide who he wants to be. He's looking forward to spending his vacation sailing to Warsaw on the sailboat he's making.

"Thinks he's somethin' owning that boat," Tom Bradley (Paul Carr) says enviously, as he watches Les walk by. Later, he's humiliated when Les knocks him ass over teakettle for picking on a little kid (Leland Mayforth). "Think you're a big fellow now, huh? Let's see how big you are. I'm gonna stomp your guts out," Tom snarls and, of course, ends up on his ass again. Les loses a week of his vacation for fighting, but he figures it was worth it.

Johnny Clancy (Thomas Carlin), who watched the fight, grinning from ear to ear, tells Les, "You gotta walk away from trouble unless there's a guaranteed pay-off." He gets a similar piece of advice from Max Cole, the school's big success story. "Now, you take two guys," Cole tells Les. "One gives and the other takes. Now, which one is going to end up the winner?" Once a resident of the school himself, Cole has since become a multi-millionaire and his visit is supposed to inspire the boys, and he enjoys flaunting his success, but he's anything but inspirational. With his beautiful wife Maureen at his side, Cole walks up to Les while he's working on his sailboat, and remarks, "It isn't much of a boat." Les replies, "No. I don't guess it isn't. But it's mine."

James Whitmore and Sal Mineo. Said Whitmore of Mineo: "He was a natural scene stealer. Even when he was standing perfectly still, he seemed to be moving. He was a pleasure to work with."

Tom Bradley shows Cole a lamp he made out of driftwood which he hopes to market. Cole punctures his dream with relish, first by denying the boy the money he'd hoped to borrow, and then by humiliating him. Cole's wife is disgusted and lays into him. Okay, okay, he'll give the boy the money he wants. Anything to shut her up. "That's what you always end up doing," she tells him. "Buying off your conscience. You'd better stop thinking of percentages and start thinking of human beings, Max, before it's too late."

Then there's Rudy Krist (James Whitmore) and his pal Doosy (Leigh Whipper), both working the nearby chain gang. And running the chain gang is a hard-as-nails character named Plug (J. Carrol Naish), who thinks respect comes from the point of a gun. When he thinks Les helped Rudy escape, and knows where he is, he backhands the boy across the face and is ready to beat him silly, when Cole walks in and knocks Plug off of his feet. Les is the only one who didn't kiss up to Cole, and is the only one he respects.

Les didn't help Rudy escape, but he was with him in the boat, when Plug shot him with a long distance rifle, too far away for Plug to know whether he'd hit him or not. Rudy flips over into the water to die, with a promise from Les that he won't tell Plug. If Plug thinks he escaped, it'll drive him mad. A friend wants to know why Les just didn't tell Plug the truth and save himself a beating. "Then, I would have been just another tough guy with a chip on his shoulder."

"If the simple, direct plot never attains real stature or power, it never succumbs to flaring melo-dramatics (even during the climactic chase), as could have happened about every ten minutes or so," said the *New York Times*. "Some of the scenes, actually vignettes, remain haunting." Exhibitor Ken Christiansen said, "Our nearby theatre does good business on this kind. We flopped, so no more for us."

"I'm just scared all of the time."

*THE YOUNG GUNS (September, 1956) Allied Artists
M Marlin Skiles, W Louis Garfinkle, P Richard V. Heermance, D Albert Band

In 1897, just as today, many public spirited citizens were aroused by the problems of delinquency among the youth of various communities... This story of one such community is based on fact.

Russ Tamblyn, on loan from M-G-M, plays Tully Rice, the son of a Wyoming desperado who can't get a break. His father's reputation makes him persona non grata in the town of Chalmers. Sheriff Peyton (Walter Coy) is willing to give the boy a chance, but his deputy (Myron Healey) and the rest of the citizens don't want him. So, he leaves for Black Crater, a lawless town full of ex-outlaws and young wannabes. Tully has to prove himself to three of these tough guys (Perry Lopez, Scott Marlowe, and Wright King), all anxious to make a name for themselves, and while he's trying to decide if he wants to participate in a robbery they're planning, Tully falls for Nora Bawdre (Gloria Talbott), the daughter of a thief who has encountered the same sort of prejudice as Tully. She tries to keep him out of trouble.

Directorial debut of Albert Band, working with writer Louis Garfinkle, the same team that created the very creepy *I Bury the Living* (1958). "Everyone was making westerns in those days," said Band. "At the same time, there was a lot of concern about juvenile delinquency. It seemed like a good idea."

"This place is getting worse than a bellyache. Nothing but old geezers and kids."

THE YOUNG STRANGER (February, 1957) RKO Radio Pictures
M Leonard Rosenman, W Robert Dozier, P Stuart Miller, D John Frankenheimer

Climbing on his high horse, Sgt. Shipley (James Gregory) lets confused and angry parent Tom Ditmar (James Daly) have it with both barrels. "Some of you smug people out in Beverly Hills seem to have the idea that delinquency wouldn't just dare happen to one of your kids!" Tom's son, Hal (James MacArthur), is in trouble with the law. He got into a fight that he claims was self-defense. The theatre manager (Whit Bissell) he decked says otherwise. And he's the one that everybody believes. Except for Hal's mother (Kim Hunter). "If he's telling the truth, you should be proud of him," she tells her husband, "but all he got from you is a lot of abuse. He's right about one thing: you don't know him. He's a stranger to you." What she says is true. Tom's a busy movie producer. The only time he sees Hal is at the dinner table.

James MacArthur makes his big screen debut, reprising his role from an episode of TV's *Climax*, "Deal a Blow." It's a low key drama, a little on the slow side, but it's sincere and credible. The incident in the movie theatre that sets the story in motion is very well played. There's a young couple (Jean Corbett and Bill Couch) sitting in front of Hal, and Hal has his feet on the seat to next to the guy. The young man attempts to hold the young lady's hand, and later tries to put his arm around her, but no matter what, she thwarts his every advance. It's his frustration with her

Bill Couch, James MacArthur, and Jeff Silver.

that makes Hal's shoe so annoying to him. He asks Hal to put his feet down and Hal's response is surly and rude, because he's got a chip on his shoulder the size of a boulder, but after some dickering he does what he should have done in the first place, and puts his feet on the floor. But now the guy isn't satisfied. He's looking for some sort of satisfaction. "Look, Mister, my feet are down," Hal tells him. "If you're so interested in watching this crummy movie, then watch it." Since the guy won't let it go, Hal puts his feet back on the chair. His blood boiling, the guy brings the manager into the mix. The manager tells Hal and his friend (Jeff Silver) to come with him, then orders them into his office, which, of course, he has no right to do. The two march out of the theatre and the usher, acting on the manager's orders, grabs Hal from behind and drags him back inside. He breaks loose, the manager tries to restrain him and that's when Hal throws a punch.

"If you want juveniles slopping in their seats, placing their feet on seats in front of them, insulting other patrons and in general making nuisances of themselves, book this film," groused exhibitor Don Holbrook. Charles E. Smith reported that he had a boy try to ape MacArthur's behavior. "We threw him out on his fanny and that's where he will stay." Mel Danner reminded everyone that the theatre manager in the picture "was no prize package."

The critics were pleased. "A simple, sensitive and thoroughly honest little picture that has to do with the temporarily strained relations between a busy father and his teen-age son," said Bosley Crowther. Thomas Schwabacher suggested how easily the film could have "slipped into a bog of sentimentality and muddy emotions" but the skill of actors, the director, and particularly the writer "saves the tone of the picture every time." *Boxoffice* singled out MacArthur as being the film's major asset, a considerable talent, "which combined with his appearance, could easily install him as a favorite among the bobby-soxers."

"Okay, champ. I'll go quiet."

Whit Bissell gets a well-deserved haymaker from James MacArthur.

SELECTED BIBLIOGRAPHY

Anastos, Ernie, with Jack Levin. *Twixt: Teens Yesterday and Today*. New York: Franklin Watts, 1983.

Barson, Michael and Steven Heller. *Teenage Confidential*. San Francisco: Chronicle Books, 1998.

Betrock, Alan. *The I Was a Teenage Juvenile Delinquent Rock 'n' Roll Horror Beach Party Movie Book*. New York: St. Martin's Press, 1986.

Caute, David. *The Great Fear: The Anti-Communist Purge under Truman and Eisenhower*. New York: Simon & Schuster, 1978.

Dixon Wheeler Winston. *Lost in the Fifties*. Illinois: Southern Illinois University Press, 2005.

Doherty, Thomas. *Teenagers & Teenpics*. Boston: Unwin Hyman, 1988.

Finch, Christopher. *Highways to Heaven*. New York: HarperCollins, 1992.

Franscella, Lawrence and Al Weisel, *Live Fast, Die Young, The Wild Ride of Making Rebel Without a Cause*. New York: Simon & Schuster, Inc. 2005.

Goldman, Eric F. *The Crucial Decade—and After: America, 1943-1960*. New York: Vintage Books (Random House), 1960.

Gunnell, John A., and Mary I. Sieber. *The Fabulous '50s: The Cars, the Culture*. Wisconsin: Krause Publications, 1992.

Halberstam, David. *The Fifties*. New York: Fawcett Columbine, 1993.

Hogan, David J. (ed.). *The Fifties Chronicle*. Illinois: Legacy Publishing, 2006.

Kleinfelder, Rita Lang. *When We Were Young: A Baby-Boomer Yearbook*. New York: Prentice Hal General Reference, 1993.

Laymen, Richard (ed.). *American Decades: 1950-1959*. Detroit: Gale Research, 1994.

Miller, Douglas T., and Marion Nowak. *The Fifties: The Way We Really Were*. New York: Doubleday, 1977.

Nashawaty, Chris. *Crab Monsters, Teenage Cavemen, and Candy Stripe Nurses*. New York: Abrams, 2013.

Palmer, Robert. *Rock and Roll*. New York: Harmony Books, 1995.

Parla, Paul and Charles P. Mitchell. *Screen Sirens Scream!* North Carolina: McFarland & Company, Inc. 1999.

Stones, Barbara. *America Goes to the Movies*. California: National Association of Theatre Owners, 1993.

Watson, Steven. *The Birth of the Beat Generation: Visionaries, Rebels, and Hipsters, 1944-1960*. New York: Pantheon Books, 1995.

Weaver, Tom. *Attack of the Monster Movie Makers*. North Carolina: McFarland & Company, Inc. 1994.

_____ *Science Fiction and Fantasy Film Flashbacks*. North Carolina: McFarland & Company, Inc. 1998.

INDEX

Ackerman, Forrest J   115
Aldrich, Henry   8-**9**
Alland, William   36
Allied Artists   26
Altman, Robert   67-69
Amboy Dukes, The novel   13
Ameican Bandstand   4, 32
American Interntational Pictures   25-26, 115
American Society of Composers, Authors and Musicias (ASCAP)   31
Anders, Luana   **135**
Andrews, Mark   **112**
Andy Hardy Series, The   5-6
Anka, Paul   **95**
April Love motion picture   24-25
April Love song   34
Are These Our Children? magazine article   17
Arkoff, Samuel Z.   25, 180
Arnold, Jack   92-93, 143
As Young as We Are   35-36
Ashley, John   **25**, 26, **74**, 75, **111**, **145**, 146
Bad Seed, The   36-38
Baddeley, Hermoine   189
Bakalyan, Richard   5, **57**, **68**, 109-110
Baker, Joyce   94
Ballyhoo   88
Bamber, Judy   74-**75**
Band, Albert   241
Barrymore, John Drew   102
Bartlet, Richard   **174**
Beat Generation, The   38-39
Bee, Molly   **96**
Belafonte, Harry   49
Bernardine   39-40
Bernds, Edward   80, 159
Berry, Chuck   98
Big Beat, The   40-41
Bissell, Whit   **116**, **118**, **242**
Blaisdell, Paul   84, 115
Blob, The   44-45
Blood of Dracula   45-46
Blue Denim   46-48
Boone, Pat   34-**35**, 39-40

Bop Girl Goes Calypso   48-50
Boys Town   14-15
Brando, Marlon   23, **230-231**, **233**
Breen, Joseph   15
Briggs, Kathleen   102
Brinkley, John   **214**
Broadcast Music Inc. (BMI)   31
Brooks, Richard   22
Brown, Myra Gale   104
Buchholz, Horst   **220**
Bucket of Blood, A   50-52
Burton, Julian   50
Byrnes, Edd "Kookie"   **135**, **158**
Cabot, Susan   **55**, **190**, 192
Cahn, Edward L.   **75**
Campbell, William   **79**, **82**
Carbone, Antony   50-51
Careless Years, The   52-53
Carey, Phil   184
Carey, Timothy   179
Carmen, Jeanne   112
Carnival Rock   53-56
Cassavettes, John   **58**
Castillo, Gloria   **120**, **158**, **180**, **216**
Chaplin, Charles   5
Chase, Kathleen   **182**
City Across the River   14, 20
Clanton, Jimmy   97
Clark, Dick   32
Clarke, Gary   **76**, **114**
Coates, Paul   5
Coates, Phyllis   **115**
Cohen, Herman   99, **114**, 117
Collins, Joan   189
Columbus Day Riot   30
Comics Code Authority   20
Condon, Eddie   3
Confidential File   5
Connors, Michael "Touch"   **136**, **186**
Contino, Dick   64
Conway, Gary   **114**, **116**, 117
Conway, Tom   181
Cool and the Crazy, The   56-58

Cooper, Jackie 8
Corday, Mara 93, **94**
Corey, Jill 182-183
Corman, Roger 53, 101, 192, 197, 208-210
Couch, Bill **242**
Courtney, Charles **218**
Crawford, Joan 11
Crayne, Dani **223**
Crime in the Streets 58-60
Cry Tough 62
Cry-Baby Killer, The 60-61
Cunningham, June 108
Curfew Breakers 62-63
Curnow, Graham **108**, 109
Cylists Raid, The 229
Daddy-O 63-64
Dale, Alan **72**
Dalton, Abby **61**, **196**
Damon, Mark **135**, **149**, **234**
Dangerous Youth 65
Danny and the Juniors **134**
Darby, Ken 137
Darren, James **86**, 87, **172**, **179**
Darro, Frankie 12
Daves, Delmer 199, 203
Davis, Bill 2
Dead End 12-13
Dead End Kids 13
Dean, James 11, 23-24, 151, **153**, **156**
deCova, Frank 209
Dee, Sandra **86**, 87, 88, **160**, 161, 200, **201**, **202**
Delicate Delinqent, The 65-67
Delinquents, The 67-69
deWilde, Brandon **47**
Diary of a High School Bride 69-70
Dickerson, Charles "Beach" 208-210
Dino 5, 70, 71
Domino, Antoine "Fats" 41, **125**
Donahue, Troy 199, **200-202**
Don't Knock the Rock 71-73
Doran, Ann **234**
Dragstrip Girl 74-76
Dragstrip Riot 76-77
Durbin, Deanna 7-8
Earth vs. the Spider 77-79
Eberhardt, Norma **136**, 161
Egan, Richard **137**, 202
Eighten and Anxious 79-80

English, Marla **180**
Escape from Red Rock 80-81
Fabulous Fifties, The 1-5, 20
Fair, Jody **111**
Field, Shirley Ann **108**
Fielder, Pat 161
Filmmakers, The 148
Flaming Teen-Age, The 81
Flanagan, Edward 14
Flippin, J.C. **233**
Ford, Constance **202**
Ford, Glenn **42**, **43**
Four Boys and a Gun 82
Fowler, Gene Jr. 117
Francis, Anne 148, **193**
Frankenstein's Daughter 82-83
Franz, Arthur 143-144
Free, William 215
Freed, Alan 31, 32, **98**
Fuller, Robert **218**, 219
Fulton, Brad 127
Garland, Fred 81
Garrett, Betty 183
Gaye, Lisa **186**
Gentle, Lili **188**, **234**
Gerard, Bernard 36
Ghost of Dragstrip Hollow 83-84
Giant Gila Monster 84-85
Gidget 86-89
Gidget: The Little Girl with Big Ideas 86
Giles, Sandra 63, **64**
Girl Can't Help It, The 89-92
Girl Gang 91-92
Girls in the Night 92-93
Girls on the Loose 93-94
Girls Town 95-96
Go, Johnny, Go! 97-99
Gobel, George 2
Godfrey, Arthur 133
Goodman, Benny 30
Gordon, Alex 5, 180-181
Gordon, Bert I. 79
Gordon, Leo 61
Gough, Michael 107
Graeff, Tom 220-221
Granvile, Bonita **10**
Great Depression, The 11-12
Great Space Adventure, The 39
Greer, Dabbs **234**

Griffith, Charles B. 164, 213
Gun Girls 99
Gurney, Robert J. 120
Haigh, Kenneth **208**
Haley, Bill **28**, 169
Hall, Huntz **10**
Halsey, Brett **195**
Hardy, Patricia 72
Harmon, Joi 134
Harris, Jack H. 44-45
Harris, Owen 30-31
Harrison, Sandra 45-**46**
Hart, Dolores **131**, 140
Hawkins, Screamin' Jay **142**
Hayes, Margaret **21**, **95**
Hays, Will 15
Haze, Jonathan 54, **166**, **197**
Headless Ghost, The 99-100
Henreid, Paul 94, **194**
Henry Aldrich Gets Glamour 8-9
High School Big Shot 100-101
High School Confidential 102-105
High School Hellcats 105-107
Holden, Joyce **93**
Hoover, J. Edgar 3
Hopper, Dennis 152
Hopper, William **154**
Horrors of the Black Museum 107-108
Hot Car Girl 109-110
Hot Rod Gang 110-111
Hot Rod Girl 112-113
Hot Rod Rumble 113
House Un-American Activities Committee 20
How to Make a Monster 114-116
Hunter, Evan 41
HypnoVista 109
I Accuse My Parents 19
I Love Lucy 47
I Was a Teenage Frankenstein 116-117
I Was a Teenage Werewolf 117-120
Invasion of the Saucer-Men 120-122
Ireland, O'Dale 77
Jackson, Anne **193**
Jaeckel, Richard **121**
Jailhouse Rock 122-124
Jamboree 124
James Dean Story, The 127
Jerry Lewis Just Stinks 67
Johnson, Dorothy **135**

Johnson, Enortis 73
Jones, Carolyn **130-131**
Jones, Dick **57**
Jones, Jack 128
Jones, Shirley 34-35
Jordan, Bobby **10**
Joseph, Jackie 195-196
Joy Ride 127-128
Juke Box Rhythm 128-129
Juvenile Jungle 129-130
Juveniles in Film (1920-1949) 7-19
Kallis, Albert 25
Kallis, Stanley 163
Kandel, Aben 100
Katzman, Sam 72
Kaye, Mary Ellen **180**
Kearney, Carolyn **236**
Kefauver, Estes 19-20, 141
Keim, Betty Lou 216, **217**
Keith, Brian **70**
Keith, Robert **233**
Kemmer, Ed 78
Kennedy, Arthur **262**
Kenney, June **78**, 110, 190, 213, **214**
Kershner, Irv 196-197
King Creole 130-132
King, Martin Luther 2
Knock on Any Door 13
Knox, Stewart 104
Koerner, Charles 17
Kohner, Kathy 86-87
Kohner, Susan 71
Kramer, Stanley 229-231
La Rosa, Julius **133**-134
Landon, Michael **118-119**
Laughlin, Tom **68**
Lederer, Francis 161
Leiber, Jerry 123
Lembec, Harvey **43**
LeRoy, Mervin 36
Let's Rock! 133-134
Lewis, Jerry **66**, 67
Lewis, Jerry Lee 103
Lewton, Val 18
Life Begins at 17 134-135
Lime, Yvonne **76**
Lindner, Robert M. 152-153
Litel, John 181
Live Fast, Die Young 136-137

Long Tall Sally song 73
Love Finds Andy Hardy 7
Love Me Tender 137-139
Loving You 28, 139-141
Lovsky, Celia 178-179
Luce, Clare Booth 22
Lumet, Sidney 58
Lund, Jana **72, 106**
Lupino, Ida 148
Lyman, Frankie **176**
Lyndon, Jimmy 8-**9**, 10
Lynley, Carol **47**
Lyon, Richard **100**
Lytel, John 181
MacArthur, James **241**, 242
Mad at the World 141
Man in the Gray Flannel Suit, The novel 2
Mancini, Henry 174
Mansfield, Jayne **89**, 90
Marlowe, Scott 56-**57, 236**
Marlowe, Steve **238**
Marquette, Jacques 217
Marr, Eddie 114
Martin, Tony 4
Matin, Dean 66-67
McCallam, David 228
McCart, Molly **211**
McCarthy, Joe 1-2
McClendon, Gordon 84
McCormack, Patty 36, **37**, 38
McGuire, Dorothy **202**
McQueen, Steve 44-45
Mell, Joseph **118**
Merlin, Jan 182
Middleton, Wallace 184
Milan, Lita **94**
Miller, Dick 50, **164**, 167, **191**, 197
Miller, Dorothy 29
Miller, Kenny 118, 120
Mineo, Sal **71, 151, 153**, 173, **239**
Mister Rock and Roll 142-143
Monster on the Campus 143-144
Moorehead, Jean 228
Moreno, Rita **194**
Morris, Barbara **51, 191**
Morrow, Jo 128-129
Motorcycle Gang 142-147
Murphy, Mary **136, 231**-232, **233**
Nader, George **224**

Natwick, Mildred **205**
Neagle, Anne 65
Nelson, Ed **166**, 209
Nelson, Lori 112, **225, 226**
Neyland, Anne **25**, 123, **145**
Nicholson, Jack **60**
Nicholson, James H. 25
Nielson, Leslie **205**
No Time to Be Young 147
O'Connor, Mary Lou 91
On the Loose 148-149
One Way Ticket to Hell 148
Only You song 164
Our Dancing Daughters 11
Paget, Debra **138**, 139
Parks, Rosa 2
Party Crashers, The 149-150
Patten, Luana **173, 174, 237, 238**
Pearson, Brian 221
Pearson, Drew 221
Pearson, Ursula 221
Perkins, Carl **126**
Perkins, Gil **126**
Persson, Gene **78**
Platters, The 163-**164**, 165
Presley, Elvis **vi**, 3, **120**, 122, 131, **137-138**
Price, Bamlet Lawrence 148
Problem Girls 32
Production Code 15
Provine, Dorothy **162**
Ram, Buck 3
Rapp, Paul 100-101
Ray, Nicholas 13, 123, 124, 152-153
Rebel Set, The 151
Rebel Without a Cause 23-24, 151-157
Reed, Ralph 158
Reefer Madness 16-17
Reform School Girl 157-159
Rennie, Michael **217**
Republic Pictures vs. American International 129
Restless Years, The 159-160
Return of Dracula, The 161-162
Reynolds, Debbie **202, 203, 205**
Rhoden Jr., Elmer 63
Richard, Dawn **119**
Richard, Little 73, **90**
Riot in Juvile Prison 162-163
Road Racers 163

Teenage Thunder

Robertson, Randy 67, 157
Rock All Night 163-166
Rock and Roll Revue 168-169
Rock Around the Clock 27-30, 169-170
Rock Around the Clock song 4
Rock Around the World 170
Rock Baby, Rock It! 170-172
Rock Pretty Baby 172-175
Rock, Rock, Rock 175-177
Rockabilly Baby 167-168
Rodann, Ziva **212**
Rogers, Ginger **217**
Rooney, Frank 229
Rooney, Mickey 5, **6**, **15**
Rudd, Enid **193**
Rumble on the Docks 177-179
Runaway Daughters 180-181
Running Wild 32- 181-182
Rusoff, Lou 110
Russell, John **225**
Russell, Rosalind 224
Rydell, Mark **58**
Sands, Anita 69
Sands, Tommy **187-188**
Saxon, John 62, **173**, **174**, **223**. **224**
Sayer, Jay 214
Schary, Dory 20-21
Schulman, Irving 153
Seduction of the Innocent 20
Seldon, Tom **237**
Senior Prom 182-183
Sex Education 49
Shadow on the Window, The 182-183
Shake, Rattle and Rock! 184-185
Shayne, Maxwell 13-15
Shayne, Robert 210
Siegel, Don 59
Silver, Jeff 241
Sims, Sylvia **208**
Sinatra, Frank 30
Sing Boy, Sing 186-188
Sixty Minute Man song 4
Slasher, The 188-189
So Young, So Bad 193-194
Sorority Girl 190-193
Sottone, Liliane 100
Soundies 168
Spain, Fay 38-39, **74**, **75**, 213
Speed Crazy 195-196

Spurlock, Geoffrey 15, 22, 38, 190-191
Stakeout on Dope Street 196-197
Steele, Tommy 170
Steiner, Max 199
Sten, Anna 180-181
Stern, Stewart 153
Stevens, Connie 150
Stewart, David J. 54, 56
Stewart, Sandy **98**
Stockwell, Dean 53
Stoller, Mike 123
Stone, Lewis **6**
Strock, Herbert L. 45, 115
Sulivan, Don 85
Sullivan, Ed 3
Summer Love 198
Summer Place, A 198-202
Swerdloff, Arthur 163
Tamblin, Russ 102-103, 123
Tammy and the Bachelor 202-206
Tammy song 205
Tashlin, Frank 89
T-Bird Gang 206-207
Teenage Bad Girl 207-208
Teenage Caveman 208-210
Teen-Age Crime Wave 210-211
Teenage Doll 212-214
Teenage Menace 15, 214-215
Teenage Monster 215-216
Teenage Rebel 216-217
Teenage Thunder 217-219
Teenage Wolfpack 219-220
Teenagers from Outer Space 220-221-222
Temple, Shirley **9-10**
Terrell, Steve **74**, **75**, **120**
Theatre Rules of Conduct 29-30
Thomas, Frankie 10
Thor, Jerome 163
Tiger, J.C. 171-172
Tiomkin, Dimitri 29
Toomey, Regis **127**
Touch of Evil 33
Tracy, Spencer 14, **15**
Troup, Bobby **49**
Turner, "Big Joe" 185
Twenty One TV show 31
Tyler, Judy **49**, **55**, **122**
Tyler, Richard 162

Unguarded Moment, The 222-225
United Artists 62
Universal Studios 40
Untamed Youth 225-227
Uris, Leon 153
Valens, Ritchie 98
Van Doren, Mamie 33, 39, **95**, **103**, **225**, **226**
Vaughn, Frankie 65
Vaughn, Robert 147, 210
Vincent, Gene **111**
Violent Playground 227-228
Violent Years, The 225-229
Wallis, Hal 140
Webster, Mary 79
Weld, Tuesday **27, 175**
Welles, Mel 102, **164**, **165**
Wendkos, Paul **88**
Wertham, Frederick 20
Wexler, Haskell 197
Wexler, Yale 196
Wheeler, Kay 172
Where Are Your Children? **19**
Whitfield, Smoki **60**
Whitmore, James **59**, 239

Wild Boys of the Road 12
Wild One, The 24, 229-233
Williams, Esther **222-224**
Wilson, Harry **83**
Wilson, Jackie 98
Wilson, Sloan 2
Wiseman, Joseph 56
Wood, Edward D. 229
Wood, Natalie **11**, 152, **153**, **154**, **156**
Wright, Teresa **160**
Yates, Herbert 129
Young and Dangerous 234
Young and the Damned, The 235
Young and Wild 236-237
Young Caprives, The 237-239
Young Don't Cry, The 238-240
Young Guns, The 240-241
Young Stranger, The 241-242
Your Hit Parade 4
Youth Runs Wild 18
Zeitlin, Rose 23
Zugsmith, Albert 27, 39, 101-102

www.ingramcontent.com/pod-product-compliance
Lightning Source LLC
Chambersburg PA
CBHW082037230426
43670CB00016B/2687